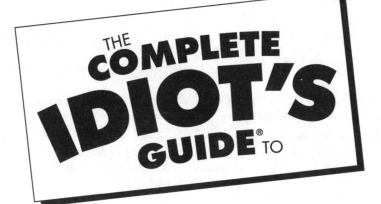

THE COMPLETE IDIOT'S GUIDE® TO

Light Desserts

by Rose Reisman

ALPHA

A Pearson Education Company

*I have a joy and zest for life. I owe this spirit to the most important people in my life—
my family. My husband, Sam, of 25 years of marriage and my four wonderful children,
Natalie, David, Laura, and Adam.*

As well as to all those who think you "can't have your cake and eat it too!" Rose

The Complete Idiot's Guide to Light Desserts published by Pearson Education, Inc, publishing as Alpha Books, Copyright © 2003 The Art of Living Well

International Standard Book Number: 0-02-864446-8
Library of Congress Catalog Card Number: 2002115305

04 03 02   8 7 6 5 4 3   2 1

Interpretation of the printing code: The rightmost number of the first series of numbers is the year of the book's printing; the rightmost number of the second series of numbers is the number of the book's printing. For example, a printing code of 02-1 shows that the first printing occurred in 2002.

Printed in the United States of America

For marketing and publicity, please call: 317-581-3722

The publisher offers discounts on this book when ordered in quantity for bulk purchases and special sales.

For sales within the United States, please contact: Corporate and Government Sales, 1-800-382-3419 or corpsales@pearsontechgroup.com.

Outside the United States, please contact: International Sales, 317-581-3793 or international@pearsontechgroup.com.

Publisher: *Marie Butler-Knight*
Product Manager: *Phil Kitchel*
Managing Editor: *Jennifer Chisholm*
Senior Acquisitions Editor: *Renee Wilmeth*
Development Editor: *Nancy D. Lewis*
Production Editor: *Katherin Bidwell*
Copy Editor: *Rhonda Tinch-Mize*
Illustrator: *Chris Eliopoulos*
Cover/Book Designer: *Trina Wurst*
Indexer: *Julie Bess*
Layout/Proofreading: *John Etchison, Rebecca Harmon*

Contents at a Glance

Contents

8 Soufflés, Caramels, and Brûlées · 141

9 Puddings, Bread Puddings, and Pudding Cakes · 153

Introduction

To most of us, myself included, desserts are an essential part of our lives—how can one celebrate a birthday without a beautiful cake? How can a summer supper on the porch be complete without a slice of luscious fruit pie? What goes better with a cup of coffee than a slice of still-warm coffee cake or a couple of cookies? What brings more oohing and aahing at a dinner party than a delectable cheesecake or a stunning dessert soufflé finale?

Desserts have always been my passion, and now that I and everyone else I know are eating lighter and healthier, reducing calories, fat grams, and cholesterol in recipes has become my vocation. At my cooking school in Toronto, the classes on light dessert making fill up first. Now you, too, can indulge in knowing that because these recipes are greatly reduced in calories, fat grams, and cholesterol, dessert can be a part of your healthy diet.

As you will see, this book is arranged in two parts—each divided into chapters devoted to broad categories. If you're new to dessert making or just want to brush up on your dessert-making techniques, you will want to peruse Part 1 so that you're familiar with the ingredients and cooking techniques that you'll be using when making the dessert recipes in Part 2.

However, if your kitchen and refrigerator look like you frequent a bakery shop and you're just wanting to know how to "lighten" your desserts to include less calories and fat, especially saturated fat and cholesterol, you can just skim Chapter 1 and then move right to the recipes and start cooking.

Keeping in mind that we all lead busy lives, I've tried to keep the recipes straight-forward and easy for the most inexperienced cook to follow. Feel free to tinker with my recipes. After all, it's a cook's undeniable right to customize a recipe. The point of making desserts is to enjoy the making as well as the eating. And because these desserts are all lower in calories, fat, saturated fat, and cholesterol, there's no reason to restrict them to special occasions. I believe moderation is the key to keeping a healthy diet every day of the week. And that includes having dessert!

Nutritional Information

All the recipes in this book have been analyzed for calories, fat, saturated fat, carbohydrate, dietary fiber, and cholesterol using ESHA Research's Food Processor Nutrition Analysis Software, Version 7.7. Results are carried to one decimal place rather than being rounded up or down to a whole number. Each recipe analysis is for one serving or item as specified. If given a choice of ingredients, such as margarine or unsalted butter, the first choice (margarine) was used for the calculation.

Before examining the nutritional analysis for each recipe, look at this table and see what the nutritional daily recommendations are for men and women aged 25 to 50.

	Women	Men
Calories	2000	2700
Total fat	67 g	90 g or less
Saturated fat	22 g or less	30 g or less
Carbohydrate	299 g	405 g
Dietary Fiber	25–35 g	25–35 g
Cholesterol	300 mg or less	300 mg or less

Now check out the recipe you're preparing, and see how it compares to your recommended daily total. You'll be surprised to see how low in calories, fat, and cholesterol these delicious desserts are and how well they fit daily into a healthy diet. Having one piece of delicious dessert is not only allowed every day, but I also recommend it!

Let's also compare a high-fat cheesecake to one of my low-fat versions. For example, this table compares a typical piece of my cheesecake with a regular one.

	Low-fat Cheesecake	High-fat Cheesecake
Calories	250	640
Total fat	7 g	32 g
Saturated fat	3 g	22 g
Carbohydrate	30 g	40 g
Dietary Fiber	1 g	1 g
Cholesterol	40 mg	120 mg

In summary, one cannot afford the calories, fat, and cholesterol of high-fat desserts on a daily basis without gaining weight or harming health. With my low-fat desserts, there is no reason you cannot enjoy dessert every day.

How This Book Is Organized

The book is divided into two parts:

Part 1, "Getting Started," steers you to choosing the right ingredients and equipment for making light desserts, and then guides you through the special cooking techniques you'll be using. You will learn how and when to substitute lower-fat ingredients for their heavier cousins so that you can then tackle and lighten your own favorite family recipes.

Part 2, "The Recipes," introduces you to desserts to tempt and please every palate from everyday fare to company special. More than 200 spectacular recipes are included for people who want to indulge their sweet tooth with a clear conscience.

Extra Bites

The sidebars in this book offer tips, inspiration, valuable knowledge, and definitions. Use these as road signs on the journey to your goal—your ideal size.

 Nutrition per Serving

The calories, fat, saturated fat, carbohydrate, dietary fiber, and cholesterol counts for each dessert to help you fit these desserts into your daily diet.

 Nutrition Watch

Like a friendly personal nutritionist, these boxes contain bits of information on how to incorporate healthy ingredients into your lifestyle.

 A Piece of Advice

Suggestions to make your desserts easier to make and more delicious.

Acknowledgments

To all the "divine" people who made this book as "delicious" as it could be.

Thanks to the entire crew at Pearson PTR Canada, including Nicole de Montbrun, Andrea Crozier, and Ed Carson, for all their care and confidence in this book, and in me. And a big thanks to Tracy Bordian, who kept this book to an incredibly tight and high-pressure schedule with ease. That's impressive!

Thanks to Martin Litkowski and Jennifer Matyczak, who have been responsible for making me visible across the country.

Thanks to an amazing editor, Madeline Koch, for forcing me—late at night—to get her my changes. She was great to work with.

As always, to my assistant Lesleigh Landry, for sampling hundreds of desserts. She not only assisted in the testing, but also helped turn my illegible handwriting into readable script. Thanks, also, for assistance in the nutritional analyses.

Thanks to the assistants in my home, Lily Lim and Ruby Reveche, who always made sure that there were ample ingredients and utensils.

Thanks to all those "great" friends, especially Susan Gordin and Kathy Kacer, who stopped by each night to pick up extra dessert for their family and friends. And who gave me honest criticism for each dessert. Sometimes too honest!

A final thanks to Renee Wilmeth and her terrific staff at Alpha Books and to Frances Towner Giedt, who capably "Americanized" the book for the United States market. You made this book possible.

Trademarks

All terms mentioned in this book that are known to be or are suspected of being trademarks or service marks have been appropriately capitalized. Alpha Books and Pearson Education, Inc., cannot attest to the accuracy of this information. Use of a term in this book should not be regarded as affecting the validity of any trademark or service mark.

Part 1

Getting Started

When you first open a new cookbook, it's very tempting to just roll up your sleeves and head for the kitchen to cook, but it's important to hold off long enough to read these chapters on techniques for lowering the fat in desserts, dessert-making ingredients, proper equipment, and cooking techniques used in making desserts.

This part of the book teaches you how to look for the sources of fat in desserts, and then how to judiciously substitute lower fat items that will produce the same flavor. You'll learn about the basic ingredients you'll be using in dessert making and what equipment is essential and helpful. Then I'll walk you through the basic cooking techniques you'll be using so that in the end making these light desserts will be "a piece of cake" … so to speak.

Chapter 1

Light Dessert Ingredients and Low-Fat Techniques

In This Chapter

◆ Stock your pantry with the basics: dry and liquid
◆ Make sure everything's very fresh
◆ From fats to eggs to milk—and then some
◆ Significantly reduce calories and fat

Dessert recipes are in essence a chemical formula that balances a number of ingredients to produce a specific end product. As with other types of recipes, that end product relies on using the freshest and best ingredients. This is not the time to scrimp and save pennies. Buy quality and don't use anything labeled "imitation."

When looking for ingredients to help reduce calories and fat, do not try to eliminate the fat entirely. Instead, try to reduce the amount by using those substitutions that will still result in an excellent dessert. Continue on with this chapter to find out more about specific ingredients and how to use them in your low-fat desserts.

Basic Dry Ingredients

In making desserts, each ingredient has a function. Dry ingredients play an important role, providing structure that binds the ingredients together as well as acting as a drier that absorbs and retains the moisture that you're adding to the dessert. This gives the dessert body. Sugar acts as a tenderizer, thereby softening the crumb.

Flour

The flour used in most of my recipes is all-purpose flour. This flour is often a blend of 80 percent plain flour and 20 percent cake flour. It's excellent for all cakes and cookies except for those that specify cake flour, which is milled from soft wheat, has a lower gluten level, and is specifically designed to produce a tender grain in cakes. You can make your own cake flour from all-purpose flour by substituting 2 tablespoons cornstarch for 2 tablespoons flour in every cup. To substitute cake flour for all-purpose flour, use 1 cup plus 2 tablespoons cake flour for every cup of all-purpose flour.

Unbleached flour is more nutritious because some of the wheat bran is retained during the milling and refining process. It tends to be a little heavier than bleached flour and is not desirable for delicate cakes.

Whole-wheat flour is not milled as finely as white flour and contains much of the bran and wheat germ, making it darker, coarser, and more nutritious. If you're going to substitute this flour for white flour, use up to 50 percent of whole-wheat flour. If you use more, the cake will be too dense.

Store flour in a cool, dry place that is well ventilated. It will absorb odors if stored next to a strongly scented product. If storing flour for a long period of time, it's best to store it in the refrigerator or freezer.

A Piece of Advice

In most recipes, there's no need to sift the flour—I never do so unless I'm making something very delicate, such as an angel food cake. The recipe will always say if sifting is necessary.

Sugar

Sugar is used in desserts to provide sweetness and to contribute to the texture of the dessert. It also helps to keep desserts fresh for longer and provides good color to many desserts, specifically for browning crusts. Its capability to caramelize adds flavor to baked goods.

Many types of sugar are available to the baker. White, dark, light brown, confectioners' sugar (sometimes called powdered sugar), and molasses are available. Each type comes from a different stage of the refining process.

White sugar is available in a variety of crystal sizes, from regular granulated to superfine to confectioners' sugar. Regular white sugar has larger granules, and confectioners' sugar has very small fine granules.

Confectioners' sugar has approximately 3 percent cornstarch added to each box to prevent lumpiness and crystallization.

A Piece of Advice

Always sift confectioners' sugar just before using.

Brown Sugar

Brown sugar is merely white sugar with the addition of molasses. It is less refined than white sugar. The darker the sugar, the more the molasses and moisture it contains. People often think it's a healthier sugar, but it is nutritionally the same as white sugar. The choice is a matter of preference.

Brown sugar tends to make a cake heavier and should be avoided in light-textured cakes.

If you want to make your own brown sugar, add 2 tablespoons unsulphured dark molasses to 1 cup granulated sugar.

If you want to cut back on the amount of sugar used in your traditional recipes, as a general rule you can cut out about one fourth to one third of the sugar without affecting the texture. You can cut out more if you use dried or puréed fruit, such as bananas, applesauce, or date purée.

In low-fat baking in which fat cannot be used for tenderizing the dessert, sugar is essential for making the dessert tender.

You don't have to sift regular sugar unless it has been sitting for a long time and has developed lumps. Confectioners' sugar should be sifted before using.

A Piece of Advice

When measuring brown sugar, always pack it firmly. To avoid lumps from forming in brown sugar, add a slice of old bread to the container and replace it every couple of weeks. If the sugar is already hard, try placing the amount of sugar needed in the microwave for 30 seconds to help soften the sugar.

Sugar Substitutes

For those who cannot consume sugar, a sugar replacement is necessary. Some of the sweeteners used in coffee are not ideal because at high baking temperatures they lose their sweetening power. One of the best on the market is Splenda, which has directions on the box; basically, you use one cup for one cup. Splenda slightly changes the flavor and texture of a dessert that traditionally uses sugar, but I find it the best substitute to date.

Leavening Agents

Leavening agents are added to desserts to make baked goods rise and to produce a light and airy texture. Baking powder and baking soda are the main ones used in baking.

 **A Piece of Advice**

If you're not sure whether your baking powder is still fresh, combine 1 teaspoon baking powder with ½ cup hot water; if it bubbles vigorously, it is still fresh. If not, toss it out.

Baking powder is a chemical leavening agent made of acid-reacting materials. There are three main types: single; fast acting or phosphate; and double acting, which is the main one used in home cooking. Baking powder contains approximately 25 percent cornstarch. Store baking powder in a cool, dark place. The average shelf life of an opened can is about one year. If it is older than a year, it might be the reason your cake is falling.

If you run out of baking powder, a good substitution is to combine 2 teaspoons cream of tartar, 1 teaspoon baking soda, and a little salt for every cup of flour.

If you use too much baking powder, the cake taste might become bitter, and it might rise rapidly and then collapse.

Also known as bicarbonate of soda, baking soda is used in baking when there is also an acid, such as buttermilk, yogurt, sour cream, molasses, honey, cocoa, or chocolate. It is needed in order to neutralize some of the acidity, as well as to leaven. Once you add baking soda to the batter, it must be baked immediately or it will begin to rise.

When a recipe calls for both baking soda and baking powder, the baking powder is needed for leavening and the soda neutralizes the acids. Baking soda can darken the color of chocolate or cocoa in a cake because it is an alkali.

Cream of tartar is an acidic by-product of winemaking. It is a white powder used to help prevent the over beating of egg whites and to help stabilize egg whites during the baking. A mixture that contains cream of tartar should not be cooked in an unlined aluminum pan because the acid reacts with the aluminum and turns the food gray.

Salt

Sodium often is confused with the term "salt." Sodium is sodium chloride, a chemical that accounts for 40 percent of salt. In low-fat baking, some flavor is removed; therefore, a small amount (as little as ⅛ teaspoon) of salt is needed to enhance the flavors left in the recipe. Salt combines with sugar to bring out and balance the sweetness. I always use salt in soy-based desserts because soy has a flat, bland taste.

Cornstarch

Cornstarch is finer than flour and is a more effective thickening agent. As a rule, you use double the flour to cornstarch to thicken a liquid.

Gelatin

Gelatin is a natural product derived from collagen, the protein found in bones and connective tissue. Unflavored gelatin is commonly used in baking and is sold in small boxes that have individual servings of approximately 1 tablespoon. Follow the directions on the package, or follow the recipe with specific instructions. The basic principle is to add approximately 2 to 3 tablespoons cold water to 1 tablespoon gelatin and let it sit for 2 minutes to allow the granules to swell; then either heat the mixture in a microwave to melt the gelatin completely or add 2 to 3 tablespoons of boiling water and stir until it is combined. Then you add it to your dessert mixture. The dessert might need as long as 2 hours to set properly.

Cookie Crumbs

Often, to replace a high-fat butter crust, I use cookie crumbs, which have much less fat and fewer calories. My favorites are chocolate wafer crumbs, vanilla wafer crumbs, and graham crumbs. If the cookies have not been ground, just place them whole in a food processor and purée until they are finely ground; then measure what you need. You can even buy your own cookies in bulk and do the same thing.

If you make your own crumbs, it helps to know how much it takes to produce 1½ cups of crumbs:

- Twelve and one-half double graham crackers
- Twenty-five 2-inch gingersnaps
- Thirty-nine 1¾-inch Sunshine Vanilla Wafers
- Forty-six and one-half 1½-inch Keebler Golden Vanilla Wafers
- Forty-six and one-half 1½-inch Nabisco Nilla wafers
- Twenty-seven 2¼-inch Nabisco Famous chocolate wafers

 **A Piece of Advice**

Because everything has a shelf life, look at the "sell by" or "use by" dates on the packages. When you're opening something like a new tin of baking powder or jar of spices that will start to deteriorate the minute it's opened, jot the date on the label so you know when to toss it and buy another.

These crusts are lower in fat because they are held together mostly with water and just a small amount of canola oil.

Quick-cooking Oats

I like to use quick-cooking oats in baking because they give desserts texture, taste, and volume without adding fat and calories. Be sure to use either quick-cooking or old-fashioned rolled oats. Do not use instant oats because they tend to make the batter sticky.

Basic Liquid Ingredients

Liquid ingredients tenderize the dessert by softening and moistening the crumb. They also keep the dessert fresh and enhance or provide the flavor of the dessert.

Sweeteners

Honey lends a specific flavor and baking quality to pastries. It's best to use it only when called for. Honey is sweeter and has a higher moisture content than granulated sugar. As a rule, use one third less honey than sugar and when possible reduce the volume of other liquids by ¼ cup for each cup of honey used.

Corn syrup is made when starch granules are extracted from corn kernels and treated with acid to break them down into a sweet syrup. It comes from the glucose from the corn sugar plus some added fructose and water. It is great in low-fat baking because it can replicate some qualities of oil.

I prefer light corn syrup for these recipes. Before measuring corn syrup, lightly grease the measuring cup so that the corn syrup will pour out easily.

Molasses is the liquid separated from sugar crystals during the first stages of refining sugar. Its color and strength depend on the stage of the separation process. The first liquid molasses drawn off is the finest quality; the second and later ones contain more impurities. The third is called blackstrap, which is the blackest and has the strongest flavor. For baking, select the dark molasses.

A Piece of Advice

When measuring liquid sweeteners, lightly grease a glass measuring cup to make sure that you get out every drop.

Pure maple syrup comes from the sap of the sugar maple tree, which is boiled down until it has evaporated and thickened. It takes about 30 gallons of maple sap to produce 1 gallon of syrup. That's why the cost is so high for pure syrup. I like to buy Grade A or Fancy Grade syrup, which is light brown in color and has a delicious delicate flavor. It is quite expensive, but it is well worth the cost. Try to avoid imitation maple syrups, which are basically corn syrup with artificial maple flavoring and color added.

Juices

Always use fresh lemon or lime juice. The bottled versions have a bitter aftertaste and are only fine if the fruit juice is not the predominant flavor in the dessert. I often squeeze more juice than I need and pour it into ice cube trays and freeze. Then pop out the cubes and store them in airtight plastic bags so they're available when you need them. One lemon produces approximately ⅓ cup juice and 1 lime approximately ¼ cup juice. One orange yields approximately ½ cup juice.

For orange juice, I'll use fresh if I've used the zest; otherwise I find the juice from frozen concentrate, bottles, or cartons to be fine for baking purposes. I also use frozen orange juice concentrate a lot because of the flavor intensity.

A Piece of Advice

I keep small cans of frozen orange juice concentrate in the freezer just for baking and cooking purposes. No need to defrost, just measure out what you need, reseal, and return the rest to the freezer.

Coffee

I like the taste of coffee in some of my desserts. Either use instant coffee or a strong brew. I always use a higher ratio of dry instant to water than would be used for drinking. Instant espresso powder is available in some groceries and produces a more intense flavor than regular instant coffee powder (but less caffeine).

Fats

Baking fats include butter, margarine, vegetable shortening, lard, and oil. For low-fat baking, I use only unsalted butter, margarine, or oil. Fats in baking tenderize, moisturize, add flakiness, and add flavor. They also add a smoother texture to the dessert.

Fats are either saturated or unsaturated. Unsaturated fats, such as oil, are liquid at room temperature. Saturated fats, such as butter, lard, and some margarine, are solid. Better-quality margarine is mostly unsaturated fat.

Dough containing butter or margarine softens in the oven and spreads quickly. Cookies, for example, are thin and crisp. Shortening cookies stay thicker because they set before the fat melts.

For the recipes in this book, you can use oil, butter, or margarine interchangeably, without losing texture or flavor.

Butter

A Piece of Advice

Because you're using less, cut your butter into small amounts and freeze it so that it won't turn rancid.

Butter has the best flavor of all fats. For cooking, it should always be unsalted. Keep in mind that butter is an animal fat, so it contains cholesterol, and it is saturated. Too much saturated fat leads to excess weight and increased cholesterol in one's blood, which can lead to heart and circulatory problems.

Margarine

A French chemist invented margarine in the late nineteenth century to provide an inexpensive fat for the army of Napoleon III. It is made from a variety of oils and solid fats that are mixed and heated. We are taught that we should only consume margarines with the least amount of saturated fats and the most monounsaturated fats. Choose soft-tub margarine, not hard. The total grams of polyunsaturated and monounsaturated fat should be no more than 6 grams. Never use reduced-calorie margarine for baking. It's always best to keep your fat intake to a minimum and not worry about the type of fat used if you're only using small amounts.

Because certain margarines can be hydrogenated, which turns them into a form of saturated fat, I prefer to use either oil or butter, or a combination of the two.

Vegetable Oils

All vegetable oils have approximately the same amount of calories and fat. Vegetable oils contain no cholesterol. They contain different amounts of polyunsaturated and monounsaturated fats. Oils high in polyunsaturated fats include safflower, sunflower, corn, soy, and cottonseed. These fats can help to lower the "bad" (LDL) cholesterol in one's blood.

Monounsaturated oils are the most desirable. They include canola oil, peanut oil, and olive oil. Most of my recipes call for canola oil.

Vegetable Oil Spray

I like to use vegetable oil spray to coat my baking pans because it is a convenient and low-fat way to keep baked desserts from sticking to the pan. Sprays are usually a mixture of oil and lecithin. I prefer a canola spray for most of my dessert making, but I do use a refrigerated butter-flavored spray when working with phyllo dough. Most of the sprays such as Pam contain canola oil, grain alcohol, and butter flavoring. You can also fill a spray pump bottle halfway with vegetable oil and use this to spray your pans.

Fat Substitutes

I don't buy artificial fat substitutes. Instead, the substitutes I work with are all natural. Using cooked or fresh fruit purées is one technique. Pureed ripe bananas give great texture and flavor to a dessert. Applesauce and purées made of cooked dried fruits such as dates, prunes, apricots, and figs are also wonderful. The rule is that you can successfully reduce the fat in a traditional recipe by as much as 75 percent and substitute the above. You must have some fat for flavor, texture, and shelf life—so don't omit all the fat.

Another technique is to use grated vegetables, such as carrots, beets, and zucchini, which also help to add moisture and texture that fat can add.

Low-fat sour cream, yogurt, and buttermilk also help to maintain texture and flavor, while greatly reducing the fat.

 **A Piece of Advice**

Store overripe bananas in the freezer. When you need them, peel, thaw, and mash or purée. One medium banana will yield ½ cup of banana purée.

Eggs

Eggs are very important in baking. They add richness and nutrition in the form of proteins, vitamins, and minerals; and they add to the texture, color, and flavor of your dessert. They also help bind a batter together: When a cake rises during baking, the proteins in the eggs combine with the proteins in the flour to keep the structure stable.

I like to use some whole eggs in my recipes not only for the taste, but also for the texture. I am careful not to use too many because of the fat and cholesterol they contain. Often I combine 1 whole egg and 2 egg whites in a dessert. The white has no fat or cholesterol, and 1 egg white only contains 15 calories and 3.5 grams of protein. It still helps bind the batter.

If you want to substitute a whole egg with egg whites, use 2 whites for every whole egg. But remember that too many egg whites can make a cake batter too dry. I often use 1 whole egg to balance the flavor and texture.

Don't get too concerned about the fat and cholesterol of the egg yolk because that one yolk, which might have 5 grams of fat, is being divided among the entire dessert, which might produce up to 12 servings.

In many of my recipes, I am able to reduce the fat, calories, and cholesterol greatly not only by adding more egg whites, but also by whipping them with cream of tartar, which helps to stabilize them, and with sugar to sweeten. This combination adds a greater volume to the dessert without adding fat.

Safety of Meringues

I once filmed an episode of my cooking show at an egg factory. The management informed me that only 1 in every 20,000 eggs will contain salmonella bacteria. Chances are this one egg is found in restaurants or establishments that work with a lot of eggs and leave them out at room temperature for hours. Usually in your home, your eggs are refrigerated. I don't worry about salmonella in my home.

If you are concerned, here is what you can do. An egg must be cooked to a temperature of 140°F for 3½ minutes or 150°F for 2 minutes. If you are beating egg whites, you can follow the recipe for Italian meringue. You combine 2 to 3 egg whites with ¼ teaspoon cream of tartar, ¼ cup water, and ¼ to ½ cup sugar in the top of a double boiler. Keep the water simmering and beat the egg white mixture for approximately 6 to 8 minutes or until the meringue is glossy and smooth and holds its shape. Remove it from the double boiler and continue beating for 1 minute. Use a stainless steel bowl, which heats faster than a glass bowl. This meringue is more stable than regular meringues.

Storing Eggs

Egg whites can be refrigerated for up to a month. Egg yolks can be refrigerated in a covered jar for 2 to 3 days. Put a drop of water over the yolks to keep them moist. To freeze leftover eggs, stir and blend them with a few grains of salt or sugar and freeze in ice cube trays. One cube equals one egg. They can be frozen for up to 1 year. Thaw them overnight in the refrigerator before using and never refreeze thawed eggs.

Egg Whites

You're probably using more egg whites than yolks rather than tossing out the yolks, giving them to your dogs, or saving them for a special rich dessert.

Most supermarkets carry powdered egg whites (in the baking aisle) and cartons of refrigerated egg whites (in the dairy section), which can be used in place of fresh egg whites. Refer to the package for substitution equivalents. When reconstituted or brought to room temperature, these products will whip like fresh egg whites.

Egg Substitutes

I prefer not to use chemically based egg substitutes. Different egg substitutes are on the market that try to duplicate the flavor and texture of egg yolks, without the fat and cholesterol. Read the ingredients thoroughly to make sure that it's not a synthetic product. Many use a host of additives and preservatives, including monosodium glutamate (MSG), artificial flavor, coloring, and modified food starches. Some natural products exist that mix 20 percent yolks to 80 percent whites and taste delicious without additives.

Milk and Milk Products

With most milk products, I like to use the low-fat versions. I save a lot of calories, fat, and cholesterol, and, because of all the other flavors in the desserts, I don't feel any taste or texture is missed. Judge for yourself. I always use low-fat milk, either 1 percent or 2 percent milkfat.

Check out the following list for information on calories and fat of specific milk products:

- 1 cup of whole milk, which is 3.5 percent milkfat, has 150 calories and 8 grams of fat.

- 2 percent milk is 125 calories per cup with 5 grams of fat; 1 percent milk has 119 calories and 3 grams of fat; and skim milk has 99 calories and less than ½ gram of fat.

- Buttermilk has 99 calories and 2 grams of fat per cup.

- Evaporated skim milk has 199 calories and 1 gram of fat per cup, compared to evaporated whole milk, which has 338 calories per cup and 19 grams of fat.

- Sweetened condensed milk has 983 calories per cup with 27 grams of fat versus low-fat condensed milk, which has 960 calories and 12 grams of fat per cup.

- Sour cream has 493 calories per cup with 48 grams of fat, compared to low-fat sour cream, which has 360 calories and 28 grams of fat. Fat-free sour cream has 360 calories per cup with 0 fat.

- Low-fat yogurt has 144 calories per cup with 4 grams of fat and non-fat yogurt has 127 calories with 0 fat.

- 2 tablespoons of full-fat cream cheese have 100 calories and 10 grams of fat versus the 50 percent less-fat version, which has 70 calories and 5 grams of fat per 2 tablespoons.

- Ricotta cheese made with whole milk has 432 calories and 32 grams of fat per cup. The lighter version has 340 calories and 20 grams of fat.

- Cottage cheese made with whole milk has 217 calories and 10 grams of fat per cup. Cottage cheese with 1 percent milkfat has 164 calories and 2 grams of fat per cup.

A Piece of Advice

You can make your own buttermilk by stirring 1 tablespoon lemon juice into 1 cup milk and letting it stand for 5 minutes before using it.

Buttermilk

Letting bacteria in regular milk thicken and create a tangy taste makes buttermilk. It creates a fat-like texture without the fat, calories, and cholesterol.

Canned Evaporated Milk

Evaporated milk comes either in whole fat, 2 percent, or skim. It is milk with 60 percent of the water removed. It has a thicker texture than regular milk and has a sweeter flavor. I often use it in place of heavy cream or whole milk in a recipe. It creates a thick, rich texture and a creamier taste. Two tablespoons of regular canned milk contain 40 calories with 2.5 grams of fat. The skim milk version has 25 calories and 0 fat.

Sweetened Condensed Milk

Sweetened condensed milk is a mixture of milk and sugar. The milk is heated until about 60 percent of the water evaporates, producing an extremely sticky and sweet milk, which is perfect for adding thickness and sweetness in desserts. It is approximately 45 percent sugar. Fortunately, it now exists in a low-fat version. Two tablespoons of regular condensed milk contain 130 calories and 3 grams of fat. The low-fat version has 120 calories and only 1.5 grams of fat.

Yogurt

Yogurt is a nutritious, low-fat, low-cholesterol product containing high levels of calcium, protein, and B vitamins. It is made from skim milk that is homogenized, pasteurized, and injected with live bacteria, including the most valuable bacteria, *Lactobacillus acidophilus*. These bacteria feed on the milk sugar to produce lactic acid. The milk is then allowed to ferment in order to coagulate into yogurt and develop that characteristic tangy flavor.

Yogurt has different levels of fat content so be sure to read the label. I usually prefer 1 percent milkfat. For a creamier texture, use 2 percent yogurt. Most recipes call for plain unflavored yogurt. The flavored yogurts are available in 1 percent milkfat or lower. I prefer to use those with sugar rather than a sugar substitute.

Low-fat yogurt is a good substitute for sour cream or heavy cream. I often use it interchangeably with low-fat sour cream.

Sour Cream

Sour cream is basically fermented heavy cream. It's made from 18 percent butterfat cream that has been injected with bacteria and allowed to thicken. Fortunately, low-fat sour creams are now available with anywhere from 5 percent milkfat or lower. I even use fat-free sour cream in my baking and don't know the difference.

Cream Cheese

Cream cheese made from milk must contain at least 33 percent butterfat and has 100 calories per ounce. Fortunately, today there is light cream cheese, which is 25 percent reduced in fat. This is not a considerable difference, but it is good enough to use light cream cheese to highlight my recipes. I will not depend on the cream cheese to make the recipe. For instance, I use a combination of either ricotta or cottage cheese along with a small amount of cream cheese. The light cream cheese gives the dessert a smoother texture and delicate flavor.

Be careful not to use the soft light cream cheese in the tub. It does not have the same properties for baking and should not be substituted. In the United States, there is fat-free cream cheese. I find its taste and texture inferior. Do not bake with it.

Cottage Cheese

Cottage cheese is a fresh, unripened cheese and one of the oldest cheeses known. It is white and has small or large curds.

A Piece of Advice

When using cottage cheese or ricotta cheese in desserts, it must be puréed until smooth for best end results. A food processor makes this easy work.

A wide variety of cottage cheeses is available, from 4 percent milkfat right down to 1 percent milkfat. I find that either 1 percent or 2 percent milkfat is best to use in desserts. If you replace ricotta with cottage cheese, remember to purée it well to smooth the curds. I don't like to use dry curd cottage cheese because the texture is too dry. If you do use it, however, add some milk to smooth it out.

Ricotta Cheese

In North America, ricotta cheese is made from whole milk or a combination of milk and whey. Ricotta cheese that is fresh and unripened has fine, moist clumps and a bland but almost nutty taste. Italian ricotta cheese is made from sheep's milk drained from the curds when provolone cheese is made.

The regular fat content is approximately 10 percent, but now 5 percent milkfat is available. Low-fat ricotta cheese is made from skim milk. I don't find a difference in baking when I use the 5 percent milkfat.

I always look for a creamy smooth ricotta cheese, not one that has been dried and pressed. If you only have the dry-pressed ricotta cheese, add 2 tablespoons water or milk and mix until it is smooth.

Because ricotta is a fresh cheese, it doesn't have a long shelf life and should be used within a few days. It can be frozen for baking purposes, which changes the texture slightly.

I use ricotta cheese in many desserts to replace some of the fat or cream cheese that might have been used traditionally.

Additional Items You'll Want Around

You'll find many of these items vital to making desserts. Besides acting as a tenderizer, fat brings flavor to the dessert. When you take some of that fat out, you need to add flavor back into the product. If you want to add soy to your diet or if you are celebrating Passover, you'll need to look in those chapters for further discussion of those special ingredients.

Soy Products

For the soy section, I used low-fat soy milk, silken tofu, or firm tofu. These products are perfect for those who have milk allergies, are lactose intolerant, are vegetarian, or are kosher. Soy is easy to digest, is low in calories, cholesterol, and sodium, and is high in protein. Look in Chapter 11 for tips on using soy in your desserts.

Passover Products

During Passover, all wheat flour products and any leavening agents must be avoided. There are many excellent products that can be used for baking during Passover. The main substitute for flour is matzo cake meal with a combination of potato starch. Look at Chapter 12 on Passover Desserts for more detail.

Flavorings

Spices, extracts, citrus zest or rind, liqueurs, coffee, and chocolate all add incredible flavor to your desserts, especially low-fat desserts, because you can't just rely on the butter, cream, or pounds of chocolate!

Spices

Once a spice is ground, its aroma fades quickly if it is exposed to air or heat or if it is around for a long period of time. Keep your spices in tightly closed jars and replace them every six months.

Extracts

Pure extracts are the concentrated natural essential oils of the flavoring agent, usually dissolved in alcohol. They are labeled either "pure" or "artificial." Only buy the pure. It's more expensive, but well worth the expense. I find that the artificial extracts usually leave a bitter aftertaste in the dessert.

Zest

Zest, or rind, is the brightly colored part of the peel of a citrus fruit. In my recipes, I call for lemon, lime, or orange rind. The zest contains the fruit's essential flavors. Be careful not to grate too much, or you'll get the white pith under the rind, which will make

 **A Piece of Advice**

One lemon yields approximately 1 tablespoon zest, 1 lime approximately 2 teaspoons, and 1 orange approximately 2 tablespoons.

the dessert bitter. I like to use a citrus zester, a kitchen gadget with a flat metal head containing five tiny sharp-edged holes. It makes grating the fruit easy and safe.

Dried Fruit

I use a wide variety of dried fruits in these desserts: dried dates, prunes, apricots, figs, cherries, raisins, cranberries, and more. They add flavor, and their natural sugar provides sweetness. Dried fruits are also a great nutritional boost because they are a valuable source of vitamins, minerals, and fiber. Be sure to buy pitted dried fruit.

Cooked and puréed dried fruit supplies an alternative to some of the fat used in the recipe. I often replace up to 75 percent of the fat in a recipe with cooked puréed dried fruit. Don't try to replace all the fat with fruit purées, or your dessert will be too dry, lack flavor, and will not have a long shelf life.

 A Piece of Advice

The easiest way to chop dried fruit is with kitchen sheers. I buy dried fruit in bulk and keep it in the freezer.

To make your own fruit purée, cut up the dried fruit and measure 1 cup. Add 1 cup water and cook over medium-low heat, taking care that enough liquid remains to prevent scorching, until the fruit is soft. Then purée the fruit in a food processor until it is smooth.

Nuts

I love to use nuts to highlight my desserts. Keep in mind that they contain a lot of calories and fat, but it is the healthy type of fat—either polyunsaturated or mono-unsaturated fat.

Toasting nuts brings out their flavor. To do this, just add nuts to a dry skillet on a high heat and toast, stirring constantly, for approximately 2 to 3 minutes or until the nuts begin to brown. Then either use them as they are or chop them to the desired consistency in a food processor.

A Piece of Advice

Nuts can go rancid quickly once opened, so I store nuts in a Ziplock freezer bag so that I can take out just what I need.

If a traditional recipe calls for a lot of nuts, try using only 25 percent of the original amount and replacing the remainder with Grape-Nuts, which is a delicious toasted wheat and barley breakfast cereal that is a great low-fat substitute for nuts.

Chocolate and Cocoa

I prefer to buy chocolate in chips rather than in blocks. It is easier to measure and melt. The 1-ounce squares are fine to use, too. The chocolate must be stored in a dry, cool place and can last for years. It might develop a white surface over time, which means that the cocoa butter has risen to the surface. It is still good to use.

Cocoa is made when chocolate liquor is pressed to remove over half the cocoa butter. One ounce of cocoa has approximately 60 calories and 4 grams of fat, compared to chocolate, which has 130 calories and 9 grams of fat per ounce. This is the reason I use cocoa in all my chocolate desserts, and occasionally I highlight the dessert with either chocolate chips or a little melted chocolate.

The following are the different types of chocolate:

◆ Semi-sweet and bitter   Both semi-sweet and bitter chocolates contain vanilla, sugar, and cocoa butter. In my recipes I only use semi-sweet, which has a wonderful sweet and creamy taste and texture.

◆ Milk   Dry milk is added to sweetened chocolate to create milk chocolate. I use milk chocolate chips in some desserts.

◆ White   White chocolate is not true chocolate because it does not contain chocolate liquor and has very little chocolate flavor, but it is nonetheless mouth watering. It contains cocoa butter, sugar, and milk. I like to use white chocolate chips to highlight some of the desserts.

◆ Compound or baking chocolate   This is an artificial chocolate that's best used for decorations. It contains vegetable fat instead of cocoa butter. Don't use it in the recipes, or you'll end up with no chocolate flavor.

A good way to melt chocolate is to place it in a bowl in the microwave and heat at either medium or high (only if you're confident). One ounce of chocolate chips equals 2 tablespoons and will take approximately 1 minute at high or 2 minutes at medium to melt. How long depends on how much cocoa butter the chocolate contains. Always err on the side of being conservative; it is better to add more cooking time than to burn the chocolate, which often cannot be salvaged. Just heat the chocolate until it appears to melt and then stir it until smooth.

One of the safest ways is to use the traditional double boiler method. Place the chocolate in the top of the double boiler over a simmering heat. Remove the top pot when the chocolate begins to melt. Stir until it is smooth.

Be careful when melting white chocolate, which tends to solidify easily and can turn lumpy. I would use a lower heat in the microwave, and use it immediately after melting.

If a little water accidentally touches your melted chocolate, it will seize up. If this happens, add 1 teaspoon vegetable oil and stir quickly. Chocolate can be melted with another liquid such as water or coffee when the correct amount in the recipe is added.

General Techniques for Lowering Fat in Desserts

First, you must know where the fat is coming from. The main sources of fat in desserts are butter, margarine, oil, eggs, sour cream, whipping cream, chocolate, nuts, and cream cheese. Do not try to eliminate the fat entirely. Instead, try to reduce the amount by using those substitutions that will still result in an excellent dessert. Nobody's interested in a dry or rubbery, tasteless dessert that even the raccoons will pass up.

Here is a list of techniques that you can use to lower the fats in your desserts:

♦ You can successfully reduce approximately 50 to 75 percent of the fat in a traditional dessert recipe using substitutions. But because fat is needed in dessert recipes for flavor and texture, you can't eliminate it all.

♦ Good substitutes for fat are plain low-fat yogurt, low-fat sour cream, buttermilk, low-fat evaporated milk, puréed fruits such as bananas or pineapple, or cooked puréed fruits such as dried dates, prunes, apricots, applesauce, and figs. A combination of low-fat ricotta or cottage cheese and a small amount of light cream cheese can replace high-fat cream cheese.

♦ For each whole egg in a recipe, you can use 2 egg whites. I like to keep some of the egg yolks in a recipe for flavor and texture. Too many egg whites will make a cake tough and rubbery.

♦ Chocolate is a high-fat ingredient, so I use unsweetened cocoa, which is much lower in fat and calories than chocolate, for the chocolatey taste. I often use a small amount of semi-sweet chocolate or chocolate chips to further highlight the chocolate taste.

♦ Instead of buttery piecrusts, I use cookie crumb crusts held together mostly with water and just a smidgen of canola oil.

♦ To make delicious crunchy toppings, I use quick-cooking oats or a crunchy cereal like Grape-Nuts to replace the nuts traditionally used. Sometimes a few nuts are kept for taste—always toasted to bring out their full flavor.

Nutrition Watch

Our bodies need some fat for good health—for life itself. The goal is to reduce the saturated fat and cholesterol (the "bad" fats) and to keep the calories from fat no higher than 30 percent of the total calories in our daily diet.

A Piece of Advice

Light or low-fat dairy products taste just as good as their higher-fat cousins in a dessert. Sometimes, to heighten the flavor, I add a little chocolate or nuts back into the recipe.

♦ Instead of using whipping cream for mousses, I use beaten egg whites in combination with a ricotta base, which gives wonderful volume and texture without excess calories and fat. A small amount of gelatin helps to hold the texture of the dessert.

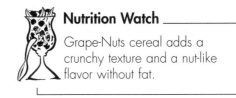

Nutrition Watch

Grape-Nuts cereal adds a crunchy texture and a nut-like flavor without fat.

♦ Using low-fat evaporated milk or low-fat condensed milk instead of heavy cream gives the dessert a creamy, rich consistency.

♦ The proper ingredients make the success of any dessert. Always check the freshness of your ingredients before storing them. If they are stale or old, they won't function properly in your dessert and might in fact destroy it.

Now that we've explored the basic ingredients you be using when making these lower-fat dessert recipes, you'll want to stock your pantry and refrigerator so that you can start making dessert memories for yourself, your family, and your friends.

The Least You Need to Know

♦ A lot of lower-fat ingredient choices exist—make use of them.

♦ Read labels carefully.

♦ Take care when toasting nuts and chocolate or melted chocolate. They can easily burn and ruin the recipe.

♦ Buy in bulk and store dried fruits and nuts in the freezer.

♦ Reduce up to 75 percent of fat in a recipe without the loss of recipe integrity or flavor.

♦ Lower-fat or not, your dessert recipes require proper ingredients for success; rotate your pantry.

Chapter 2

Essential Equipment and Special Cooking Techniques

In This Chapter

- ◆ Invest in the proper equipment
- ◆ Know your oven and its hot spots
- ◆ Measure correctly or you might ruin your dessert
- ◆ Brush up on your basic mixing and folding techniques
- ◆ Proper freezing and defrosting techniques

I've written the recipes in this book with the basic assumption that your kitchen has the essential equipment needed for making the desserts and that you have some cooking experience. Read through the recipe completely before you begin to make sure you have the right equipment and that you understand what you will be doing.

Essential Equipment

As with any other type of recipe, the preparation of desserts is made easier with the right equipment. So, do a kitchen inventory and add the utensils and pans you are missing. Of course, some of your equipment such as wooden spoons, rubber spatulas, knives, zester, and so forth will be doing double duty as you use them in everyday cooking. But some, such as bundt cake pans and pie plates, are dessert specific. If necessary, rearrange your cabinets so that all of that equipment is together and easily accessible.

When choosing new electric appliances such as a food processor or electric mixer, do some homework. Read up on these to see which are rated best and why. Ask around. If a colleague or friend has a particular brand, find out what she or he likes about it and what's not liked. If still in doubt, ask to try it out before you buy. A food processor won't help you make better desserts if you're wary about using it. If necessary, take a class.

Baking Pans

Here is a list of the pans I recommend for your kitchen:

- Three 8-inch round and square metal nonstick pans
- Three 9-inch round and square metal nonstick pans
- One 9-inch by 13-inch nonstick baking pan
- Two 8-inch springform pans
- Two 9-inch springform pans
- Two 10-inch springform pans
- Two 9-inch nonstick Bundt pans
- One 10-inch nonstick tube pan with removable bottom
- Three 9-inch glass pie plates
- Two 15-inch by 10-inch jelly roll pans
- Two 9-inch by 5-inch loaf pans
- Two 8-inch tart pans with removable bottom
- Two 9-inch tart pans with removable bottom
- Eight 6-ounce ovenproof ramekins or custard cups
- Three large nonstick baking sheets
- Small, medium, and large nonstick saucepans
- Small, medium, and large nonstick skillets

A Piece of Advice

Now that you've gotten all of this baking equipment together, you have to find a place to store it. Consider the investment of having a section of lower cabinet shelves converted to slots. Pans won't be stacked one upon another, making it infinitely easier to get at what's needed.

Baking pans can be made of metal or glass, but cakes bake slightly faster in glass pans. I always recommend checking your baked desserts 5 to 10 minutes before the specified baking time because of different qualities of pans and differences in oven temperatures.

Utensils and Special Equipment

Here are some more items for your "need" list:

◆ Assorted mixing bowls

◆ Metal and plastic spatulas and whisks

◆ Knives: chefs, slicing, serrated

◆ Wooden spoons

◆ Measuring cups for liquids and dry ingredients

◆ Measuring spoons

◆ Kitchen scale

◆ Citrus zester

◆ Parchment paper

◆ Wooden or metal cake testers

Electric Equipment

A wide variety of electric mixers are available today. Kitchen Aid is a popular brand and the one I used on my television show. The wire whisk or flat paddle-type beater is used most for all general-purpose cake baking. However, because low-fat baking doesn't require creaming butter, sugar, and eggs, I don't find this piece of equipment very necessary. I generally use a food processor, handheld electric beater, and whisk for all my baking.

I love food processors, but they must be treated with respect. I recommend buying an extra work bowl and metal blade for dessert making. You'll find a food processor indispensable for mixing cakes, chopping nuts, making cookie crumb crusts, and blending mixtures. For these tasks, I only use the metal blade. Wet ingredients cannot be overbeaten, but be careful not to overbeat the flour. When the flour and other dry ingredients are added to the wet, you should use the pulse or on/off feature just until the flour is incorporated. Then, with a wooden spoon, mix until everything is well blended. Overmixing will toughen your cake or cookies.

A Piece of Advice

Handheld electric mixers are great for beating egg whites and mixing ingredients in general.

Ovens

Each oven is different. If I use three different ovens, I have different times and results with each. Know your oven well, whether it's electric, gas, or convection. I have to be honest: I use an electric oven and get great results every time because I always check the dessert 5 to 10 minutes before the specified baking time.

Convection ovens are ideal for baking cheesecakes because they distribute the heat evenly throughout the oven. As a general rule, reduce the recommended temperature by 25°F to 50°F and the recommended baking time by 20 to 30 percent. But you must always check the dessert.

Know your oven's hot spots. I prefer to bake in the middle of the oven to get the best overall results. Have your oven checked every two years because the temperatures can fluctuate with use. Always check your baked dessert 5 to 10 minutes before the time in the recipe is up, just to be sure. If your oven is not properly calibrated, it can affect your dessert. I check my ovens every so often with a Taylor oven thermometer to make sure that they are not off.

Don't open the door before you check the dessert. Cold air can cause a cake to fall or crack. When a cake is done, the color of the top should often be golden brown, the edges should just begin to pull away from the sides, and the dessert cake should appear firm, not loose. Always use a cake tester and insert it into the center. It should come out clean and dry.

A Piece of Advice

For baking, I use a microwave only to defrost, melt, or warm. I don't bake my desserts here. Remember, a microwave oven's efficiency is diminished if your oven's not clean. Keep it spotless!

Special Cooking Techniques for Light Desserts

Before making desserts from this book, read this section on special cooking techniques so that when you get to the recipes you'll know what I'm saying. If you're new to baking, brush up on your skills before you start. You don't need to use ingredients to practice a whisking or folding motion. An empty bowl and a wire whisk or a rubber spatula will suffice.

Measuring

When measuring dry ingredients, use dry measuring cups and always level them off with a knife. When measuring liquid ingredients, use glass measuring cups suited for liquid ingredients. Have the cup sitting on a level surface and at eye level—no looking down into the cup.

Beating, Blending, and Whisking

Beating, blending, and whisking are all ways to mix ingredients rapidly either with a whisk, wooden spoon, or electric mixer. Blending means stirring or mixing ingredients until they are well combined. Whisking means to beat ingredients with a hand-held whisk until the ingredients are mixed completely.

Beating Egg Whites

The trick to beating egg whites properly is to use a clean bowl and clean beaters. Use a hand beater or an electric mixer with a large balloon beater. I find that egg whites at room temperature beat best and to the greatest volume. They tend to separate best when cold. If any foreign material is in your bowl, especially fat (perhaps from a drop of egg yolk) or even water, the egg whites will not beat, no matter how long you beat them.

There is one way you might salvage the egg whites. Try adding 2 teaspoons of lemon juice for every 2 egg whites. This sometimes helps to beat them properly. If this fails, you'll have to try again with fresh egg whites, but with clean and dry bowls and beaters.

To beat egg whites, begin beating them with a bit of cream of tartar until they are foamy; gradually add the sugar and keep beating until the whites are glossy and smooth. Be sure that the sugar granules are completely dissolved in the egg whites, especially for meringues, which will "weep" during baking when undissolved sugar granules melt and ooze out. To test whether the sugar is dissolved, pinch some of the beaten egg whites between your thumb and forefinger. If it feels grainy, the sugar granules are still whole; if it is smooth, the sugar is dissolved. Continue beating until stiff peaks almost form.

You should be able to turn the bowl upside down without the whites losing their shape. At this point, the egg whites are stiff, but not dry. Avoid overbeating the whites, or you'll destroy the texture: The whites will become lumpy and dry, and they'll move with liquid at the bottom of the bowl.

 **A Piece of Advice**

A good way to get rid of any grease in a bowl is to wipe it with a paper towel dampened with white vinegar. Avoid plastic bowls when beating egg whites because they can never be cleaned completely of grease residue.

 **A Piece of Advice**

You can salvage over-beaten whites by adding one more egg white to the beaten ones and beating again. Discard the portion you don't need (1 beaten egg white equals 2 tablespoons) for the recipe and continue.

Folding

Folding egg whites into the batter must be done correctly to maintain volume in the mixture. Use a rubber spatula and insert the lighter mixture into the middle of the bowl containing the heavier mixture; drag it down through the mixture toward you, gently scraping the bottom of the bowl and lifting the mixture from the bottom to the top. Just be careful of overfolding because you can deflate the whites and end up with a poor volume.

Marbleizing Cakes

A marbling is done by alternating different flavored or different colored batter or by blending in various fillings.

Here are three techniques I use, each resulting in a different marbled appearance:

- ◆ Alternate layers of batter and filling. This gives the least marbleized effect.
- ◆ Run a knife through the alternate layers of batter and filling. This gives a moderate marbleized effect.
- ◆ Gently fold the one into the other until just "streaked" with color. This gives the most marbleized effect.

In order to keep the second flavor or filling from sinking to the bottom of the pan, keep in mind that chocolate batter is heavier than vanilla batter and textured fillings are heavier than cake batter. Follow the recipe because I've taken this into consideration when telling you how to form the layers and how to achieve the finished marbled appearance.

Water Bath/Bain-Marie

A water bath (or bain-marie) is a large pan of water into which you place your dessert pan. This allows the dessert to bake more evenly and keeps the texture smoother. It is often used with custards, brûlées, crème caramels, soufflés, and pudding cakes.

When baking cheesecakes, I like to place a pan of water on the lowest rack to make more moisture in the oven, which prevents the cheesecake from cracking and keeps its consistency smooth.

Cooling Cakes

Remove the pan from the oven and set it on a cooling rack away from cold drafts. Always cool a cake completely before icing or placing in the refrigerator or freezer. This method often prevents cracking, especially with cheesecakes.

 **A Piece of Advice**

To avoid damaging cakes with toppings, cover the cake pan snugly with aluminum foil, and then invert the cake onto the rack. When the cake (with foil) is then inverted onto the serving platter and the foil is removed, your topping will still be in place.

Ingredients at Room Temperature

Every cookbook says that ingredients should be at room temperature. I confess that I don't always follow this rule because I'm often in a hurry. But ingredients are easier to incorporate when they are at room temperature.

Freezing Cakes and Desserts

Many desserts can be frozen and stored for later use. After the cake has cooled on the wire rack, wrap it in plastic wrap or foil and place it inside a plastic freezer bag. Make sure that you get as much of the air out of the bag as possible. You can freeze an iced cake by first placing it on a baking sheet in the freezer until the icing is firm, approximately 20 minutes. Then wrap as stated.

Do not freeze custards, brûlées, soufflés, desserts made with cottage cheese, or those with a lot of beaten egg whites.

Thawing Cakes and Desserts

Unfrosted cakes can be defrosted in the oven, which makes them taste freshly baked. They can also be thawed at room temperature or in the refrigerator overnight.

A frosted cake is best defrosted in the refrigerator. Allow at least 12 hours for it to defrost before you plan on serving it.

A Piece of Advice

As with other foods, the smaller the dessert, the quicker it defrosts. If you're in doubt, test to see if it's thawed by inserting a clean straw twig. If the item is still partially frozen, let it finish thawing at room temperature.

The Least You Need to Know

- ◆ Baking pans can be made of metal or glass, but cakes bake slightly faster in glass pans.

- ◆ A food processor is indispensable for mixing cakes, chopping nuts, making cookie crumb crusts, and blending mixtures.

- ◆ Know your oven's hot spots; have your oven checked every two years because the temperatures can fluctuate with use.

- ◆ Use the correct measuring cups—dry for dry ingredients and liquid for liquid ingredients; measure at eye level, not looking down into the measuring cup.

- ◆ Take extra care when folding beaten egg whites into a mixture—overfolding will deflate the egg whites, giving you less volume and poor end results.

- ◆ To avoid freezer burn, properly wrap cakes and desserts for freezing; some desserts should not be frozen—custards, brûlées, soufflés, desserts made with cottage cheese, or those with a lot of beaten egg whites.

Part 2

The Recipes

This part of the book lists more than 190 dessert recipes—each of which has been kitchen tested no less than four times. Only those recipes that meet my strict dessert-lover's standards are included. Just because they are light, doesn't mean that they have a wimpy flavor—in fact, most of the time you'll find these desserts so delicious that no one will believe you when you tell them they are low-fat desserts to enjoy everyday without a guilty conscience.

When testing and developing the recipes, I endeavored to cut out the excessive fat in a recipe but preserve taste. Some of the recipes are new and original; some are makeovers of family recipes or classic favorites. The result is a unique collection of dessert recipes that are low in fat but high in style and taste.

Chapter 3

Layer Cakes

In This Chapter

- ◆ Cakes with poppy seeds
- ◆ Dense chocolate cakes
- ◆ Italian meringue to top it off
- ◆ Rich and creamy cakes

Bake a cake, and you can change a simple meal into a festive occasion. Can you even imagine celebrating a birthday without a layer cake? These cakes are the most simple to make, yet I'm astonished at how many good cooks think they can't bake a good layer cake from scratch. Not so. Follow my recipes carefully and you, too, will become known for your great layer cakes.

These cakes are baked in 8- or 9-inch round or square pans. Always spray the pans with vegetable cooking spray. It doesn't matter if you use glass or metal pans, but check the baking times because glass might cook faster. If you use a different size pan than the recipe calls for, adjust the baking time accordingly. A cake baked in a 8-inch pan takes more time than one in a 9-inch pan—add or subtract 10 minutes per inch.

Always bake cakes in the center of a preheated oven and don't be tempted to open the oven door to see how the cake is doing. If that's done too soon, it can cause the cake to fall. By the time you can smell the cake, take a peak through the oven window. If your oven doesn't have a window, wait until three fourths of the specified baking time has lapsed before opening the door. The cake is done when it begins to pull away from the sides of the pan and a toothpick or tester inserted into the center of the cake comes out clean, without any batter clinging to it.

When you remove the cake from the oven, set the pan on a wire rack to cool, away from drafts. If it looks like any part of the cake is sticking to the sides of the pan, run a small knife around the edge of the cake to prevent it from tearing as it cools. Cool cakes completely before icing. A good way to ice a layer cake is to use a springform: place one layer in the pan, ice the middle, and then place the other layer cake over top. Let the pan sit in the freezer for 10 minutes to set the icing, and then remove the springform pan sides and continue to ice the entire cake.

Italian Meringue Icing is a delicious low-fat icing made by beating egg whites with sugar and water over a very low heat. This process kills any bacteria in the egg whites and makes an icing that lasts much longer and is more stable than regular meringue toppings. Use it with any cake or muffin recipe. You can create a variety of icings by adding flavorings such as almond extract, orange juice concentrate, or cocoa.

Be the first in your neighborhood to dispel the "I can't bake layer cakes from scratch" notion. With my delicious lower-fat recipes, you and your family will be happy you did.

Poppy Seeds in Cakes

Poppy seeds, which are harvested from white poppies, have been used for centuries for baked goods, particularly in central Europe, the Middle East, and India. In pastry, they are frequently ground to a fine meal or, as I have done here, used whole. In these cakes, poppy seeds add a sweet, nutty flavor.

Lemon Poppy Seed Cake with Lemon Curd Filling

Lemon, lemon, and more lemon! That's my definition of divine. Orange juice gives the lemon curd a rich color even though the traditional combination of egg yolks and butter is not used.

Prep time: 20 minutes • Cook time: 18 to 20 minutes • Serves 14

Vegetable cooking spray

Lemon Curd

⅔ cup fresh orange juice

2 tsp. finely grated lemon zest

⅓ cup fresh lemon juice

1 cup granulated sugar

¼ cup cornstarch

Cake

1¼ cups granulated sugar

⅓ cup canola oil

1 large egg

1 large egg white

2 tsp. finely grated lemon zest

¼ cup fresh lemon juice

2 tsp. poppy seeds

1⅓ cups all-purpose flour

1½ tsp. baking powder

½ tsp. baking soda

⅔ cup low-fat sour cream

2 large egg whites

¼ tsp. cream of tartar

3 TB. granulated sugar

Position a rack in the center of the oven and preheat the oven to 350°F. Lightly coat two 9-inch round cake pans with cooking spray.

Make lemon curd: In a small saucepan off the heat, whisk together orange juice, lemon rind and juice, sugar, and cornstarch until smooth. Cook over medium heat, whisking constantly, for 8 minutes or until the mixture is clear, thickened, and bubbling. Transfer to a bowl. Place a piece of plastic wrap directly on surface of lemon curd. Chill the curd in the refrigerator while you prepare the cakes.

Make cake: In a large bowl and using a whisk or electric mixer, beat sugar, oil, egg, egg white, lemon rind, lemon juice, and poppy seeds.

 A Piece of Advice

To get the most volume when beating egg whites, have the egg whites at room temperature and always use a clean and dry bowl and beaters. Any foreign substance will prevent the whites from foaming. If this does happen, try adding 2 teaspoons lemon juice for every 2 egg whites and continue beating.

In another bowl, stir together flour, baking powder, and baking soda. With a wooden spoon, stir the flour mixture into the sugar mixture in batches, alternating with sour cream, just until combined.

In another bowl, using an electric mixer or balloon wire whisk, beat egg whites with cream of tartar until foamy. Gradually add 3 tablespoons sugar and whip until stiff but not dry. Stir one fourth of egg whites into the cake batter. Gently fold in remaining egg whites until just blended. Divide the mixture evenly between the prepared pans.

Nutrition Watch

Lemons are an excellent source of vitamin C, but they start to lose their vitamin power soon after being squeezed.

Bake for 18 to 20 minutes or until a tester comes out clean. Let the pans cool on a wire rack.

Place one cake layer on a cake platter. Spread some curd over top. Place the second cake layer on top of the first and top with the remaining curd.

 Nutrition per Serving

Calories: 270	Fat (total): 6.6 g	Carbohydrate: 49 g
Protein: 3 g	Fat (saturated): 1.1 g	Dietary Fiber: 0.5 g
Cholesterol: 18 mg		

Banana Poppy Seed Layer Cake with Chocolate Icing

Bananas and chocolate make an incredible combination in a dessert. For this cake, use bananas so ripe that they can almost be "poured" from the skin. It will give the cake incredible flavor. I keep my overripe bananas in the freezer so I can thaw them to use in any dish requiring puréed bananas.

Prep time: 20 minutes   •   Cook time: 15 to 20 minutes   •   Serves 14

Vegetable cooking spray

Cake

⅓ cup canola oil

1 large egg

1 large egg white

1 large ripe banana, mashed (about ½ cup)

2 tsp. vanilla extract

1 cup granulated sugar

2 tsp. poppy seeds

1¼ cups all-purpose flour

2 tsp. baking powder

½ tsp. baking soda

⅔ cup plain low-fat yogurt

Icing

2 oz. light cream cheese, softened

1 cup smooth 5% ricotta cheese

1½ cups confectioners' sugar

¼ cup unsweetened cocoa

1 small ripe banana

Position a rack in the center of the oven and preheat the oven to 350°F. Lightly coat two 9-inch round cake pans with cooking spray.

Make cake: In a large bowl and using a whisk or electric mixer, beat oil, egg, egg white, banana, vanilla, sugar, and poppy seeds.

In another bowl, stir together flour, baking powder, and baking soda. With a wooden spoon, stir the dry ingredients into the poppy seed mixture in batches, alternating with yogurt, mixing until just combined. Divide the mixture evenly between the prepared pans.

Bake for 15 to 20 minutes or until a tester inserted in the center comes out dry. Let the pans cool on a wire rack.

Make icing: In a food processor, beat cream cheese, ricotta cheese, confectioners' sugar, and cocoa until the mixture is smooth.

Place one cake layer on a cake platter. Spread icing over the top. Slice the banana and place the slices on the iced cake layer. Place the second cake layer on top and ice the top and sides.

 **A Piece of Advice**

You can substitute low-fat sour cream for the yogurt. Either product comes in 1 percent milkfat or less.

 Nutrition Watch

Bananas are loaded with potassium and are an excellent source of carbohydrates and vitamin C. Enjoy them as a nutritious snack any time of the day.

 **Nutrition per Serving**

Calories: 269   Fat (total): 8.4 g   Carbohydrate: 42 g
Protein: 5.4 g   Fat (saturated): 2.1 g   Dietary Fiber: 1.3 g
Cholesterol: 24 mg

Chocolate Cakes

For lower-fat baking, cocoa is a godsend as it imparts the intense taste of solid chocolate with only a trace of saturated fat. Since you're counting on the cocoa for flavor, use the best brand you can afford. To further the semblance of chocolate, sometimes I add a bit of solid chocolate or a few chocolate chips to a cocoa-based recipe as I did for the Sour Cream Chocolate Cake.

Banana-Chocolate Fudge Layer Cake

I don't know anyone who doesn't love the combination of banana and chocolate. This layer cake is divinely moist and tender—even the icing is lovely and light.

Prep time: 25 minutes • Cook time: 15 to 20 minutes • Serves 12

Vegetable cooking spray

Banana Cake

3 TB. margarine or unsalted butter

⅓ cup granulated sugar

1 large egg

1 large ripe banana, mashed (about ½ cup)

1 tsp. vanilla extract

¾ cup all-purpose flour

½ tsp. baking soda

¼ cup plain low-fat yogurt

Chocolate Fudge Cake

3 TB. margarine or unsalted butter

¾ cup packed light brown sugar

1 large egg

3 TB. unsweetened cocoa

½ cup all-purpose flour

½ tsp. baking soda

½ tsp. baking powder

⅓ cup plain low-fat yogurt

Frosting

1½ cups smooth 5% ricotta cheese

¾ cup confectioners' sugar

¼ cup unsweetened cocoa

½ of a large banana

Place a rack in the center of the oven and preheat the oven to 350°F. Lightly coat two 8-inch round cake pans with cooking spray.

Nutrition Watch

This layer cake is light because it uses puréed bananas and low-fat sour cream to reduce the fat content, and the icing uses low-fat yogurt instead of butter or margarine.

Make banana cake: In a food processor or large bowl using an electric mixer, combine margarine and sugar; mix until smooth. Add the egg, banana, and vanilla and mix until everything is well combined. In a small bowl, stir together flour and baking soda; add this mixture to the banana mixture in batches, alternating with the yogurt, mixing until just combined. Pour the mixture into a prepared pan.

Make chocolate fudge cake: In a large bowl, combine margarine, sugar, and egg and mix until everything is well combined. (The mixture might look curdled.) In a small bowl, stir together cocoa, flour, baking soda, and baking powder. Add the mixture to the sugar mixture, alternating with the yogurt, mixing until just combined. Pour the mixture into a prepared pan.

Bake both cakes for 15 to 20 minutes or until a tester inserted in the center comes out clean.

Make frosting: In a food processor or large bowl, using an electric mixer, beat ricotta cheese, confectioners' sugar, and cocoa until smooth.

 A Piece of Advice

This makes a heavenly birthday cake. It's delicious—and healthier than most. For a special effect, double the recipe and create a four-layer extravaganza. The ricotta cheese gives the frosting its smooth butter-like texture. Eliminate the cocoa for white frosting. You might have to cut back on the confectioners' sugar, though.

Assemble cake: Put the banana cake on a cake platter; top with one fourth of the frosting. Thinly slice the banana and place slices over top. Put the chocolate cake on top and use the remaining frosting to frost the sides and top.

 Nutrition per Serving

Calories: 265   Fat (total): 9 g   Carbohydrate: 39 g
Protein: 8 g   Fat (saturated): 3 g   Dietary Fiber: 2 g
Cholesterol: 42 mg

Sour Cream Chocolate Cake

With its sour cream topping, this rich and dense chocolate cake is definitely for an adult crowd. If the sour cream icing is not to your taste, try the Brownie Fudge Cake (see Chapter 5) with a more traditional chocolate frosting.

Prep time: 15 minutes • Cook time: 20 to 25 minutes • Serves 16

Vegetable cooking spray

Cake

¾ cup packed light brown sugar

½ cup granulated sugar

½ cup unsweetened cocoa powder

⅓ cup canola oil

2 large eggs

½ cup water

2 tsp. vanilla extract

1¼ cups all-purpose flour

1½ tsp. baking powder

½ tsp. baking soda

1 cup low-fat sour cream, at room temperature

Icing

1 cup low-fat sour cream

1¼ cups confectioners' sugar

3 TB. unsweetened cocoa

1½ oz. semi-sweet chocolate or 3 TB. semi-sweet chocolate chips

Position a rack in the center of the oven and preheat the oven to 350°F. Lightly coat a 9-inch square cake pan with cooking spray.

Make cake: In a large bowl and using a whisk or electric mixer, beat brown sugar, sugar, cocoa, oil, eggs, water, and vanilla.

In another bowl, stir together flour, baking powder, and baking soda. With a wooden spoon, stir the dry ingredients into the cocoa mixture in batches, alternating with the sour cream, and mixing until just combined. Pour the mixture into the prepared pan.

Bake for 20 to 25 minutes or until a tester comes out dry. Let the pan cool on a wire rack.

Make icing: In a microwavable bowl, heat the chocolate on high for 30 seconds. Stir until smooth. In a food processor, beat sour cream, confectioners' sugar, cocoa, and melted chocolate together until the mixture is smooth. Pour over the top and sides of the cake.

Nutrition Watch

Substitute low-fat sour cream, 1 percent milkfat or less, for the regular sour cream, which has 14 percent milkfat, in all your recipes. The texture and taste remain excellent.

Nutrition per Serving

Calories: 256
Protein: 3.6 g
Cholesterol: 37 mg

Fat (total): 8.6 g
Fat (saturated): 2.8 g

Carbohydrate: 41 g
Dietary Fiber: 1.7 g

Cakes with Italian Meringue

In traditional cake recipes, sweetened whipped cream is frequently used as a frosting. Italian meringue frosting is a low-fat treat that gives the illusion of whipped cream without the milkfat. It merely requires beating egg whites with sugar and water over very low heat. You can jazz up the frosting by adding a variety of flavorings such as maple, almond or lemon extract, orange juice concentrate, or unsweetened cocoa.

Black Forest Cake with Italian Meringue

From the Black Forest of Germany, this chocolate cake is usually made with butter, flavored with Kirsch, a clear brandy distilled from the juice and pits of cherries, decorated with sour cherries, and then layered and frosted with whipped cream. My version is far lower in fat and calories.

Prep time: 20 minutes • Cook time: 15 minutes • Serves 12

Vegetable cooking spray

Cake

2 tsp. instant coffee granules

¼ cup hot water

¾ cup granulated sugar

⅓ cup canola oil

1 large egg

1 large egg white

1½ tsp. vanilla extract

¾ cup all-purpose flour

⅓ cup unsweetened cocoa

1½ tsp. baking powder

½ tsp. baking soda

¼ tsp. salt

¾ cup low-fat sour cream

Icing

3 large egg whites

¾ cup granulated sugar

¼ cup water

¼ tsp. cream of tartar

¼ cup raspberry jam

¼ cup dried cherries

½ oz. semi-sweet chocolate, grated

Position a rack in the center of the oven and preheat the oven to 350°F. Lightly coat two 8-inch round cake pans with cooking spray.

Make cake: Dissolve instant coffee in hot water and cool.

In a large bowl, using a whisk or electric mixer, beat cooled coffee, sugar, oil, egg, egg white, and vanilla.

 **A Piece of Advice**

I like to use dried cherries because sour cherries are not easy to find and are often not pitted. By all means use sour cherries if they're available, and pit them.

In another bowl, stir together flour, cocoa, baking powder, baking soda, and salt. With a wooden spoon, stir the dry ingredients into the sugar mixture in batches, alternating with the sour cream, and mixing until just combined. Divide the mixture evenly between the prepared pans.

Nutrition Watch _____

Whipped cream contains 35 percent milkfat, compared to this Italian meringue icing, which contains no fat at all. Once you've tried it, you might well choose the meringue as regular icing for all your cakes.

Bake for 15 minutes or until a tester inserted in the center comes out with just a few crumbs clinging to it. Let the pans sit on a wire rack for 10 minutes. Remove the cakes from the pans and set them on racks to cool.

Make icing: In the top of a double boiler or in a glass or metal bowl that fits over the top of a saucepan of simmering water, combine egg whites, sugar, water, and cream of tartar. Place the pan over medium-low heat. With an electric mixer, beat for 8 minutes or until mixture thickens and soft peaks form. Remove pan from heat; beat the mixture for 1 minute or until stiff peaks form.

To assemble: Place one cake layer on a cake platter. On the stovetop or in the microwave, heat the jam; spread it over the cake layer. Sprinkle with dried cherries. Spread some icing over top. Place the second cake layer on top of the first and ice the top and sides. Sprinkle with the grated chocolate.

 Nutrition per Serving

Calories: 253   Fat (total): 8.4 g   Carbohydrate: 41 g
Protein: 3.4 g   Fat (saturated): 1.8 g   Dietary Fiber: 1.1 g
Cholesterol: 23 mg

Coconut Layer Cake with Italian Meringue Icing

I used to avoid coconut desserts because coconut milk contains saturated fat. Now that light coconut milk, which is 75 percent reduced in fat, is available, I even add it where it's not called for!

Prep time: 25 minutes   •   Cook time: 15 minutes   •   Serves 14

Vegetable cooking spray

Cake

1 cup granulated sugar

¾ cup light coconut milk

⅓ cup vegetable oil

2 large eggs

1½ tsp. vanilla extract

1¼ cups all-purpose flour

1½ tsp. baking powder

¼ tsp. salt

5 TB. shredded coconut, toasted (divided use)

2 large egg whites

¼ tsp. cream of tartar

¼ cup granulated sugar

Icing

3 large egg whites

¾ cup granulated sugar

¼ cup water

¼ tsp. cream of tartar

Position a rack in the center of the oven and preheat the oven to 350°F. Lightly coat two 9-inch round cake pans with cooking spray.

Make cake: In a large bowl and using a whisk or electric mixer, beat sugar, coconut milk, oil, eggs, and vanilla.

In another bowl, stir together flour, baking powder, salt, and 2 tablespoons toasted coconut. With a wooden spoon, stir the dry ingredients into the coconut milk mixture, mixing until just combined.

In a separate bowl, beat egg whites with cream of tartar until they are foamy. Gradually add sugar, beating until stiff peaks form. Stir one fourth of egg whites into the cake batter. Gently fold in the remaining egg whites. Divide the mixture evenly between the prepared pans.

Bake for approximately 15 minutes or until a tester inserted into the center comes out dry. Let the pans cool on a wire rack.

Nutrition Watch

Coconut is one of the few fruits that contain saturated fat, so use it sparingly to highlight a dessert. That's why light coconut milk is a great idea in baking and cooking.

A Piece of Advice

Toasting heightens the flavor of coconut. To toast it, brown in a dry skillet over a high heat for approximately 2 to 3 minutes, stirring constantly. Be careful because it can quickly go from light golden brown to burnt.

Make icing: In the top of a double boiler or in a glass or metal bowl over the top of a saucepan of simmering water, combine egg whites, sugar, water, and cream of tartar. Place over medium heat. With an electric mixer, beat for 6 to 8 minutes or until thickened and soft peaks form. Remove from heat; and beat for 1 minute or until stiff peaks form. Stir in 2 tablespoons toasted coconut.

Place one cake layer on a cake platter. Spread some icing over top. Place the second cake layer on top of the first and ice the top and sides. Sprinkle the top with remaining toasted coconut.

 **Nutrition per Serving**

Calories: 238   Fat (total): 7.8 g   Carbohydrate: 38 g
Protein: 3.2 g   Fat (saturated): 2.2 g   Dietary Fiber: 0.7 g
Cholesterol: 30 mg

Dreamy, Rich, and Creamy

There's no doubt that almost everyone loves the smooth, creamy texture and mild flavor of cream cheese. It's marvelous in frostings and when put into the cake it gives the crumb a smooth, velvety texture. Regular cream cheese, however, ranges from 35 to 40 percent fat. To lower the fat, I use a small amount of low-fat cream cheese, along with smooth 5 percent ricotta cheese for a rich, creamy texture.

Orange Layer Cake with Cream Cheese Frosting

A dream of a cake with a creamy cheese-based icing, light and fluffy as a cloud. Frozen orange juice concentrate gives the cake its intense orange flavor. I keep small cans of it in my freezer for making cakes like this.

Prep time: 20 minutes   •   Cook time: 15 to 20 minutes   •   Serves 14

Vegetable cooking spray

Cake

1 cup granulated sugar

⅓ cup canola oil

2 large eggs

⅓ cup orange juice concentrate

1 TB. finely grated orange zest

1¼ cups all-purpose flour

1½ tsp. baking powder

1 tsp. baking soda

1 cup plain low-fat yogurt

Frosting

1¼ cups smooth 5% ricotta cheese

2½ oz. light cream cheese, softened

¾ cup granulated sugar

1½ TB. orange juice concentrate

2 tsp. finely grated orange rind

Position a rack in the center of the oven and preheat the oven to 350°F. Lightly coat two 9-inch round cake pans with cooking spray.

Make cake: In a large bowl and using a whisk or electric mixer, beat sugar, oil, eggs, orange juice concentrate, and orange zest.

In another bowl, stir together flour, baking powder, and baking soda. With a wooden spoon, stir dry ingredients into the sugar mixture in batches, alternating with yogurt, mixing until just combined. Divide the mixture evenly between the prepared pans.

Nutrition Watch

Regular cake frosting contains mostly butter, lard, or vegetable shortening—2 tablespoons of frosting have 150 calories and 8 grams of fat. The frosting for this cake is made from 5 percent ricotta cheese and a small amount of low-fat cream cheese, so the fat and calorie content is very low.

 **A Piece of Advice**

When zesting an orange or lemon, be sure not to grate the white pith beneath the brightly colored layer of the peel. This zest contains all of the essential oils or flavor of the peel. The pith is bitter and will destroy the taste of your dessert.

Bake for 15 to 20 minutes or until a tester comes out dry. Let pans cool on a wire rack.

Make frosting: In a food processor, combine ricotta cheese, cream cheese, sugar, orange juice concentrate, and orange zest; purée until smooth. Transfer the mixture to a bowl and cover with plastic wrap. Chill until the cakes are fully cooled.

To assemble: Place one cake layer on a cake platter. Spread some frosting over top. Place the second cake layer on top of the first and frost the top and sides.

 Nutrition per Serving

Calories: 263
Protein: 6.2 g
Cholesterol: 41 mg

Fat (total): 8.5 g
Fat (saturated): 2.4 g

Carbohydrate: 40 g
Dietary Fiber: 0.4 g

Boston Cream Pie

Boston Cream Pie came to North America in the mid-1850s when a German pastry chef, who worked at the Parker House Hotel in Boston, made his version of a popular cake known as pudding cake pie. Traditionally this delicious "pie" is made with sponge cake layers, a filling of vanilla custard, and a thin layer of chocolate icing, making a very rich cake filled with fat and calories. My version uses a combination of ricotta, low-fat cream cheese, and orange to heighten the heavenly flavor.

Prep time: 20 minutes • Cook time: 12 to 15 minutes • Serves 12

Vegetable cooking spray

Custard

½ cup smooth 5% ricotta cheese

2 oz. light cream cheese

⅓ cup granulated sugar

2 TB. thawed frozen orange juice concentrate

2 tsp. grated orange zest

Cake

1 cup granulated sugar

¼ cup canola oil

1 large egg

2 large egg whites

1½ tsp. vanilla extract

1¼ cups all-purpose flour

2 tsp. baking powder

⅛ tsp. salt

¾ cup plain low-fat yogurt

Glaze

3 TB. semi-sweet chocolate chips

1½ TB. water

Position a rack in the center of the oven and pre-heat the oven to 350°F. Lightly coat two 9-inch round cake pans with cooking spray.

Make custard: In a food processor, combine ricotta, cream cheese, sugar, orange juice concentrate, and rind. Purée until the mixture is smooth. Chill while you prepare the cake.

Make cakes: In a large bowl and using a whisk or electric mixer, beat sugar, oil, egg, egg whites, and vanilla. In another bowl, stir together flour, baking powder, and salt. With a wooden spoon, stir the dry ingredients into the sugar mixture in batches, alternating with the yogurt, and mixing until just combined. Divide the mixture evenly between the prepared pans.

Bake for 12 to 15 minutes or until a tester inserted in the center comes out dry. Let the pans cool on a wire rack.

Place one cake layer on a cake platter. Spread the chilled custard over top. Place the second cake layer on top of the first.

 Nutrition Watch

Custards contain egg yolks, butter, and cream, all loaded with saturated fat. This is the fat that has been linked to heart disease, certain types of cancer, and stroke. It's healthier to use lower-fat versions for the custard like this one.

 A Piece of Advice

If you're in a hurry, you can make the custard while the cakes are cooking. Chill it for a few minutes in the freezer, stirring occasionally.

To make the glaze: Place the chocolate chips and water in a microwave safe dish. Microwave on high for 20 seconds or just until the chocolate begins to melt. Stir until it is smooth and pour over top in a marble design. Serve the cake immediately or chill until ready to serve.

 Nutrition per Serving

Calories: 257　　　Fat (total): 8 g　　　Carbohydrate: 41 g
Protein: 5.2 g　　　Fat (saturated): 2.3 g　　Dietary Fiber: 0.6 g
Cholesterol: 24 mg

The Least You Need to Know

- ◆ Luscious doesn't have to mean high in fat and cholesterol. With my precise use of low-fat cream cheese, ricotta cheese, and yogurt, excess eggs, heavy cream, and butter are not needed—and there's no loss of flavor or texture.

- ◆ Tiny poppy seeds add a sweet, nutty flavor to lower-fat cakes.

- ◆ Chocolate is high in saturated fat, but I get the intense taste of chocolate flavor with only a trace of saturated fat by using cocoa powder. Because you're counting on it for flavor, use the best cocoa powder that you can afford.

- ◆ Italian Meringue, made from egg whites, sugar, and water, makes a great substitute for whipped cream frosting—without a drop of fat.

- ◆ Coconut is also high in saturated fat, but light coconut milk is not and it adds wonderful coconut flavor to my baking. After you've tried this wonderful product, you're likely to find yourself adding it to recipes when it's not called for—just for its lovely coconut flavor.

Chapter 4

Cheesecakes

In This Chapter

- ◆ Luscious fruit-swirled cheesecakes
- ◆ New York–style cheesecakes
- ◆ Decadent creamy cheesecakes
- ◆ Miscellaneous cheesecakes

Cheesecakes have been around for centuries, popular in Europe long before here in the United States. Just saying the word "cheesecake" conjures up the idea of something creamy, decadent, and beloved. Cheesecakes are the most sensuous of desserts, but because they are traditionally made with cream cheese—which is at least 33 percent butterfat and contains one hundred calories per ounce—how do they fit into light desserts? Can you really remove all of that butterfat and still have a rich, creamy cheesecake? I emphatically say "yes!"

There are two main styles of cheesecake: what is commonly called New York style, made with cream cheese, and Italian or curd cheese style, made with ricotta cheese and occasionally, cottage cheese. Fortunately, we have healthier dairy products at our fingertips so now you can make guilt-free cheesecakes in any style you want—with a smooth, velvety, dense texture or with a lighter and fluffier texture.

In reduced-fat cheesecakes, I've replaced regular cream cheese with low-fat cream cheese, sometimes adding low-fat ricotta or cottage cheese. Read each recipe carefully before you start to make sure that you have all the required ingredients and substitutions, preferably at room temperature. This is particularly true if the recipe calls for low-fat cream cheese, as lumps are very difficult to eliminate once they have formed. However, if you're rushed and don't have time to set everything out beforehand, just be sure to beat the ingredients thoroughly to get the desired smooth consistency. Preheat your oven to the correct temperature and position the rack in the center of the oven.

Because both ricotta and cottage cheese have a grainy texture, it's necessary to remove as much of the whey (liquid) from the cheese as possible and then purée the dry curds in a food processor or blender. A hand or electric beater does not always make a smooth batter. I also use fewer eggs and more whites in proportion to yolks to further reduce the fat content. When sour cream is called for, in the cake or as a topping, I use low-fat or nonfat sour cream or substitute drained plain nonfat yogurt. Even with all these lower-fat substitutions, these recipes will be among the higher calories-from-fat recipes in this book.

Traditionally cheesecakes are baked in a springform pan, which is a metal pan with a removable bottom. Most of my recipes call for a 9-inch pan. If you must use a different size, you'll need to adjust the cooking time accordingly—for a smaller pan, add 10 minutes per inch, and for a larger pan, subtract 10 minutes per inch. Because springform pans are not watertight, set the pan on a baking sheet to catch any liquid that might leak out during baking.

Up until the time when the beaten egg whites are added to cheesecake batter, don't worry about over mixing; keep processing the batter, scraping down the sides until the batter looks smooth and velvety. Egg whites give cheesecakes a light and fluffy texture. When beating them, always be sure that the bowl and beater are totally clean or they will not foam properly. If that should happen, try adding 2 teaspoons lemon juice for every 2 egg whites. If they still don't set up properly, start over. Add the beaten egg whites into the rest of the batter slowly in stages, gently folding just enough to incorporate them. Over mixing at this point can cause the delicate structure of the beaten egg whites to collapse and produce a soggy cheesecake.

Cheesecakes are notorious for cracking. Cracks occur because the cake gives off a considerable amount of moisture as it bakes. If it gives off too much too quickly, the cake can crack. To help solve this problem, increase the humidity of the oven by placing a pan of water on the bottom rack in the oven. Never open the oven door until the cheesecake is almost done. Do not place a cheesecake fresh out of the oven in a cool or drafty place. To prevent cracking during the cooling process, run a knife around the sides of the pan to release the tension and allow the cake to pull away freely as it contracts. If all else fails and your cheesecake does crack, toss a cup of berries or some sliced fruit on top of the cake to hide the flaw.

A cheesecake is done when the 2-inch diameter at the center is slightly loose. If it bakes until it is firm in the center, the cheesecake will be too dry. Over baking can also cause the cheesecake to crack. Remember, the cake will harden as it cools. After the cheesecake is baked, let it cool to room temperature and then chill it for at least 2 hours. Cheesecake tastes best when it is thoroughly chilled.

A Piece of Advice

Cutting the cake—here's a trade secret. Use a long strand of dental floss. Waxed or plain is fine—just no mint flavor, please. Stretch the floss taut and gently press it through the cake. Release one end and pull the floss out. Alternatively, use a cake knife, dipping the knife in hot water between slices.

You can freeze cheesecakes that do not contain whipped egg whites. Wrap the cake carefully in plastic wrap or foil and place it in a freezer bag for up to three months. Defrost in the refrigerator before serving.

Take your pick. They're all here—a low-fat cheesecake for every taste, whether you crave chocolate or you'd rather have fruit and cream or any one of the other thirteen exotic flavors.

Give It a Swirl

Marbled cheesecakes not only have a striking appearance, but they offer a taste of two or more different flavors in every forkful. Don't strive for perfection when you're making the swirls; it's the randomness of the marbleized design that makes it so attractive.

Mango Swirl Cheesecake

Cheesecakes with fruit are luscious. In this version, a seductive purée of mango is swirled through the cheesecake. If you love mangos like I do, serve the cheesecake with Mango Coulis for even more mango flavor.

Prep time: 15 minutes • Cook time: 55 minutes • Chill time: at least 2 hours • Serves 16

Vegetable cooking spray

Purée

1 large half-ripe mango, peeled and pitted

Crust

1¾ cups graham cracker crumbs

2 TB. granulated sugar

3 TB. water

1 TB. honey

1 TB. canola oil

Filling

2 cups 2% cottage cheese, drained

4 oz. light cream cheese, softened

1 cup granulated sugar

¾ cup low-fat sour cream

1 large egg

2 large egg whites

¼ cup all-purpose flour

2 tsp. finely grated orange zest

1½ tsp. vanilla extract

Position a rack in the center of the oven and preheat the oven to 350°F. Lightly coat a 9-inch springform pan with cooking spray.

Nutrition Watch

Mangoes are rich in vitamins A, C, and D, as well as high in potassium and dietary fiber. Fresh mangoes are in season from May to September, and thanks to overnight air freight, imported mangoes are frequently available in stores throughout the rest of the year. Mango purée can be found fresh in some natural food stores, as well as Indian and Mexican markets. Also look for frozen mango purée in many supermarkets.

Make purée: In a food processor or blender, purée mango. Set aside.

Make crust: In a bowl, stir together graham crumbs, sugar, water, honey, and oil until well mixed. Pat the mixture onto the bottom and sides of the prepared pan.

Make filling: In the clean work bowl of a food processor, combine cottage cheese, cream cheese, sugar, sour cream, egg, egg whites, flour, orange zest, and vanilla; process until smooth. Pour the mixture into the crust. Dollop puréed mango over the top of the batter and, using a knife, swirl it around to create a marbleized effect.

Place a pan of hot water on the bottom rack of the oven. Set the cheesecake on a baking sheet and bake for 55 to 60 minutes or until it is slightly loose at the center. Remove the cake from the oven and run a knife around the edge of the cake. Let the cake cool in its pan on a wire rack to room temperature. Chill.

To unmold the cake, run the blade of a long thin knife between the top edge of the cake and the pan. Loosen the spring and carefully lift off the sides, leaving the cake on the pan bottom. Slice and serve.

 **A Piece of Advice**

You can replace cottage cheese with ricotta cheese for a creamier texture. Be sure to process it well to get rid of any lumps.

 Nutrition per Serving

Calories: 198
Protein: 7 g
Cholesterol: 23 mg

Fat (total): 5.1 g
Fat (saturated): 2.1 g

Carbohydrate: 3.1 g
Dietary Fiber: 0.6 g

Cranberry Swirl Cheesecake

For best flavor and texture, use canned, whole-berry cranberry sauce—not the jellied version— for this colorful cake. When I tried whole cranberries, they fell to the bottom of the pan and provided too tart a flavor. This cheesecake will brighten any holiday feast.

Prep time: 15 minutes • Cook time: 45 minutes • Chill time: at least 2 hours • Serves 16

Vegetable cooking spray

Purée

½ cup canned whole-berry cranberry sauce

Crust

2 cups vanilla wafer crumbs

1 TB. canola oil

2 TB. water

Filling

1½ cup smooth 5% ricotta cheese

3 oz. light cream cheese, softened

⅔ cup low-fat sour cream

1 large egg

2 tsp. vanilla extract

¾ cup granulated sugar

3 TB. all-purpose flour

Position a rack in the center of the oven and preheat the oven to 350°F. Lightly coat a 9-inch springform pan with cooking spray.

Make purée: In a food processor or blender, purée cranberry sauce. Set aside.

Make crust: In a bowl, stir together wafer crumbs, oil, and water until well mixed. Pat the mixture onto the bottom and sides of the prepared pan.

 Nutrition Watch

Ricotta is a good source of calcium and now comes in 5 percent milkfat. I use it in place of cream cheese, so I can reduce the amount of fat by as much as half.

A Piece of Advice

Vanilla wafers come whole in a box. To make the crumbs, place the wafers in the food processor and pulse until they are finely ground; then you can measure them. It will take about 52 Sunshine Vanilla Wafers or 62 Keebler Golden Vanilla Wafers or 62 Nabisco Nilla wafers to make 2 cups crumbs. If you substitute graham cracker crumbs, add 2 tablespoons sugar.

Make filling: In the clean work bowl of a food processor, combine ricotta cheese, cream cheese, sour cream, egg, vanilla, sugar, and flour; process until smooth. Pour the mixture into the crust. Dollop puréed cranberry sauce over the top of the batter and use a knife to swirl it around to create a marbleized effect.

Place a pan of hot water on the bottom rack of the oven. Set the cheesecake on a baking sheet and bake for 45 minutes or until it is slightly loose at the center. Remove the cheesecake from the oven and run a knife around the edge of the cake. Let the cake cool in its pan on a wire rack to room temperature. Chill.

To unmold the cake, run the blade of a long thin knife between the top edge of the cake and the pan. Loosen the spring and carefully lift off the sides, leaving the cake on the pan bottom. Slice and serve.

Nutrition per Serving

Calories: 187
Protein: 4.5 g
Cholesterol: 28 mg

Fat (total): 6.8 g
Fat (saturated): 2.8 g

Carbohydrate: 27 g
Dietary Fiber: 0.4 g

Apricot Swirl Cheesecake

When dried fruit is rehydrated, it makes a wonderful purée. Here dried apricots lend their intense flavor to this incredibly delicious cheesecake.

Prep time: 25 minutes • Cook time: 50 to 55 minutes • Chill time: at least 2 hours •
Serves 16

Vegetable cooking spray

Apricot Swirl

3 oz. (½ cup) chopped dried apricots

1 cup water

3 TB. granulated sugar

Crust

1¾ cups graham cracker crumbs

3 TB. granulated sugar

¼ cup water

1 TB. canola oil

Filling

2 cups 2% cottage cheese

4 oz. light cream cheese, softened

½ cup low-fat sour cream

1 large egg

1 tsp. vanilla extract

1 tsp. finely grated lemon zest

1 TB. fresh lemon juice

1 cup granulated sugar (divided use)

¼ cup all-purpose flour

2 large egg whites

¼ tsp. cream of tartar

Position a rack in the center of the oven and preheat the oven to 350°F. Lightly coat a 9-inch springform pan with cooking spray.

Make apricot swirl: In a small saucepan, combine apricots, water, and sugar. Bring to a boil. Reduce heat to medium low and simmer for 12 to 15 minutes or until apricots are tender. In a food processor or blender, purée the mixture until smooth. Set aside.

Make crust: In a bowl, stir together graham crumbs, sugar, water, and oil until combined. Pat the mixture onto the bottom and sides of the prepared pan.

Make filling: In a clean work bowl of a food processor, combine cottage cheese, cream cheese, sour cream, egg, vanilla, lemon zest, lemon juice, ¾ cup sugar, and flour; process until smooth. Transfer to a large bowl and set aside.

In a clean bowl and using an electric mixer, beat egg whites with the cream of tartar until foamy. Gradually add remaining ¼ cup sugar, continuing to beat until stiff peaks form. Gently fold the egg white mixture into the cheese mixture just until combined. Pour the mixture into the prepared crust. Dollop puréed apricot over the top of the batter and swirl it around using a knife.

 A Piece of Advice

Ricotta can replace cottage cheese for a creamier, denser cake. Buy dried apricots in bulk and keep them in the freezer; you can use scissors to cut them into pieces. If you can find them, buy Turkish dried apricots, which have a pure, tart flavor. They are available at most specialty food stores, natural food stores, and Middle Eastern markets.

Nutrition Watch

Apricots are rich in vitamin A and are a valuable source of iron and calcium. They are a concentrated form of energy, so they make a great energizing snack anytime.

Place a pan of hot water on the bottom rack of the oven. Set the cheesecake pan on a baking sheet and bake for 50 to 55 minutes or until it is slightly loose at the center. Remove the cake from the oven and run a knife around the edge of the cake. Let the cake cool in its pan on a wire rack to room temperature. Chill.

Unmold the cake by running the blade of a long thin knife between the top edge of the cake and the pan. Loosen the spring and carefully lift off the sides, leaving the cake on the pan bottom. Slice and serve.

Nutrition per Serving

Calories: 211   Fat (total): 4.8 g   Carbohydrate: 35 g
Protein: 7 g   Fat (saturated): 1.9 g   Dietary Fiber: 0.9 g
Cholesterol: 2.2 mg

Peanut Butter Chocolate Swirl Cheesecake

Your little angels will leave the peanut butter and jam sandwiches behind after they try this version of cheesecake. What a combination! Serve it with my Chocolate Sauce (see Chapter 16).

Prep time: 20 minutes   •   Cook time: 45 to 50 minutes   •   Chill time: at least 2 hours   •
Serves 16

Vegetable cooking spray

Crust

1¾ cups chocolate wafer crumbs

1 TB. honey

1 TB. canola oil

2 TB. water

Filling

2 cups smooth 5% ricotta cheese

¾ cup low-fat sour cream

3 oz. light cream cheese, softened

1 large egg

⅓ cup smooth peanut butter

2 tsp. vanilla extract

⅓ cup + 3 TB. granulated sugar (divided use)

3 TB. all-purpose flour

2 large egg whites

¼ tsp. cream of tartar

Chocolate Swirl

¼ cup semi-sweet chocolate chips

1 TB. water

Position a rack in the center of the oven and preheat the oven to 350°F. Lightly coat a 9-inch springform pan with cooking spray.

Make crust: In a bowl, stir together wafer crumbs, honey, oil, and water until mixed. Pat the mixture onto the bottom and sides of the prepared pan.

Make filling: In a food processor, combine ricotta, sour cream, cream cheese, egg, peanut butter, vanilla, ⅔ cup sugar, and flour; process until smooth. Transfer the mixture to a large bowl.

In another bowl and using an electric mixer, beat egg whites with the cream of tartar until foamy. Gradually add the remaining 3 tablespoons sugar, continuing to beat until stiff peaks form. Gently fold the egg mixture into the cheese mixture just until blended and pour into the prepared crust.

Make chocolate swirl: In a microwavable bowl, heat chocolate chips with water on high for 40 seconds. Stir until smooth. Dollop chocolate over the top of batter and, using a knife, swirl it around.

Place a pan of hot water on the bottom rack of the oven. Place the cheesecake pan on a baking sheet and bake for 45 to 50 minutes or until it is slightly loose at the center. Remove the cake from the oven and run a knife around the edge of the cake. Let the cake cool in its pan on a wire rack to room temperature. Chill.

To unmold the cake, run the blade of a long thin knife between the top edge of the cake and the pan. Loosen the spring and carefully lift off the sides, leaving the cake on the pan bottom. Slice and serve.

Nutrition Watch

Peanut butter is a great source of protein when combined with a grain, as in bread—perfect for children who don't consume enough protein in their diets. Although it's high in fat, it contains monounsaturated fat, which is the healthy fat. Always buy natural smooth peanut butter. The commercial brands can have hydrogenated fat and added sugar.

Nutrition per Serving

Calories: 246
Protein: 7.7 g
Cholesterol: 29 mg

Fat (total): 11 g
Fat (saturated): 4.1 g

Carbohydrate: 29 g
Dietary Fiber: 1 g

Miniature Raspberry Swirl Cheesecakes

These individual desserts are a wonderful way to indulge your guests. I love to serve them with fresh fruit and Raspberry Coulis (see Chapter 16). When fresh raspberries are in season, use a few to decorate each cake.

Prep time: 15 minutes • Cook time: 20 to 25 minutes • Chill time: at least 2 hours • Serves 12

1¼ cups smooth 5% ricotta cheese

1¼ cups 2% milkfat cottage cheese

⅓ cup low-fat sour cream

1 large egg

2 tsp. vanilla extract

1 cup granulated sugar

¼ cup all-purpose flour

⅓ cup raspberry jam

1/3 cup fresh raspberries for garnish (optional)

 **A Piece of Advice**

Cottage cheese makes these cheesecakes light and fluffy. Process it well for a smooth batter, and be sure to place a large pan filled with water in the oven to prevent the cakes from falling during baking, as well as to keep them moist.

Nutrition Watch

Use 2 percent cottage cheese, rather than 1 percent, for better flavor and texture. Because the recipe is divided into 12 cheesecakes, the calories and fat won't vary much.

Position a rack in the center of the oven and preheat the oven to 350°F. Line one 12-cup muffin tin with paper muffin liners.

In a food processor, combine ricotta cheese, cottage cheese, sour cream, egg, vanilla, sugar, and flour; process until smooth. Divide the mixture among the prepared muffin cups. Place a dollop of raspberry jam in each muffin cup and use a knife to swirl it around gently.

Set the muffin tin in a larger pan. Pour enough hot water into the larger pan to come halfway up the sides of the muffin cups.

Bake for 20 to 25 minutes or just until the muffins are set. Remove the muffin tin from its water bath. Let the tin cool on a wire rack to room temperature. Chill. Unmold onto serving plates. If using, sprinkle the cakes with a few fresh raspberries and serve.

 **Nutrition per Serving**

Calories: 171
Protein: 7.2 g
Cholesterol: 36 mg

Fat (total): 3.4 g
Fat (saturated): 2 g

Carbohydrate: 28 g
Dietary Fiber: 0.6 g

New York Style

The richest of the traditional cheesecakes, New York cheesecake is made of pounds of cream cheese, lots of eggs and extra egg yolks, sugar, and heavy cream, plus flavoring. No wonder that a slice of the famous Lindy's New York cheesecake contained over 500 calories, 40 grams of fat (over half of them saturated fat), and around 230 milligrams of cholesterol. The characteristic texture of a New York–style cheesecake is dense, smooth, and velvety.

New York–Style Mocha Cheesecake

Traditional New York cheesecake is dense, heavy, and oh so rich! Yes, it is delicious, but it is also loaded with calories, fat, and cholesterol. Thanks to beaten egg whites, this mocha version is so light that you'll feel free to treat yourself to this cheesecake more often. Serve it with a fruit coulis or chocolate sauce (see Chapter 16).

Prep time: 20 minutes   •   Cook time: 55 to 60 minutes   •   Chill time: at least 2 hours   •   Serves 16

Vegetable cooking spray

Crust

1 cup chocolate wafer crumbs

¾ cup graham cracker crumbs

3 TB. granulated sugar

3 TB. water

1 TB. canola oil

Filling

1 TB. instant coffee granules

2 TB. hot water

1½ cups smooth 5% ricotta cheese

3 oz. light cream cheese, softened

2 large eggs, separated

1½ tsp. vanilla extract

¾ cup plain low-fat yogurt

1 cup + 3 TB. sugar (divided use)

¼ cup all-purpose flour

¼ teaspoon cream of tartar

Chocolate Swirl

¼ cup semi-sweet chocolate chips

1 TB. hot water

Position a rack in the center of the oven and preheat the oven to 350°F. Lightly coat a 9-inch springform pan with cooking spray.

Make crust: In a bowl, stir together wafer crumbs, graham crumbs, sugar, water, and oil until mixed. Pat the mixture onto the bottom and sides of the prepared pan.

Make filling: Dissolve coffee granules in hot water. Place it in a food processor along with ricotta cheese, cream cheese, egg yolks, vanilla, yogurt, 1 cup sugar, and flour; process until smooth. Transfer the mixture to a large bowl.

In another bowl and using an electric mixer, beat egg whites with cream of tartar until foamy. Gradually add remaining 3 tablespoons sugar, continuing to beat until stiff peaks form. Gently fold the egg white mixture into the cheese mixture just until blended. Pour it into the prepared crust.

Nutrition Watch

With the amount of cheese and yogurt in this recipe, it is a good source of calcium and protein. Dessert can be nutritious!

A Piece of Advice

If you don't have instant coffee on hand, use 2 tablespoons strong brewed coffee left over from breakfast.

Make chocolate swirl: In a microwavable bowl, heat chocolate chips with water on high for 40 seconds. Stir the mixture until smooth. Place dollops over top of the filling and use a knife to swirl it around.

Place a pan of hot water on the bottom rack of the oven. Set the cheesecake pan on a baking sheet and bake for 55 to 60 minutes or until it is slightly loose at the center. Run a butter knife around the edge of the cake. Let it cool on a wire rack until it is room temperature. Chill.

To unmold the cake, run the blade of a long thin knife between the top edge of the cake and the pan. Loosen the spring and carefully lift off the sides, leaving the cake on the pan bottom. Slice and serve.

Nutrition per Serving

Calories: 218   Fat (total): 7 g   Carbohydrate: 33 g
Protein: 5.8 g   Fat (saturated): 2.9 g   Dietary Fiber: 0.6 g
Cholesterol: 37 mg

New York–Style Cheesecake with Glazed Strawberry Topping

This is one of my favorite cheesecake recipes. It's light and airy yet tastes rich and satisfying. Serve this with Strawberry Coulis (see Chapter 16).

Prep time: 20 minutes • Cook time: 55 to 60 minutes • Chill time: at least 2 hours • Serves 16

Vegetable cooking spray

Crust

1¾ cups vanilla wafer crumbs

2 TB. granulated sugar

2 TB. water

1 TB. margarine or unsalted butter

Filling

1½ cups smooth 5% ricotta cheese

1 cup plain low-fat yogurt

4 oz. light cream cheese, softened

2 large eggs, separated

1½ tsp. vanilla extract

1 cup + 2 TB. sugar (divided use)

¼ cup all-purpose flour

⅛ tsp. salt

¼ tsp. cream of tartar

Topping

2 cups sliced fresh strawberries

2 TB. red currant jelly or apple jelly

Position a rack in the center of the oven and preheat the oven to 350°F. Lightly coat a 9-inch springform pan with cooking spray.

Make crust: In a bowl, stir together wafer crumbs, sugar, water, and margarine until mixed. Pat the mixture onto the bottom and sides of the prepared pan.

Make filling: In a food processor, combine ricotta cheese, yogurt, cream cheese, egg yolks, vanilla, 1 cup sugar, flour, and salt; process until smooth. Transfer mixture to a large bowl.

In another bowl and using an electric beater, beat egg whites with cream of tartar until foamy. Gradually add remaining 2 tablespoons sugar, continuing to beat until stiff peaks form. Gently fold the egg white mixture into the cheese mixture just until incorporated. Pour it into the prepared crust.

Place a pan of hot water on the bottom rack of the oven. Set the cheesecake pan on a baking sheet and bake for

 **A Piece of Advice**

Sometimes I use low-fat vanilla yogurt in this cheesecake in place of the plain yogurt. See the tip following the earlier Cranberry Swirl Cheesecake recipe to get an idea as to how many vanilla wafers to grind for the crumbs. You can always substitute graham cracker crumbs.

Nutrition Watch _____

Strawberries are an excellent source of vitamin C, and they provide potassium and iron. They also supply folate, one of the B vitamins, and might play a role in the prevention of certain cancers and heart disease.

55 to 60 minutes or until it is slightly loose at the center. Run a knife around the edge of the cake. Let it cool on a wire rack until it is room temperature.

To unmold the cake, run the blade of a long thin knife between the top edge of the cake and the pan. Loosen the spring and carefully lift off the sides, leaving the cake on the pan bottom. Slice and serve.

Make topping: Arrange strawberries on top of cheese-cake. In a microwave or on the stovetop, heat jelly until melted. Brush over the berries. Chill.

Nutrition per Serving

Calories: 210
Protein: 5.7 g
Cholesterol: 40 mg

Fat (total): 6.6 g
Fat (saturated): 2.8 g

Carbohydrate: 32 g
Dietary Fiber: 0.7 g

Creamy Smooth

Lighter in texture than New York style cheesecake, these cheesecakes are often referred to as Italian or curd cheese style. They are a bit tricky to make as they contain so much moisture, but if you follow my directions carefully, you shouldn't have any problems.

Bailey's Irish Cream Cheesecake

Coffee cream liqueurs add a subtle flavor to desserts. Using Bailey's Irish Cream in a chocolate creamy cheesecake is not just delicious—it's decadent. Serve this with one of the chocolate or raspberry sauces in Chapter 16.

Prep time: 15 minutes   •   Cook time: 60 minutes   •   Chill time: at least 2 hours   •
Serves 16

Vegetable cooking spray

Crust

2¼ cups chocolate wafer crumbs

3 TB. water

1 TB. canola oil

Filling

2 cups smooth 5% ricotta cheese

¾ cup plain low-fat yogurt

4 oz. light cream cheese

1 large egg

1 large egg white

2 TB. Bailey's Irish Cream or other coffee cream liqueur

2 tsp. vanilla extract

1¼ cups granulated sugar

½ cup unsweetened cocoa

3 TB. all-purpose flour

Topping

1¼ cups low-fat sour cream

2 TB. granulated sugar

1 TB. Bailey's Irish Cream or other coffee cream liqueur

Position a rack in the center of the oven and preheat the oven to 350°F. Lightly coat a 9-inch springform pan with cooking spray.

Make crust: In a bowl, stir together wafer crumbs, water, and oil until mixed. Pat the mixture onto the bottom and sides of the prepared pan.

Make filling: In a food processor, combine ricotta cheese, yogurt, cream cheese, egg, egg white, liqueur, vanilla, sugar, cocoa, and flour; process until smooth. Pour the mixture into the prepared crust.

 Nutrition Watch

Low-fat ricotta cheese, yogurt, and sour cream are excellent sources of protein and calcium, and they're low in calories, fat, and cholesterol.

A Piece of Advice

Feel free to substitute a liqueur of your choice. Try a combination of coffee and chocolate! An orange liqueur, such as Grand Marnier, or the intense black raspberry flavor of Chambord are also wonderful with chocolate.

Place a pan of hot water on the bottom rack of the oven. Set the cheesecake pan on a baking sheet and bake for 50 minutes. The cake will still be quite loose.

Meanwhile, make topping: In a bowl, stir together sour cream, sugar, and liqueur. Carefully pour a thin stream of this mixture over the top of the hot cheesecake, smoothing it with a knife. Return the cake to the oven and bake for another 10 minutes. The topping will be loose and will set as the cake cools. Remove the cake from the oven and run a knife around the edge of the cake. Let the cake cool in its pan on a wire rack to room temperature. Chill.

To unmold the cake, run the blade of a long thin knife between the top edge of the cake and the pan. Loosen the spring and carefully lift off the sides, leaving the cake on the pan bottom. Slice and serve.

Nutrition per Serving

Calories: 277
Protein: 8 g
Cholesterol: 34 mg

Fat (total): 9.9 g
Fat (saturated): 4.6 g

Carbohydrate: 39 g
Dietary Fiber: 1.5 g

Coconut Cream Cheesecake

I would never have made this delicious cheesecake with regular coconut milk, which is laden with calories, saturated fat, and cholesterol. But now that light coconut milk is available in my grocery, I can indulge. It has 75 percent less fat.

Prep time: 20 minutes • Cook time: 55 to 60 minutes • Chill time: at least 2 hours • Serves 16

Vegetable cooking spray

Crust

2¼ cups vanilla wafer crumbs

2 TB. sugar

2 TB. shredded coconut, toasted

¼ cup water

1 TB. canola oil

Filling

2 cups smooth 5% ricotta cheese

4 oz. light cream cheese, softened

¾ cup light coconut milk

1 large egg

1 large egg white

2 tsp. vanilla extract

¾ cup + 2 TB. granulated sugar (divided use)

¼ cup all-purpose flour

⅛ tsp. salt

5 TB. shredded coconut, toasted (divided use)

2 large egg whites

¼ tsp. cream of tartar

Position a rack in the center of the oven and preheat the oven to 350°F. Lightly coat a 9-inch springform pan with cooking spray.

Make crust: In a bowl, stir together wafer crumbs, sugar, coconut, water, and oil until mixed. Pat the mixture onto the bottom and sides of the prepared pan.

Make filling: In a food processor, combine ricotta cheese, cream cheese, coconut milk, egg, egg white, vanilla, ¾ cup sugar, flour, and salt; purée until smooth. Transfer to a large bowl. Stir in ¼ cup coconut.

In another bowl and using an electric mixer, beat egg whites with cream of tartar until they are foamy. Gradually add 2 tablespoons sugar, continuing to beat until stiff peaks form. Gently fold the egg white mixture into the cheese mixture just until blended. Pour into the prepared crust.

Place a pan of hot water on the bottom rack of the oven. Set the cheesecake pan on a baking sheet and bake for 55 to 60 minutes or until it is slightly loose at the center. Remove the cake from the oven and run a knife around the edge of the cake. Let the cake cool in its pan on a wire rack to room temperature. Chill. When ready to serve, garnish with the remaining 1 tablespoon toasted coconut.

Nutrition Watch

Coconut is high in fat, so use small amounts to highlight, not dominate, a recipe. Coconut is also high in potassium.

Nutrition per Serving

Calories: 230   Fat (total): 9.5 g   Cholesterol: 28 mg
Protein: 6.2 g   Fat (saturated): 4.7 g   Dietary Fiber: 0.8 g
Carbohydrate: 30 g

Sour Cream Brownie Cheesecake

This cake is sinfully delicious—a thick layer of brownie topped with a creamy cheesecake layer and a light sour cream layer make it irresistible to kids and adults alike. To make the brownie mocha-flavored, add 1 teaspoon instant coffee dissolved in 1 tablespoon hot water or add 1 tablespoon strong brewed coffee, or to taste.

Prep time: 20 minutes   •   Cook time: 50 minutes   •   Chill time: at least 2 hours   •
Serves 12

Vegetable cooking spray

Brownie Layer

⅔ cup granulated sugar

¼ cup canola oil

1 large egg

1 tsp. vanilla extract

⅓ cup all-purpose flour

⅓ cup unsweetened cocoa

1 tsp. baking powder

¼ cup low-fat sour cream

Cheesecake Layer

1 cup smooth 5% ricotta cheese

½ cup granulated sugar

⅓ cup light cream cheese

¼ cup low-fat sour cream

1 large egg

2 TB. all-purpose flour

1 tsp. vanilla extract

2 TB. semi-sweet chocolate chips

Topping

1 cup low-fat sour cream

2 TB. granulated sugar

1 tsp. vanilla extract

1 TB. semi-sweet chocolate chips

Position a rack in the center of the oven and preheat the oven to 350°F. Lightly coat an 8½-inch springform pan with cooking spray.

Make brownie layer: In a bowl, beat together sugar, oil, egg, and vanilla. In another bowl, stir together flour, cocoa, and baking powder. Stir the wet mixture into the dry mixture just until combined. Stir in sour cream. Pour the mixture into prepared pan.

Make cheesecake layer: In a food processor, combine ricotta cheese, sugar, cream cheese, sour cream, egg, flour, and vanilla; process until smooth. Stir in chocolate chips. Pour the mixture on top of brownie layer.

Place a pan of hot water on the bottom rack of the oven. Set the cheesecake pan on a baking sheet and bake for 40 minutes.

Meanwhile, make topping: In a small bowl, stir together sour cream, sugar, and vanilla. When the cake layers have cooked for 40 minutes, carefully pour the topping mixture over top, smoothing it with the back of a wooden spoon, and sprinkle chocolate chips over the top. Bake 10 more minutes. Remove from the oven and let cool in its pan on a wire rack to room temperature. Chill.

To unmold the cake, run the blade of a long thin knife between the top edge of the cake and the pan. Loosen the spring and carefully lift off the sides, leaving the cake on the pan bottom. Slice and serve.

Nutrition Watch

Cheesecakes are often forbidden if you're trying to reduce calorie and fat intake. Usually they contain high-fat cream cheese, which has 35 percent milkfat, and regular sour cream, which has 14 percent milkfat, as well as many eggs. I've used low-fat sour cream, ricotta cheese, and light cream cheese to significantly reduce calories and fat.

Nutrition per Serving

Calories: 225
Protein: 7 g
Cholesterol: 47 mg

Fat (total): 8 g
Fat (saturated): 3 g

Carbohydrate: 31 g
Dietary Fiber: 1 g

Miscellaneous Exotic Creations

I love cheesecake so much that I couldn't stop developing new recipes, each so special it deserved to be in a section of exotic flavors. With so many kinds of cheesecake, it's no wonder that cheesecake is most everybody's favorite cake.

Molasses and Ginger Cheesecake

I love the flavor of gingerbread, whether it's in a cookie or cake. When added to a cheesecake, it's exceptional.

Prep time: 20 minutes • Cook time: 60 to 65 minutes • Chill time: at least 2 hours • Serves 16

Vegetable cooking spray

Crust

1¾ cups ladyfinger crumbs

2 TB. granulated sugar

½ tsp. ground cinnamon

¼ cup water

1 TB. honey

1 TB. canola oil

Filling

2 cups smooth 5% ricotta cheese

3 oz. light cream cheese

1 large egg

¾ cup low-fat sour cream

⅓ cup molasses

⅔ cup packed light brown sugar

⅓ cup + ¼ cup granulated sugar (divided use)

3 TB. all-purpose flour

1 tsp. ground cinnamon

¼ tsp. ground ginger

2 large egg whites

¼ tsp. cream of tartar

A Piece of Advice

Buy firm, Italian packaged ladyfingers and process them in a food processor until the crumbs are fine. You can substitute vanilla wafer or graham cracker crumbs—add just enough water for the crumbs to come together, keeping in mind that ladyfinger crumbs need more moisture.

Position a rack in the center of the oven and preheat the oven to 350°F. Lightly coat a 9-inch springform pan with cooking spray.

Make crust: In a bowl, stir together ladyfinger crumbs, sugar, cinnamon, water, honey, and oil until mixed. Pat the mixture onto the bottom and sides of the prepared pan.

Make filling: In a food processor, combine ricotta cheese, cream cheese, egg, sour cream, molasses, brown sugar, ⅓ cup granulated sugar, flour, cinnamon, and ginger; purée until smooth. Transfer the mixture to a large bowl.

In another bowl and using an electric mixer, beat egg whites with cream of tartar until foamy. Gradually add remaining ¼ cup granulated sugar, continuing to beat until stiff peaks form. Gently fold the egg white mixture into the cheese mixture just until combined. Pour it into the prepared crust.

Place a pan of hot water on the bottom rack of the oven. Set the cheesecake pan on a baking sheet and bake for 60 to 65 minutes or until it is slightly loose at the center. Remove the cheesecake from oven and run a knife around the edge of the cake. Let the cake cool in its pan on a wire rack to room temperature. Chill.

Nutrition Watch

Molasses is rich in iron, calcium, and phosphorus. You'll want to buy dark molasses, not blackstrap molasses, which is too bitter for this recipe. Unsulphured molasses has a cleaner sugar-cane flavor.

To unmold the cake, run the blade of a long thin knife between the top edge of the cake and the pan. Loosen the spring and carefully lift off the sides, leaving the cake on the pan bottom. Slice and serve.

Nutrition per Serving

Calories: 223   Fat (total): 6.3 g   Carbohydrate: 35 g
Protein: 6.6 g   Fat (saturated): 3.2 g   Dietary Fiber: 0.3 g
Cholesterol: 69 mg

Lemon Curd Cheesecake

Lemon is one of my favorite flavors in baking. Instead of using ordinary lemon juice in the cheesecake, I thought a marbled lemon curd would be delicious. It is!

Prep time: 25 minutes • Cook time: 60 minutes • Chill time: at least 2 hours • Serves 16

Vegetable cooking spray

Lemon Curd

⅓ cup granulated sugar

1 TB. cornstarch

⅔ cup water

1 tsp. finely grated lemon zest

2 TB. fresh lemon juice

1 large egg

Crust

1¾ cups graham cracker crumbs

3 TB. granulated sugar

¼ cup water

1 TB. vegetable oil

Filling

2 cups smooth 5% ricotta cheese

4 oz. light cream cheese, softened

1 large egg

1 large egg white

½ cup plain or lemon-flavored low-fat yogurt

2 tsp. finely grated lemon zest

¼ cup fresh lemon juice

1⅓ cups granulated sugar

¼ cup all-purpose flour

Position a rack in the center of the oven and preheat the oven to 350°F. Lightly coat a 9-inch springform pan with cooking spray.

Nutrition Watch

I keep a large bowl of lemons on the kitchen counter because they're always in use, having become an essential part of my baking and cooking. At room temperature, they'll keep for three or four days. Refrigerated in a plastic bag, they'll stay fresh for up to one month. Bring lemons to room temperature before juicing and use immediately because they start to lose their vitamin power as soon as they are squeezed.

Make curd: In a small saucepan off the heat, combine sugar, cornstarch, water, zest, and juice until smooth. Cook over medium heat, whisking constantly, for 4 minutes or until thickened. Remove from heat. In a bowl, beat egg. Whisk lemon mixture into egg. Return the mixture to the saucepan and cook over lowest heat, stirring constantly, for 3 minutes or until curd is smooth and thickened. Transfer it to a clean bowl. Place a piece of plastic wrap on the surface of the curd. Chill while you mix the cheesecake.

Make crust: In a bowl, stir together graham crumbs, sugar, water, and oil until mixed. Pat the mixture onto the bottom and sides of the prepared pan.

Make filling: In a food processor, combine ricotta cheese, cream cheese, egg, egg white, yogurt, lemon zest and juice, sugar, and flour; process until smooth.

Pour it into the prepared crust. Dollop lemon curd on top of the filling and use a knife to swirl it around.

Place a pan of hot water on the bottom rack of the oven. Set the cheesecake pan on a baking sheet and bake for approximately 60 minutes or until it is slightly loose at the center. Remove from the oven and run a knife around the edge of the cake. Let cool in its pan on a wire rack to room temperature. Chill.

To unmold the cake, run the blade of a long thin knife between the top edge of the cake and the pan. Loosen the spring and carefully lift off the sides, leaving the cake on the pan bottom. Slice and serve.

 **A Piece of Advice**

For the best flavor, use fresh lemon juice. In fact, you won't find bottled lemon juice in my kitchen. If a recipe's worth making, it also merits spending the few extra pennies for fresh lemons. To get the most juice from a lemon, heat it gently in the microwave for 30 seconds.

 Nutrition per Serving

Calories: 239
Protein: 6.8 g
Cholesterol: 34 mg

Fat (total): 6.6 g
Fat (saturated): 2.8 g

Carbohydrate: 38 g
Dietary Fiber: 0.5 g

Rocky Mountain Miniature Chocolate Cheesecakes

I find that individual cheesecakes are elegant to serve, especially these, which are almost mousse-like in texture. Serve these with Chocolate Sauce (see Chapter 16).

Prep time: 10 minutes • Cook time: 25 minutes • Chill time: at least 2 hours • Serves 12

1¾ cups smooth 5% ricotta cheese

3 oz. light cream cheese, softened

½ cup low-fat sour cream

1 large egg

¾ cup granulated sugar

3 TB. unsweetened cocoa

1½ TB. all-purpose flour

⅓ cup miniature marshmallows

3 TB. semi-sweet chocolate chips

Position a rack in the center of the oven and preheat the oven to 350°F. Line one 12-cup muffin tin with paper muffin liners.

In a food processor, combine ricotta cheese, cream cheese, sour cream, egg, sugar, cocoa, and flour; process until smooth. Divide the mixture among the prepared muffin cups.

A Piece of Advice

If you only have large marshmallows, use scissors to cut them into small pieces. You can replace the ricotta with 2 percent cottage cheese—just be sure to process it well for a smooth batter.

Set the muffin tin in a larger pan. Pour enough hot water into the larger pan to come halfway up the sides of the muffin cups.

Bake for 20 minutes. Sprinkle marshmallows and chocolate chips evenly over the cheesecakes. Bake for 5 minutes longer or until marshmallows and chocolate chips begin to melt.

Remove the muffin tin from its water bath. Let tin cool on a wire rack to room temperature. Chill. Unmold onto serving plates.

 Nutrition per Serving

Calories: 161
Protein: 6.2 g
Cholesterol: 36 mg

Fat (total): 6.2 g
Fat (saturated): 3.8 g

Carbohydrate: 20 g
Dietary Fiber: 0.6 g

The Least You Need to Know

- Judiciously use light cream cheese, low-fat sour cream, and low-fat yogurt to reduce calories and fat.
- Drain whey from ricotta cheese and cottage cheese and purée for smoother texture.
- A pan of hot water in the oven during baking reduces surface cracks.
- Set the springform pan on a baking sheet to catch any leaks.
- Cheesecake is done when the 2-inch diameter at the center is slightly loose.
- As long as the cheesecakes does not contain whipped egg whites, it can be frozen.
- Use a long strand of dental floss (waxed or plain is fine; just not mint flavored) to cut the cheesecake.

Coffeecakes, Crumb Cakes, Pound Cakes, and Snack Cakes

In This Chapter

- ◆ Fragrant coffeecakes laced with fruit and chocolate
- ◆ Old-fashioned coffeecakes with delicious crumb toppings
- ◆ Luscious pound cakes
- ◆ Great cakes for snacking

Can you think of anything more wonderful than the fragrance of a hot, just-baked coffeecake filled with luscious fruit, a coffeecake dusted with crisp crumbs, a dense, finely textured pound cake, or an eat-out-of-hand snack cake cooling on the counter on a cold winter day? Add a carafe of freshly brewed coffee, a pot of perfectly steeped tea, or a glass of cold milk and you're ready for something special to happen. The models for my cakes are old family favorites from years past when eggs, cream, and butter were still part of everyday life.

To save calories and fat, I have added a lot of fruit; used canola oil in place of butter; replaced regular sour cream with low-fat sour cream or yogurt; and spiked the flavor with dashes of exotic spices, intensely flavored extracts, and fresh citrus zest. When nuts are included in the recipes, they are used in small amounts as a topping or added to the batter for texture.

Rarely are these special cakes frosted. Instead, a light dusting of sugar or a crunchy topping of nutritious cereal such as Grape-Nuts Flakes, quick-cooking oats, or low-fat granola supply texture and flavor without the fat.

Many of these coffeecakes and crumb cakes are baked in a 8- or 9-inch spring-form pan with a removable bottom. As with other cakes, lightly spritz the pan with vegetable cooking spray to ensure easy removal and always preheat the oven. Place the pan in the center of the oven and check for doneness by inserting a toothpick or tester into the center of the cake. The tester should come out dry and clean. Cool the cake in its pan on a rack until it is room temperature. My pound cakes are baked in a loaf pan while snack cakes are usually baked in a square cake pan and cut into squares to eat out of hand.

Some of these cakes have puréed cooked dried fruit spooned over the top for flavor and texture. Cook the fruit with the recommended amount of water and mash or purée it until smooth. Spoon it over the top of the batter and gently swirl it in. Do not mix it in thoroughly, or the fruit will sink to the bottom.

Coffeecakes

Sometimes described as muffin batter baked in one pan, coffeecakes are so easy to make and so loved by most everyone. Their very name invites you to grab a mug of hot coffee, slow down, and enjoy the day. Usually eaten for breakfast or brunch, many of these recipes are so special that they're lovely with afternoon tea.

Orange Upside-Down Coffeecake

This looks so beautiful with the orange slices caramelized on top. The cake beneath is moist and delicious.

Prep time: 30 minutes • Cook time: 30 minutes • Cool time: 20 minutes • Serves 16

Vegetable cooking spray

⅔ cup packed light brown sugar

¼ cup light corn syrup

1 TB. margarine or unsalted butter, softened

2 large navel oranges

⅔ cup granulated sugar

zest of 1 orange, finely grated

½ cup plain low-fat yogurt

⅓ cup fresh orange juice

¼ cup canola oil

1 large egg

2 large egg whites

1⅓ cups all-purpose flour

1½ tsp. baking powder

⅛ tsp. salt

Position a rack in the center of the oven and preheat oven to 350°F. Lightly coat a 9-inch square cake pan with cooking spray.

In the prepared pan, stir together brown sugar, corn syrup, and margarine. Place the pan in the oven for 5 minutes. Stir the mixture until it is well mixed. It will be sticky and thick.

Using a sharp paring knife, cut the zest and pith away from the oranges. Slice oranges crosswise into ¼-inch thick slices. Place the slices in a single layer in the bottom of the pan.

In a bowl and using a whisk or electric mixer, beat sugar, orange zest, yogurt, orange juice, oil, egg, and egg whites. In another bowl, stir together flour, baking powder, and salt. With a wooden spoon, stir the dry ingredients into the orange mixture just until everything is combined. Pour the batter into the pan.

Bake for 30 minutes or until a tester comes out dry. Let cake cool in its pan on a wire rack for 20 minutes. Carefully invert the cake onto a serving platter. Cut into 2¼-inch squares and serve.

 Nutrition Watch

Oranges are an excellent source of vitamin C. But after being squeezed, they begin losing some of their nutritional benefit and good taste.

 A Piece of Advice

Be sure to use sweet oranges, or the cake will be bitter—taste them before you use them! When you're removing the peel and pith, do so over a bowl to catch any juice. If you have a specialty produce store nearby, ask for Cara Cara oranges, a type of navel orange with a dark pink or red flesh. Use light corn syrup for this cake because you want sweetness but no flavor—dark corn syrup has been flavored with caramel.

 **Nutrition per Serving**

Calories: 184   Fat (total): 4.7 g   Carbohydrate: 33 g
Protein: 2.5 g   Fat (saturated): 0.6 g   Dietary Fiber: 0.8 g
Cholesterol: 14 mg

Cranberry Sour Cream Coffeecake

Cranberries have a tartness that goes well with a sweet cake like this wonderful delight, especially combined with orange juice and a crunchy topping.

Prep time: 15 minutes   •   Cook time: 55 to 60 minutes   •   Serves 16

Vegetable cooking spray

Cake

1 TB. finely grated orange zest

½ cup fresh orange juice

½ cup low-fat sour cream

⅓ cup canola oil

1 large egg

2 large egg whites

2 tsp. vanilla extract

1 cup granulated sugar

1¾ cups all-purpose flour

2 tsp. baking powder

1 tsp. baking soda

1 cup canned whole-berry cranberry sauce

Topping

¼ cup Grape-Nuts cereal

3 TB. packed light brown sugar

3 TB. all-purpose flour

2 tsp. water

2 tsp. canola oil

Position a rack in the center of the oven and preheat the oven to 350°F. Lightly coat a 9-inch springform pan with cooking spray.

Make cake: In a large bowl and using a whisk or electric mixer, beat orange zest and juice, sour cream, oil, egg, egg whites, vanilla, and granulated sugar.

Nutrition Watch

Cranberries are a very good source of vitamin C. Dried cranberries make a great midday snack—their nutrients and calories are concentrated and supply a quick energy source.

In another bowl, stir together flour, baking powder, and baking soda. With a wooden spoon, stir the flour mixture into the orange mixture just until combined. Pour the mixture into the prepared pan.

In a food processor, purée cranberry sauce until smooth. Dollop it over the batter and using a knife, swirl it around gently.

Make topping: In a small bowl, stir together cereal, brown sugar, flour, water, and oil just until crumbly. Scatter over the cake batter.

Bake for 55 to 60 minutes or until a tester inserted in the center of the cake comes out clean. Let the cake cool in its pan on a wire rack.

To unmold the cake, run the blade of a long thin knife between the top edge of the cake and the pan. Loosen the spring and carefully lift off the sides, leaving the cake on the pan bottom. Slice and serve.

A Piece of Advice

Canned cranberry sauce made with whole berries gives a better texture to the cake than whole fresh cranberries on their own. Be careful not to buy jellied cranberry sauce.

Nutrition per Serving

Calories: 215
Protein: 2.9 g
Cholesterol: 16 mg

Fat (total): 6.1 g
Fat (saturated): 0.9 g

Carbohydrate: 37 g
Dietary Fiber: 0.9 g

Orange Apple Sour Cream Coffeecake

Coffeecakes are a simple, delicious cake to have any time of day, but this one puts coffeecakes in a different league completely. I like to serve it when I'm entertaining, and it's especially good for nibbling on a holiday morning.

Prep time: 20 minutes • Cook time: 45 to 50 minutes • Serves 16

Vegetable cooking spray

Topping

⅓ cup packed light brown sugar

3 TB. chopped pecans

1½ TB. all-purpose flour

2 tsp. margarine or unsalted butter

½ tsp. ground cinnamon

Filling

2 cups peeled, chopped apples

½ cup dark raisins

1 TB. granulated sugar

1 tsp. ground cinnamon

Cake

⅔ cup packed light brown sugar

½ cup granulated sugar

⅓ cup canola oil

2 large eggs

1 TB. grated orange zest

2 tsp. vanilla extract

1⅔ cups all-purpose flour

2 tsp. baking powder

1 tsp. baking soda

½ cup fresh orange juice

½ cup low-fat sour cream

Position a rack in the center of the oven and preheat the oven to 350°F. Lightly coat a 10-inch springform pan with cooking spray.

Nutrition Watch

Traditional coffeecakes appear low in fat because many people don't think they are high in fat. But beware! Most contain loads of butter, regular sour cream, and a lot of eggs.

A Piece of Advice

Another time, try chopped fresh pears or peaches in place of apples. To increase the fiber in your diet, use ⅔ cup whole-wheat flour and 1 cup all-purpose flour. If you don't want to layer the cake, mix the apples with the batter and then add the topping.

Make topping: In a small bowl, combine brown sugar, pecans, flour, margarine, and cinnamon until crumbly. Set aside.

Make filling: In a bowl, mix together apples, raisins, sugar, and cinnamon. Set aside.

Make cake: In a large bowl and using a whisk or electric mixer, beat together brown sugar, granulated sugar, and oil. Add eggs, one at a time, beating well after each addition. Mix in orange zest and vanilla. In a separate bowl, stir together flour, baking powder, and baking soda. In another bowl, stir together orange juice and sour cream. Add the flour mixture to the sour cream mixture in batches, alternating with the beaten sugar mixture, mixing just until it is all blended. Spoon half of the batter into the prepared pan. Top with half of the apple mixture. Spoon remaining batter into the pan. Top with remaining apple mixture; sprinkle with topping.

Bake for 45 to 50 minutes or until a tester inserted in the center comes out clean. Let the cake cool in its pan on a wire rack.

To unmold the cake, run the blade of a long thin knife between the top edge of the cake and the pan. Loosen the spring and carefully lift off the sides, leaving the cake on the pan bottom. Slice and serve.

Nutrition per Serving

Calories: 248	Fat (total): 7.8 g	Carbohydrate: 42 g
Protein: 3.5 g	Fat (saturated): 0.8 g	Dietary Fiber: 1.2 g
Cholesterol: 31 mg		

Raspberry Coffeecake with Granola Topping

Serve this great cake at your next coffee klatch or office meeting. The tart raspberries go so well with the sweet, crunchy granola topping.

Prep time: 20 minutes • Cook time: 40 to 45 minutes • Serves 16

Vegetable cooking spray

Topping

⅓ cup packed light brown sugar

¼ cup low-fat granola

¼ cup all-purpose flour

2 tsp. water

2 tsp. canola oil

Cake

1¼ cups granulated sugar

⅓ cup canola oil

2 large eggs

1 tsp. vanilla extract

1⅓ cups + 2 tsp. all-purpose flour (divided use)

1½ tsp. baking powder

1 tsp. baking soda

⅛ tsp. salt

¾ cup plain low-fat yogurt

2 cups raspberries, fresh or frozen, thawed and drained

2 tsp. all-purpose flour

Position a rack in the center of the oven and preheat the oven to 350°F. Lightly coat a 9-inch square cake pan with cooking spray.

Make topping: In a small bowl, mix together brown sugar, granola, flour, water, and oil until crumbly. Set aside.

Make cake: In a large bowl and using a whisk or electric mixer, beat granulated sugar, oil, eggs, and vanilla. In another bowl, stir together 1⅓ cups flour, baking powder, baking soda, and salt. With a wooden spoon, stir the dry ingredients into the sugar mixture in batches, alternating with the yogurt, making two additions of dry and one of wet. Mix just until combined.

Toss raspberries with remaining 2 teaspoons flour and fold them into the batter. Pour the mixture into the prepared pan. Sprinkle with reserved topping.

Bake for 40 to 45 minutes or until a tester inserted in the center comes out clean. If you are using frozen berries, bake for an extra 5 to 10 minutes. Remove the cake from the oven and cool in its pan on a wire rack. Cut into 2¼-inch squares and serve.

A Piece of Advice

This recipe works well with either fresh or frozen raspberries, blueberries, or blackberries. If you are using frozen berries, measure them before defrosting and then drain them well. Note the difference in baking time when using frozen berries.

Nutrition Watch

Be sure to buy low-fat granola (any flavor is fine) because regular granola is loaded with fat, calories, and cholesterol. Raspberries contain iron, potassium, and vitamins A and C.

Nutrition per Serving

Calories: 204   Fat (total): 6.2 g   Carbohydrate: 34 g
Protein: 3 g   Fat (saturated): 0.7 g Dietary Fiber: 1.5 g
Cholesterol: 27 mg

Orange Marmalade Coffeecake

Marmalade has a distinct tartness that goes well with this coffeecake and crunchy oatmeal topping. Serve it with Mango Coulis (see Chapter 16).

Prep time: 20 minutes • Cook time: 45 to 50 minutes • Serves 16

Cake

¾ cup granulated sugar

2 tsp. finely grated orange zest

½ cup fresh orange juice

⅓ cup canola oil

1 large egg

2 large egg whites

1 tsp. vanilla extract

1¾ cups all-purpose flour

1½ tsp. baking powder

½ tsp. baking soda

¾ cup buttermilk

⅔ cup orange marmalade

Topping

⅓ cup packed light brown sugar

⅓ cup quick-cooking oats

¼ cup all-purpose flour

½ tsp. ground cinnamon

1 TB. water

2 tsp. canola oil

 **A Piece of Advice**

Another time, use apricot or peach jam in place of the orange marmalade. You can also substitute plain low-fat yogurt for buttermilk or make your own buttermilk by adding 1 tablespoon lemon juice to 1 cup low-fat milk, and letting it sit for 5 minutes. If you use buttermilk sporadically in your cooking, it also comes in a dry powder that will keep for months on your pantry shelf.

Position a rack in the center of the oven and preheat the oven to 350°F. Lightly coat a 9-inch springform pan with cooking spray.

Make cake: In a large bowl and using a whisk or electric mixer, beat sugar, orange zest and juice, oil, egg, egg whites, and vanilla.

In another bowl, stir together the flour, baking powder, and baking soda. With a wooden spoon, stir the dry ingredients into the sugar mixture in batches—alternating with the buttermilk, making two additions of dry and one of wet, and stirring just until combined. Pour the mixture into the prepared pan. Melt marmalade in a microwave or on the stove. Dot over batter and gently swirl it around.

Make topping: In a small bowl, stir together brown sugar, oats, flour, cinnamon, water, and oil until crumbly. Sprinkle over the batter.

Bake for 45 to 50 minutes or until a tester comes out dry. Let the cake cool in its pan on a wire rack.

To unmold the cake, run the blade of a long thin knife between the top edge of the cake and pan. Loosen the spring and carefully lift off the sides, leaving the cake on the pan bottom. Slice and serve.

Nutrition Watch

Despite its name, buttermilk contains no butter—it is just low-fat milk with a special bacteria added to give it a slightly thickened texture and tangy flavor. It's great to use in low-fat cooking.

 Nutrition per Serving

Calories: 217   Fat (total): 5.8 g   Carbohydrate: 38 g
Protein: 3.2 g   Fat (saturated): 0.6 g   Dietary Fiber: 0.7 g
Cholesterol: 14 mg

Upside-Down Apple and Cranberry Coffeecake

Upside-down cakes are attractive to serve. This one, dotted with dried cranberries, makes a very festive dessert.

Prep time: 15 minutes   •   Cook time: 25 to 35 minutes   •   Serves 16

Vegetable cooking spray

Topping

¼ cup light corn syrup

¾ cup packed light brown sugar

1 TB. margarine or unsalted butter

½ tsp. ground cinnamon

¼ cup thinly sliced, peeled apples

¼ cup dried cranberries

Cake

¾ cup granulated sugar

⅓ cup unsweetened applesauce

¼ cup canola oil

1 large egg

2 large egg whites

2 tsp. vanilla extract

1 tsp. ground cinnamon

1¼ cups all-purpose flour

½ tsp. baking powder

½ cup plain low-fat yogurt

Position a rack in the center of the oven and preheat the oven to 350°F. Lightly coat a 9-inch square cake pan with cooking spray.

Make topping: In the cake pan, stir together corn syrup, brown sugar, margarine, and cinnamon. Place in the oven for 3 minutes or until mixture is melted. Stir. The mixture will be sticky. Arrange apples and cranberries on top.

Nutrition Watch _____

Between the apples and cranberries, you get vitamins A and C and a good source of dietary fiber and carbohydrate with this cake.

 A Piece of Advice _____

Feel free to use other dried fruits—such as dried cherries, raisins, chopped apricots, or dates—in this yummy cake.

Make cake: In a large bowl and using a whisk or electric mixer, combine sugar, applesauce, oil, egg, egg whites, vanilla, and cinnamon. In another bowl, stir together flour and baking powder. Stir the dry ingredients into the applesauce mixture in batches, alternating with the yogurt, making two additions of dry and one of wet. Stir just until combined. Spread the cake batter over the fruit in the pan.

Bake for 25 to 35 minutes or until a tester comes out dry.

Let the cake cool in its pan on a wire rack for 20 minutes, and then carefully turn out on a large platter. To serve, cut into 2¼-inch squares.

 Nutrition per Serving

Calories: 192   Fat (total): 4.7 g   Carbohydrate: 35 g
Protein: 2.3 g   Fat (saturated): 0.6 g   Dietary Fiber: 0.8 g
Cholesterol: 14 mg

Prune-Swirled Coffeecake

I find that the combination of prunes and coffee produces a great tasting coffeecake. I love a slice in the morning with a cup of coffee or, actually, any time of day.

Prep time: 25 minutes   •   Cook time: 45 minutes   •   Serves 16

Vegetable cooking spray

Prune Swirl

3 oz. (½ cup) pitted prunes, chopped

⅔ cup water

2 TB. granulated sugar

Cake

2 TB. instant coffee granules

⅓ cup hot water

1 cup granulated sugar

⅓ cup canola oil

1 large egg

1 large egg white

1 tsp. vanilla extract

1½ cups all-purpose flour

1½ tsp. baking powder

½ tsp. baking soda

¾ cup low-fat sour cream

Position a rack in the center of the oven and preheat oven to 350°F. Lightly coat an 8-inch square cake pan with cooking spray.

Make prune swirl: In a small saucepan, combine prunes, water, and sugar. Bring to a boil; reduce the heat to simmer and cook for 10 minutes. Transfer to a food processor or blender and purée.

Meanwhile, make cake: Dissolve instant coffee in hot water. In a large bowl and using a whisk or electric mixer, beat sugar, oil, egg, egg white, vanilla, and coffee. In another bowl, stir together flour, baking powder, and baking soda. With a wooden spoon, stir the dry ingredients into the sugar mixture in batches, alternating with sour cream, making two additions of dry and one of wet. Stir just until combined. Set aside ½ cup of the batter. Pour the remaining batter into the prepared pan.

In a small bowl, stir together prune purée and reserved batter. Dot this mixture over the batter in the pan and swirl it around gently using a knife.

Bake for 45 minutes or until a tester inserted in the center comes out clean. Let the cake cool in its pan on a wire rack.

A Piece of Advice

Whenever I'm using dried fruits, such as prunes or dates, I buy them in a bulk food store and keep them in large bags in the freezer so that I never run out. The sour cream can be replaced with low-fat plain yogurt with 1 percent milkfat or less.

Nutrition Watch

Prunes provide high energy and fiber, and when they're puréed they make a fabulous no-fat substitute in baking, adding moisture and texture.

 Nutrition per Serving

Calories: 175
Protein: 2.4 g
Cholesterol: 17 mg

Fat (total): 5.7 g
Fat (saturated): 0.9 g

Carbohydrate: 28 g
Dietary Fiber: 0.7 g

Date Oatmeal Coffeecake

If you have a weakness for date squares, you'll love this coffeecake. It's so moist, with a satisfying crunchy oatmeal topping.

Prep time: 30 minutes • Cook time: 50 to 55 minutes • Serves 16

Vegetable cooking spray

Cake

6 oz. (1¼ cups) pitted dates, chopped

1¼ cups water

1 cup granulated sugar

2 large eggs

2 tsp. vanilla extract

1 cup buttermilk

⅓ cup vegetable oil

1⅓ cups all-purpose flour

1½ tsp. baking powder

1 tsp. ground cinnamon

½ tsp. baking soda

Topping

½ cup packed light brown sugar

½ cup quick-cooking oats

¼ cup all-purpose flour

½ tsp. ground cinnamon

1 TB. margarine or unsalted butter, melted

1 TB. water

Position a rack in the center of the oven and preheat oven to 350°F. Lightly coat a 9-inch springform pan with cooking spray.

In a saucepan, combine dates and water. Bring the liquid to a boil; reduce the heat to medium and simmer, uncovered, for 5 to 8 minutes, stirring occasionally. Remove from heat. Mash. Set aside to cool.

Meanwhile, make topping: In a small bowl, stir together brown sugar, oats, flour, cinnamon, margarine, and water until crumbly.

In a large bowl and using a whisk or electric mixer, beat together sugar, eggs, vanilla, buttermilk, and oil. In another bowl, stir together flour, baking powder, cinnamon, and baking soda.

Nutrition Watch

Dates are a good source of protein and iron. When they are cooked and puréed, they can replace up to 75 percent of the fat in a baked dessert. For every cup of fat in a recipe, substitute ¾ cup fruit purée, which equals 25 percent fat.

Pour the wet ingredients over the dry ingredients and with a wooden spoon, stir until just combined. Pour the batter into prepared pan. Dot cooled date mixture on top. Sprinkle with topping.

Bake for 50 to 55 minutes or until a tester inserted in the center comes out clean. Let the cake cool in its pan on a wire rack.

To unmold the cake, run the blade of a long thin knife between the top edge of the cake and the pan. Loosen the spring and carefully lift off the sides, leaving the cake on the pan bottom. Slice and serve.

 **Nutrition per Serving**

Calories: 226   Fat (total): 6.3 g   Carbohydrate: 39 g
Protein: 3.2 g   Fat (saturated): 0.8 g   Dietary Fiber: 1.5 g
Cholesterol: 27 mg

Mocha Coffeecake

What can go wrong when you mix coffee with chocolate? I love a slice of this celestial cake with a cappuccino or caffé latte in the afternoon, especially when the cake is served with Crème Anglaise or Vanilla Cream (see Chapter 16).

Prep time: 20 minutes • Cook time: 30 to 35 minutes • Serves 16

Vegetable cooking spray

Topping

½ cup packed light brown sugar

3 TB. semi-sweet chocolate chips

4 tsp. unsweetened cocoa

Cake

1¼ cups granulated sugar

⅓ cup canola oil

⅓ cup brewed strong coffee

1 large egg

2 large egg whites

1 tsp. vanilla extract

1¼ cups all-purpose flour

⅓ cup unsweetened cocoa

1½ tsp. baking powder

½ tsp. baking soda

⅔ cup low-fat sour cream

Position a rack in the center of the oven and pre-heat oven to 350°F. Lightly coat a 9-inch square cake pan with cooking spray.

Make topping: In a small bowl, stir together brown sugar, chocolate chips, and cocoa.

Make cake: In a large bowl and using whisk or electric mixer, beat together sugar, oil, coffee, egg, egg whites, and vanilla. In another bowl, stir together flour, cocoa, baking powder, and baking soda. With a wooden spoon, stir the dry ingredients into the coffee mixture in batches, alternating with sour cream, making two additions of dry and one of wet. Stir until just combined. Pour the batter into the prepared pan. Sprinkle with topping.

Nutrition Watch

The calories, fat, and cholesterol are reduced in this recipe by using mostly cocoa instead of chocolate. Cocoa has only 3 grams of fat per ounce, compared to 9 grams of fat in chocolate. With this kind of saving, I can splurge by adding a few chocolate chips to the topping.

Bake for 30 to 35 minutes or until a tester inserted in the center comes out clean. Let the cake cool in its pan on a wire rack. Cut into 2¼-inch squares and serve.

 Nutrition per Serving

Calories: 205   Fat (total): 6.5 g   Carbohydrate: 34 g
Protein: 2.7 g   Fat (saturated): 1.5 g   Dietary Fiber: 1.1 g
Cholesterol: 17 mg

Cream Cheese–Filled Coffeecake

This is one of my favorite coffee cakes. The combination of a layer of light cream cheese and strawberry jam is incredible. Try serving this with Raspberry Coulis in Chapter 16.

Prep time: 25 minutes   •   Cook time: 55 to 60 minutes   •   Serves 16

Vegetable cooking spray

Filling

¾ cup smooth 5% ricotta cheese

2 oz. light cream cheese, softened

1 large egg yolk

¼ cup granulated sugar

2 tsp. all-purpose flour

1 tsp. vanilla extract

Topping

⅓ cup Grape-Nuts cereal

3 TB. all-purpose flour

3 TB. packed light brown sugar

¼ tsp. ground cinnamon

2 tsp. canola oil

2 tsp. water

Cake

¾ cup granulated sugar

3 TB. canola oil

1 large egg

1 large egg white

2 tsp. vanilla extract

1 cup all-purpose flour

1½ tsp. baking powder

½ tsp. ground cinnamon

¾ cup light sour cream

⅓ cup strawberry jam

Nutrition Watch

Grape-Nuts, a wheat and toasted barley cereal that makes a nutritious breakfast, gives a crunchy nutlike texture to desserts without adding excess fat or calories.

Position a rack in the center of the oven and preheat oven to 350°F. Lightly coat an 8½-inch springform pan with cooking spray.

Prepare filling: In a food processor, combine ricotta cheese, cream cheese, egg yolk, sugar, flour, and vanilla; process until smooth.

Make topping: In a small bowl, stir together cereal, flour, brown sugar, cinnamon, oil, and water until crumbly.

Make cake: In a large bowl and using a whisk or electric mixer, beat together sugar, oil, egg, egg white, and vanilla. In another bowl, stir together flour, baking powder, and cinnamon. With a wooden spoon, stir the dry ingredients into the sugar mixture in batches, alternating with sour cream, making two additions of dry and one of wet. Stir just until combined. Pour the batter into the prepared pan.

Melt jam in a microwave or on the stovetop. Spread it over cake batter. Pour the filling over the top, spreading it to cover the batter. Sprinkle with topping.

Bake for 55 to 60 minutes or until a tester inserted in the center comes out clean. Let the cake cool in its pan on a wire rack.

To unmold the cake, run the blade of a long thin knife between the top edge of the cake and the pan. Loosen the spring and carefully lift off the sides, leaving the cake on the pan bottom. Slice and serve.

 **A Piece of Advice**

Another time, substitute raspberry, blackberry, or peach jam for the strawberry. Low-fat cottage cheese can replace the ricotta cheese, but process it well until the mixture is free of lumps.

 Nutrition per Serving

Calories: 196	Fat (total): 6.2 g	Carbohydrate: 31 g	
Protein: 4.1 g	Fat (saturated): 2 g	Dietary Fiber: 0.5 g	

Brownie Fudge Coffeecake

You can tell that I love chocolate desserts. A combination of a brownie and a cake, this makes a great basic cake because it is quite moist and full of delicious chocolate flavor. This is one of the few recipes in this section that I feel is better iced. You can serve it with coffee, but it's spectacular for afternoon tea.

Prep time: 15 minutes • Cook time: 30 to 35 minutes • Serves 16

Vegetable cooking spray

Cake

¼ cup semi-sweet chocolate chips

2 TB. water

1 cup granulated sugar

½ cup unsweetened cocoa

1 large egg

2 large egg whites

¾ cup low-fat sour cream

½ cup dark corn syrup

¼ cup canola oil

2 tsp. vanilla extract

1¼ cups all-purpose flour

1½ tsp. baking powder

Icing

⅔ cup confectioners' sugar

1 TB. unsweetened cocoa

5 tsp. water

Nutrition Watch

There is no difference in calories or nutrition between dark or light corn syrup. Dark corn syrup is flavored with caramel and is used when its color and moistness is desired. Light corn syrup is flavorless and has been clarified to remove all color and cloudiness.

A Piece of Advice

Be sure not to burn your chocolate. If you're uncertain, microwave it on the defrost cycle for a shorter time, just until the chips begin to melt, and check it more often. If the frosting thickens, add a few drops of warm water or heat it gently in the microwave

Position a rack in the center of the oven and preheat oven to 350°F. Lightly coat a 9-inch square baking pan with cooking spray.

Make cake: In a small microwavable bowl, combine chocolate chips and water. Cook on high for 30 seconds or just until the chips begin to melt. Stir the mixture until it is smooth.

In a large bowl and using a whisk or electric mixer, beat together sugar, cocoa, egg, egg whites, sour cream, corn syrup, oil, vanilla, and melted chocolate.

In another bowl, stir together flour and baking powder. With a wooden spoon, stir the dry ingredients into the sour cream mixture just until everything is combined. Pour the mixture into the prepared pan.

Bake for 30 to 35 minutes or until a tester comes out dry. Let the cake cool in its pan on a wire rack.

Make icing: In a bowl and using a whisk or electric mixer, beat confectioners' sugar, cocoa, and water until the mixture is smooth. Spread it over the cake. Cut the cake into 2¼-inch squares and serve.

 **Nutrition per Serving**

Calories: 216   Fat (total): 5.8 g   Carbohydrate: 38 g
Protein: 2.9 g   Fat (saturated): 1.6 g   Dietary Fiber: 1.4 g
Cholesterol: 17 mg

Double Chocolate Chip Banana Coffeecake

This has to be the best chocolate cake I've ever baked. The combination of the two fruits and a surprise vegetable keeps the cake moist, and the cocoa and sprinkling of chocolate chips give it a superb, dense chocolate flavor. Although it's superb for dessert, I frequently serve this special cake when I'm having a Sunday brunch.

Prep time: 20 minutes   •   Cook time: 40 to 45 minutes   •   Serves 16

Vegetable cooking spray

Cake

1 cup packed dark brown sugar

½ cup granulated sugar

⅓ cup canola oil

1 ripe medium banana, mashed (about ⅓ cup)

1 tsp. vanilla extract

2 large eggs

2 cups finely chopped or grated peeled zucchini

½ cup canned crushed pineapple, drained

2 cups all-purpose flour

⅓ cup unsweetened cocoa

1½ tsp. baking powder

1½ tsp. baking soda

⅓ cup semi-sweet chocolate chips

¼ cup low-fat sour cream

Chocolate Cream Cheese Icing

⅓ cup light cream cheese, softened

1 cup confectioners' sugar

1 TB. unsweetened cocoa

1 TB. low-fat milk

Position a rack in the center of the oven and preheat oven to 350°F. Lightly coat a 12-cup Bundt pan with cooking spray.

Make cake: In a food processor, combine brown sugar, granulated sugar, oil, banana, vanilla, and eggs; process the mixture until smooth. Add zucchini and pineapple; process the mixture just until everything is combined.

 Nutrition Watch

Zucchini is an extremely low-fat vegetable and the surprise ingredient in this recipe. Like the banana and pineapple, it adds moisture without adding fat.

In a bowl, stir together flour, cocoa, baking powder, and baking soda. Stir the wet ingredients into the dry ingredients just until they are mixed. Stir in chocolate chips and sour cream. Spoon the mixture into the prepared pan.

Bake 40 to 45 minutes or until a tester inserted in the center comes out clean. Let the cake cool in its pan on a wire rack. Unmold onto a serving plate.

Make icing: With an electric mixer or food processor, cream together cream cheese, confectioners' sugar, cocoa, and milk. Spread the mixture over the cooled cake. Slice and serve.

 Nutrition per Serving

Calories: 270　　Fat (total): 7.5 g　　Carbohydrate: 63 g
Protein: 3.7 g　　Fat (saturated): 2.2 g　　Dietary Fiber: 2.2 g
Cholesterol: 30 mg

Orange Poppy Seed Bundt Cake

This is a dense orange coffeecake, delicious with a strong citrus flavor.

Prep time: 20 minutes　•　Cook time: 30 to 35 minutes　•　Serves 14

Vegetable cooking spray

Cake

1⅓ cups granulated sugar

2 large eggs

1 cup smooth 5% ricotta cheese

⅔ cup plain low-fat yogurt

⅓ cup canola oil

3 TB. orange juice concentrate

1 TB. finely grated orange zest

1⅓ cups all-purpose flour

2¼ tsp. baking powder

2 tsp. poppy seeds

½ tsp. baking soda

Icing

2 oz. light cream cheese, softened

⅔ cup confectioners' sugar

1 TB. orange juice concentrate

Position a rack in the center of the oven and preheat oven to 350°F. Lightly coat a 9-inch Bundt pan with cooking spray.

 Nutrition Watch

Light cream cheese is reduced by 25 percent fat from regular cream cheese, which has 35 percent fat. It is not a low-fat product, so use it carefully.

Make cake: In a food processor, combine sugar, eggs, ricotta cheese, yogurt, oil, orange juice concentrate, and orange zest; purée the mixture until it is smooth. Transfer it to a large bowl.

In another bowl, stir together flour, baking powder, poppy seeds, and baking soda. With a wooden spoon, stir the dry ingredients into the orange mixture just until everything is combined. Pour the mixture into the prepared pan.

Bake for 30 to 35 minutes or until a tester inserted in the center comes out clean. Let the cake cool in its pan on a wire rack until room temperature. Unmold the cake onto a serving plate.

Make icing: Using the food processor or electric mixer, beat cream cheese, confectioners' sugar, and orange juice concentrate until the mixture is smooth. Drizzle it over the cake.

 **A Piece of Advice**

Be sure to beat the ricotta mixture well to get it as smooth as possible. A food processor lets you achieve a good consistency.

 Nutrition per Serving

Calories: 213	Fat (total): 6.9 g	Carbohydrate: 32 g
Protein: 4.6 g	Fat (saturated): 1.6 g	Dietary Fiber: 0.3 g
Cholesterol: 20 mg		

Carrot Cake with Cream Cheese Frosting

While technically not a coffeecake, I just love this cake from my first cookbook, *Toronto's Dessert Scene.* It was the carrot cake from a recipe given to me by Carole Ogus, of Carole's Cheesecakes. It is fabulous but loaded with fat and calories. This light version greatly reduces the fat by replacing a lot of the oil or butter with pineapple, using more carrots and low-fat yogurt. The frosting uses a small amount of low-fat cream cheese and spreads nicely over the cake. Invite your friends or neighbors over for coffee and serve this gem of a cake. They will all be asking for the recipe.

Prep time: 25 minutes • Cook time: 40 to 45 minutes • Serves 16

Vegetable cooking spray

Cake

⅓ cup margarine or unsalted butter

1 cup granulated sugar

2 large eggs

1 tsp. vanilla extract

1 large ripe banana, mashed

2 cups grated carrots

⅔ cup golden raisins

½ cup canned crushed pineapple, drained

½ cup plain low-fat yogurt

2 cups all-purpose flour

1½ tsp. baking powder

1½ tsp. baking soda

1½ tsp. ground cinnamon

¼ tsp. ground nutmeg

Frosting

⅓ cup light cream cheese, softened

⅔ cup confectioners' sugar

1 TB. low-fat milk or water

1 TB. grated carrots for garnish (optional)

Nutrition Watch

People often think carrot cake is healthier than other desserts. Not so! Most of these cakes use a batter made of oil, butter, eggs, and regular sour cream. The frosting is based on butter or vegetable shortening. Be careful of recipes that sound healthy, but aren't!

A Piece of Advice

Very ripe bananas can be kept frozen for up to 1 year. Raisins can be replaced with chopped, pitted dates; apricots; prunes; or currants. Use a food processor to mix the batter, but take care not to over process it.

Position a rack in the center of the oven and preheat oven to 350°F. Lightly coat a 9-inch Bundt pan with cooking spray.

Make cake: In a large bowl, cream together margarine and sugar until they are smooth; add eggs and vanilla, and beat well. (The mixture might look curdled.) Add banana, carrots, raisins, pineapple, and yogurt; stir until everything is well combined.

In a bowl, stir together flour, baking powder, baking soda, cinnamon, and nutmeg until combined. Add them to the carrot mixture; stir just until everything is combined. Pour the mixture into prepared pan.

Bake for 40 to 45 minutes or until a tester inserted in the center comes out clean. Let the cake cool in its pan for 10 minutes before inverting the cake onto a serving plate.

Make frosting: In a bowl or food processor, beat together cream cheese, confectioners' sugar, and milk until the mixture is smooth; drizzle over top of the cake. If using, decorate the cake with grated carrots.

Nutrition per Serving

Calories: 223
Protein: 4 g
Cholesterol: 30 mg

Fat (total): 5 g
Fat (saturated): 1 g

Carbohydrate: 41 g
Dietary Fiber: 1 g

Crumb Cakes

When a coffeecake is dusted with a crisp crumb topping, it's referred to as a crumb cake. These are old-fashioned cakes that date back to early days. Several books on kitchen management published back in the 1800s take a page or more describing how to make crumb cakes. Those were made with butter, eggs, and cream. My recipes are equally delicious but with a fraction of the calories, fat, and cholesterol.

Chocolate Chip Crumb Cake

If I had to name my number-one dessert of all time, this crumb cake would be it. I created this recipe for my earlier book, *Enlightened Home Cooking*, and even today I whip it up all the time. My children can now bake it blindfolded!

Prep time: 20 minutes   •   Cook time: 35 to 40 minutes   •   Serves 16

Vegetable cooking spray

Cake

8 oz. smooth 5% ricotta cheese

⅓ cup margarine or unsalted butter

1¼ cups granulated sugar

2 large eggs

2 tsp. vanilla extract

1½ cups all-purpose flour

2 tsp. baking powder

½ tsp. baking soda

¾ cup plain low-fat yogurt

½ cup semi-sweet chocolate chips

Filling

½ cup packed light brown sugar

4 tsp. unsweetened cocoa

½ tsp. ground cinnamon

Confectioners' sugar for dusting (optional)

Position a rack in the center of the oven and preheat oven to 350°F. Lightly coat a 9-inch Bundt pan with cooking spray.

Make cake: In a food processor, beat together ricotta cheese, margarine, and sugar, mixing well. Add eggs and vanilla, mixing well. Combine flour, baking powder, and baking soda. Add the dry ingredients to the bowl in batches, alternating with yogurt, mixing just until everything is incorporated. Stir in chocolate chips. Pour half the batter into prepared pan.

Nutrition Watch

I adapted this recipe from a cake sold at The Silver Palate food shop in New York City. By using cocoa, low-fat ricotta, and low-fat yogurt, I was able to reduce the amount of fat and calories for a version that won't clog your arteries so quickly! Even though chocolate is higher in fat and cholesterol than cocoa, ½ cup spread over 16 slices is acceptable. Here's proof that you don't have to give up chocolate when you eat light!

A Piece of Advice

A 9-inch springform pan can be used instead of a Bundt pan. Check the cake after 30 to 40 minutes baking time to see if it needs to cook a few minutes longer.

Prepare filling: Combine brown sugar, cocoa, and cinnamon in a small bowl. Sprinkle half over batter in the pan. Add the remaining batter and top with the remaining filling.

Bake for 35 to 40 minutes or until a tester inserted in the center comes out dry. Let the cake cool in its pan on a wire rack. After it has cooled, unmold onto a serving platter and dust cake with confectioners' sugar, if using.

 Nutrition per Serving

Calories: 226
Protein: 5 g
Cholesterol: 42 mg

Fat (total): 7 g
Fat (saturated): 4 g

Carbohydrate: 36 g
Dietary Fiber: 2 g

White Chocolate Chip Crumb Cake

When one is constantly developing recipes as I do, you tend to never "leave well enough alone." That's why I adapted my favorite Chocolate Chip Crumb Cake into a new version, dotted with white chocolate chips. It's so good!

Prep time: 30 minutes • Cook time: 35 to 40 minutes • Serves 16

Vegetable cooking spray

Cake

1⅓ cups granulated sugar

⅓ cup unsweetened cocoa

1 cup smooth 5% ricotta cheese

1 large egg

2 large egg whites

⅓ cup canola oil

1 tsp. vanilla extract

1¼ cups all-purpose flour

⅓ cup white chocolate chips

2 tsp. baking powder

½ tsp. baking soda

Crumb Filling

½ cup packed light brown sugar

4 tsp. unsweetened cocoa

Position a rack in the center of the oven and preheat oven to 350°F. Lightly coat a 9-inch Bundt pan with cooking spray.

Make cake: In a food processor, combine sugar, cocoa, ricotta cheese, egg, egg whites, oil, and vanilla; process until smooth. Transfer to a large bowl.

In another bowl, stir together flour, white chocolate chips, baking powder, and baking soda. With a wooden spoon, stir the dry ingredients into the sugar mixture just until combined.

Make crumb filling: In a small bowl, stir together brown sugar and cocoa.

Pour half of the batter into prepared pan. Sprinkle with half of the crumb mixture. Pour rest of the batter into pan and sprinkle with the remaining crumb mixture.

Bake for 35 to 40 minutes or until a tester comes out dry. Let the cake cool in its pan on a wire rack. Unmold onto a large serving plate.

 **A Piece of Advice**

I like to use a food processor when working with ricotta cheese so that I can make the batter as smooth as possible. If the cheese seems very dry, add 2 tablespoons milk to make it softer and smoother.

Nutrition Watch

Traditionally, a coffeecake like this one would be filled with much more fat, eggs, chocolate, and sour cream. By using ricotta cheese, cocoa, and just a smidgeon of white chocolate chips, the amount of fat and calories is greatly reduced, but the full chocolate flavor prevails.

 Nutrition per Serving

Calories: 225
Protein: 4.2 g
Cholesterol: 19 mg

Fat (total): 7.6 g
Fat (saturated): 2.1 g

Carbohydrate: 35 g
Dietary Fiber: 1 g

Date Crumb Cake with Coconut Topping

Cooking dates so that they soften to the point where they become a purée makes a great addition to a dessert because it gives flavor and moisture. This cake is outstanding with the coconut topping, which prettily decorates the cake.

Prep time: 30 minutes • Cook time: 35 to 40 minutes • Serves 16

Vegetable cooking spray

Cake

12 oz. (2½ cups) chopped, pitted dried dates

1¾ cups water

¼ cup margarine or unsalted butter

1 cup granulated sugar

2 large eggs

1½ cups all-purpose flour

1½ tsp. baking powder

1 tsp. baking soda

Topping

⅓ cup shredded unsweetened coconut

¼ cup packed light brown sugar

3 TB. low-fat milk

2 TB. margarine or unsalted butter

Position a rack in the center of the oven and preheat oven to 350°F. Lightly coat a 9-inch square cake pan with cooking spray.

Make cake: Place dates and water in a saucepan; bring to a boil, cover, and reduce heat to low. Cook for 10 minutes, stirring often, or until dates are soft and most of the liquid has been absorbed. Set pan aside to cool for 10 minutes.

Meanwhile, in a large bowl or food processor, beat together margarine and sugar. Add eggs and mix well. Add the cooled date mixture and mix everything well.

In a bowl, combine flour, baking powder, and baking soda. Stir the dry ingredients into the date mixture just until blended. Pour the mixture into the prepared pan.

Bake for 35 to 40 minutes or until a tester inserted in the center comes out dry. Let the cake cool in its pan on a wire rack.

Make topping: In a small saucepan, combine coconut, brown sugar, milk, and margarine; cook the mixture over medium heat, stirring, for 2 minutes, or until the sugar dissolves. Pour topping over the cake and spread evenly. Cut into 2¼-inch squares and serve.

Nutrition Watch

Dates are often used in desserts to lower the fat. They have a buttery taste when puréed and give the cake the moisture that fat would supply. They are a good source of protein and iron, too.

Nutrition per Serving

Calories: 217

Protein: 3 g

Cholesterol: 27 mg

Fat (total): 5 g

Fat (saturated): 2 g

Carbohydrate: 41 g

Dietary Fiber: 2 g

Pound Cakes

Traditional pound cakes are made of equal weights of flour, sugar, butter, and eggs. The original pound cakes didn't contain any leavening such as baking powder or baking soda, so the batter had to be beaten a very long time in order to get the cake to rise. With chemical leavenings and today's modern appliances, the making of a pound cake is easy. By using lower-fat substitutes for all the butter and eggs, pound cake can be enjoyed once again without guilt.

White and Dark Marble Pound Cake

The flavor and texture of this pound cake are heavenly. By removing a small amount of the batter and mixing it with the cocoa mixture, you produce a beautiful marbled appearance.

Prep time: 20 minutes   •   Cook time: 40 to 45 minutes   •   Serves 16

Vegetable cooking spray

Cake

1¼ cups granulated sugar

2 oz. light cream cheese, softened

¼ cup canola oil

1 large egg

1 large egg white

1 TB. vanilla extract

⅔ cup plain low-fat yogurt

1⅓ cups all-purpose flour

2 tsp. baking powder

Marble

2 TB. granulated sugar

4 tsp. unsweetened cocoa

4 tsp. water

Topping (optional)

2½ TB. packed light brown sugar

½ tsp. unsweetened cocoa

2 TB. semi-sweet chocolate chips

Position a rack in the center of the oven and preheat oven to 350°F. Lightly coat a 9-inch by 5-inch loaf pan with cooking spray.

Make cake: In a large bowl and using a whisk or electric mixer, beat together sugar, cream cheese, oil, egg, egg white, vanilla, and yogurt until mixture is smooth. In another bowl, stir together flour and baking powder. With a wooden spoon, stir the dry ingredients into the cream cheese mixture just until everything is combined. Remove ⅓ cup batter and set aside. Pour the remaining batter into prepared pan.

Make marble: In a small bowl, stir together reserved batter, sugar, cocoa, and water. Pour this over the top of the batter in the pan. Using a knife, swirl the dark batter through the light batter to create a marbled effect.

Nutrition Watch

Low-fat yogurt (1 percent milk-fat or less) gives this cake its low-fat characteristics without affecting the moisture and texture. You can substitute low-fat sour cream as well.

A Piece of Advice

You can use a food processor to mix this cake, but be careful not to over mix when the flour is added or the cake will become dry.

Prepare topping (if using): Stir together brown sugar, cocoa, and chocolate chips. Sprinkle the mixture over the batter.

Bake for 40 to 45 minutes or until a tester comes out dry. Let the cake cool in its pan on a wire rack.

Remove the cake from the pan and cut into 8 slices. Cut each slice in half to serve.

Nutrition per Serving

Calories: 161
Protein: 2.7 g
Cholesterol: 16 mg

Fat (total): 4.7 g
Fat (saturated): 0.9 g

Carbohydrate: 27 g
Dietary Fiber: 0.4 g

Banana Chocolate Chip Pound Cake with Streusel Topping

This banana cake beats all the others. The moist texture comes from the bananas and yogurt. The cake has a delicious crunchy topping, with a few chocolate chips thrown in.

Prep time: 20 minutes • Cook time: 40 to 45 minutes • Serves 16

Vegetable cooking spray

Cake

¾ cup granulated sugar

1 ripe large banana, mashed (½ cup)

¼ cup canola oil

1 large egg

1 large egg white

2 tsp. vanilla extract

1 cup plain low-fat yogurt

1⅔ cups all-purpose flour

1½ tsp. baking powder

½ tsp. baking soda

⅓ cup semi-sweet chocolate chips

Topping

⅓ cup Grape-Nuts cereal

¼ cup packed light brown sugar

1 TB. all-purpose flour

1½ tsp. canola oil

1 tsp. water

Position a rack in the center of the oven and preheat oven to 350°F. Lightly coat a 9-inch by 5-inch loaf pan with cooking spray.

Make cake: In a large bowl and using a whisk or electric mixer, combine sugar, banana, oil, egg, egg white, vanilla, and yogurt. In another bowl, stir together flour, baking powder, baking soda, and chocolate chips. With a wooden spoon, stir the dry ingredients into the banana mixture just until everything is combined. Pour mixture into prepared pan.

To prepare topping: In a bowl, stir together cereal, brown sugar, flour, oil, and water until combined. Sprinkle evenly over the batter.

Bake for 40 to 45 minutes or until a tester comes out dry.

Let the cake cool in its pan on a wire rack.

Remove the cake from the pan and cut into 8 slices. Cut each slice in half to serve.

 A Piece of Advice

For best results, use the ripest bananas you can find. In fact, keep overripe bananas in the freezer so that they're handy for baking—just defrost and mash them. The intensity of their flavor is superb.

Nutrition per Serving

Calories: 194
Protein: 3 g
Cholesterol: 18 mg

Fat (total): 6.4 g
Fat (saturated): 1.8 g

Carbohydrate: 31 g
Dietary Fiber: 1 g

Snack Cakes

"Snack time!" Those words are heard in most every home, every day. Because pre-packaged snacks and chips are usually so high in fat, I make sure that my home has a steady supply of snacks that are not high in fat, yet so full of flavor that my kids will pick my snacks—especially my snack cakes—every time. These are cakes to be cut into squares and eaten out of hand. My kids love to take these cakes to school in their lunch boxes; my husband and I frequently indulge with a cold glass of milk before bed.

Milk Chocolate Fudge Snack Cake

This is a dense chocolate cake that uses very little flour. The flavor is so heavenly that you'll never believe it's low in fat. I love to serve this cake with a chocolate or raspberry sauce (see Chapter 16).

Prep time: 20 minutes • Cook time: 30 to 35 minutes • Chill time: at least 30 minutes • Serves 12

Vegetable cooking spray

½ cup milk chocolate chips

3 TB. water

1 TB. chocolate liqueur

¾ cup + 3 TB. sugar (divided use)

½ cup unsweetened cocoa

3 TB. all-purpose flour

2 large egg yolks

¾ cup evaporated skim milk

2 large egg whites

¼ tsp. cream of tartar

Nutrition Watch _____

All chocolate, whether it's white, dark, or milk chocolate, has approximately the same amount of fat and calories. One ounce has about 130 calories and 9 grams of fat.

Position a rack in the center of the oven and preheat oven to 350°F. Lightly coat an 8-inch springform pan with cooking spray.

In a small microwavable bowl, combine chocolate chips, water, and liqueur. Microwave the mixture on high for 40 seconds. Stir it until it is smooth.

In a large bowl, whisk together ¾ cup sugar, cocoa, flour, egg yolks, and evaporated milk. Whisk in the chocolate mixture.

In another bowl and using an electric mixer, beat egg whites with cream of tartar until they are foamy. Gradually add remaining 3 tablespoons sugar, beating until stiff peaks form. Fold the mixture into the batter just until blended. Pour the batter into the prepared pan.

Bake for 30 to 35 minutes or until the cake is just set at the center. Let the cake cool in its pan on a wire rack. Chill for at least 30 minutes.

To unmold the cake, run the blade of a long thin knife between the top edge of the cake and the pan. Loosen the spring and carefully lift off the sides, leaving the cake on the pan bottom. Slice and serve.

 **Nutrition per Serving**

Calories: 150   Fat (total): 3.5 g   Carbohydrate: 26 g
Protein: 3.5 g   Fat (saturated): 1.8 g Dietary Fiber: 1.7 g
Cholesterol: 36 mg

Molasses and Ginger Chiffon Snack Cake

Chiffon cakes have a lovely light texture like angel food cake, but a more enjoyable crumb. This heavenly one relies on whipped egg whites for its airiness. "Chiffon" merely means the cake is made with oil instead of a solid shortening. I chose to make this snack cake in a tube pan instead of a square pan. It's great for snacking and eating out of hand.

Prep time: 25 minutes   •   Cook time: 30 to 35 minutes   •   Serves 12

1 TB. instant coffee granules

3 TB. hot water

¾ cup + ⅓ cup sugar (divided use)

¾ tsp. ground ginger

2 large egg yolks

¼ cup dark molasses

3 TB. canola oil

6 large egg whites, about ¾ cup

½ tsp. cream of tartar

1 cup cake flour

1½ tsp. baking powder

Position a rack in the center of the oven and preheat oven to 325°F. Set aside an ungreased 10-inch tube pan. Dissolve the instant coffee in the hot water. Set aside to cool.

In a large bowl, whisk together ¾ cup sugar, ginger, egg yokes, molasses, oil, and cooled coffee. In another bowl, beat egg whites with cream of tartar until they are foamy. Gradually add remaining ⅓ cup sugar, beating until stiff peaks form.

In a separate bowl, sift cake flour with baking powder. Gently fold the dry ingredients into the molasses mixture. Gently fold in egg whites. Pour the mixture into the pan.

Nutrition Watch

The traditional chiffon cakes sound like they are low in fat, but most have as many as 6 egg yolks, which add greatly to the fat and cholesterol. This version only uses 2, with more whites. You won't notice the difference.

Bake for 30 to 35 minutes or until a tester comes out dry. Invert the cake immediately onto a wire rack, taking care so that the cake does not crack. Let it rest until it is completely cool. Take the cake out of the pan carefully, using a knife to separate it from the sides of pan.

 Nutrition per Serving

Calories: 169   Fat (total): 4.4 g   Carbohydrate: 29 g
Protein: 3.3 g   Fat (saturated): 0.5 g   Dietary Fiber: 0.8 g
Cholesterol: 35 mg

Gingerbread Snack Cake with Molasses Cream Cheese Frosting

Gingerbread, whether in a cookie, cake, or any dessert, has a unique combination of flavors. The molasses, cinnamon, and ginger give it that distinctive taste and aroma. Take this cake to your next picnic.

Prep time: 25 minutes   •   Cook time: 20 to 25 minutes   •   Serves 16

Vegetable cooking spray

Cake

1 cup packed dark brown sugar

1 tsp. ground cinnamon

½ tsp. ground ginger

1 large egg

2 large egg whites

¾ cup plain low-fat yogurt

½ cup dark molasses

3 TB. canola oil

1⅓ cups all-purpose flour

1 tsp. baking powder

½ tsp. baking soda

Frosting

2 oz. light cream cheese, softened

⅓ cup confectioners' sugar

2 tsp. dark molasses

1½ tsp. water

Nutrition Watch

Molasses is rich in iron, calcium, and phosphorous. Be sure to buy dark molasses for your baking. Contrary to belief, blackstrap is only marginally more nutritious than regular molasses.

Position a rack in the center of the oven and preheat oven to 350°F. Lightly coat a 13-inch by 9-inch cake pan with cooking spray.

Make cake: In a large bowl and using a whisk or electric mixer, beat brown sugar, cinnamon, ginger, egg, egg whites, yogurt, molasses, and oil.

In another bowl, stir together flour, baking powder, and baking soda. With a wooden spoon, stir the dry ingredients into the molasses mixture just until everything is combined. Pour the mixture into the prepared pan.

Bake for 20 to 25 minutes or until a tester comes out dry. Let the cake cool in its pan on a wire rack.

Make frosting: Using a food processor or electric mixer, beat cream cheese, confectioners' sugar, molasses, and water until the mixture is smooth. Spread over the cooled cake.

A Piece of Advice

If your brown sugar becomes hard, try microwaving it for a few seconds and then add a piece of bread to your container. That always keeps it moist.

Nutrition per Serving

Calories: 178	Fat (total): 3.8 g	Carbohydrate: 33 g
Protein: 2.9 g	Fat (saturated): 0.8 g	Dietary Fiber: 0.4 g
Cholesterol: 16 mg		

Maple Apple Cinnamon Snack Cake

This cake resembles a light apple coffeecake. The applesauce sweetens the cake, as well as giving it moisture, so you don't need much fat. It's great for afternoon tea or as a special treat while you're watching a special video.

Prep time: 25 minutes • Cook time: 35 to 40 minutes • Serves 16

Vegetable cooking spray

Cake

½ cup packed light brown sugar

1 tsp. ground cinnamon

1 large egg

2 large egg whites

1 cup unsweetened applesauce

½ cup pure maple syrup

½ cup plain low-fat yogurt

⅓ cup canola oil

2 tsp. vanilla extract

2 cups + 1 TB. all-purpose flour (divided use)

1½ tsp. baking powder

1 tsp. baking soda

1 cup diced, peeled apples

2 TB. granulated sugar

Icing

1 cup confectioners' sugar

2 TB. pure maple syrup

1 TB. water

A Piece of Advice

Be sure to buy unsweetened applesauce, and choose small jars because the sauce goes bad quickly after opening. Always use a clean utensil in the jar to keep out bacteria.

Nutrition Watch

Applesauce is simply cooked and puréed apples. It's a wonderful low-fat ingredient to use in baking as a substitute for some of the fat. You can reduce the fat by as much as 75 percent by using applesauce or another cooked puréed fruit.

Position a rack in the center of the oven and preheat oven to 350°F. Lightly coat a 9-inch Bundt pan with cooking spray.

Make cake: In a large bowl and using a whisk or electric mixer, beat together brown sugar, cinnamon, egg, egg whites, applesauce, maple syrup, yogurt, oil, and vanilla.

In another bowl, stir together 2 cups flour, baking powder, and baking soda. With a wooden spoon, stir the dry ingredients into the applesauce mixture just until everything is combined.

In another bowl, toss together apples, sugar, and the remaining 1 tablespoon flour. Stir the mixture into the batter. Pour it into the prepared pan.

Bake for 35 to 40 minutes or until a tester comes out dry. Let the cake cool in its pan on a wire rack. Unmold onto a large serving plate.

Make icing: In a bowl and using an electric mixer, beat together confectioners' sugar, maple syrup, and water. Add additional water as needed to achieve spreading consistency. Spread the icing over the cake.

Nutrition per Serving

Calories: 218
Protein: 2.9 g
Cholesterol: 14 mg

Fat (total): 5.2 g
Fat (saturated): 0.5 g

Carbohydrate: 40 g
Dietary Fiber: 0.8 g

Pumpkin Orange Maple Snack Cake

The combination of orange, pumpkin, and maple syrup is fabulous in this snacking cake. I pack these squares in the kids' lunches; they are also great as a midnight snack.

Prep time: 15 minutes • Cook time: 35 minutes • Serves 16

Vegetable cooking spray

Cake

1 cup packed light brown sugar

1½ tsp. ground cinnamon

¼ tsp. ground ginger

1 large egg

2 oz. light cream cheese, softened

½ cup pumpkin purée

½ cup plain low-fat yogurt

2 tsp. finely grated orange zest

⅓ cup fresh orange juice

¼ cup canola oil

3 TB. pure maple syrup

1½ cups all-purpose flour

1½ tsp. baking powder

½ tsp. baking soda

2 large egg whites

¼ tsp. cream of tartar

¼ cup granulated sugar

Icing

½ cup confectioners' sugar

2 TB. pure maple syrup

1½ tsp. water

Position a rack in the center of the oven and pre-heat oven to 350°F. Lightly coat a 9-inch square cake pan with cooking spray.

Make cake: In a large bowl and using a whisk or electric mixer, beat brown sugar, cinnamon, ginger, egg, cream cheese, pumpkin purée, yogurt, orange zest, orange juice, oil, and maple syrup. In another bowl, stir together flour, baking powder, and baking soda. With a wooden spoon, stir the dry ingredients into the pumpkin mixture just until everything is combined.

In a separate bowl and using clean beaters, beat egg whites with cream of tartar until they are foamy. Gradually add sugar, beating until stiff peaks form. Stir ¼ of egg whites into the batter. Gently fold in remaining egg whites just until blended. Pour the mixture into the prepared pan.

Bake for 35 minutes or until a tester comes out dry. Let the cake cool in its pan on a wire rack.

Make icing: In a bowl and using an electric mixer, beat together confectioners' sugar, maple syrup, and water. Spread the mixture over top of the cooled cake.

Nutrition Watch

Cooked, puréed pumpkin is a great fruit to use as a fat sub-stitute in baking—you can reduce the fat by as much as 75 percent. Be sure not to buy pumpkin pie filling, which has sugar and spices already added.

A Piece of Advice

For the best flavor, use pure maple syrup, not the artifi-cial kind. Artificial or pancake syrups are nothing more than corn syrup and artificial flavoring and color.

 **Nutrition per Serving**

Calories: 189   Fat (total): 4.6 g   Carbohydrate: 34 g
Protein: 3 g   Fat (saturated): 0.8 g   Dietary Fiber: 0.8 g
Cholesterol: 16 mg

The Least You Need to Know

◆ Coffeecakes, crumb cakes, pound cakes, and snack cakes needn't be loaded with fat and cholesterol—you can use canola oil in place of butter and low-fat sour cream or yogurt for superb texture.

◆ Spike the flavor of these luscious cakes with spices, flavoring extracts, and fresh citrus zest.

◆ These cakes are rarely frosted—instead lightly dusted with confectioners' sugar or given a crunchy, sometimes nutty, topping.

◆ Bake the cakes in the center of the oven until a tester inserted in the middle comes out clean. Cool in their pan on a wire rack.

Chapter 6

Cobblers, Crisps, and Crumbles

In This Chapter

- Luscious fruit cobblers with a light biscuit toppings
- Light fruit crisps with crunchy toppings
- British-style crumbles with crumbly toppings

I don't know anyone who doesn't love a cobbler … or a crisp … or a crumble. These homey desserts are superb while still warm from the oven, but I find myself eating leftovers for breakfast or lunch the next day.

A mainstay dessert during the early frontier days, cobblers and the like are among the simplest desserts to make, consisting of little more than fruit with a crust (when the cook had time to make it) or a crumbly topping (when she didn't). These are desserts with only one secret—their simplicity.

Although most splendid in the summertime when the flavors are bursting from the fresh fruits and berries, thanks to modern freezing techniques, frozen fruits and berries can be used year round. If you are using frozen, measure the fruit or berries when still frozen, and then defrost and drain well before using.

Do yourself a favor when making these desserts. Experiment a little if you must, but keep to very few ingredients. The fruit is supposed to be the primary flavor so avoid adding more spices or making a more complicated crust. Depending on what you have on hand, though, do feel free to mix and match these recipes, using a filling from one recipe and a crust or topping from another.

Cobblers

A cobbler is a baked deep-dish fruit dessert topped with a thick biscuit crust, often sprinkled with sugar. The toppings in these recipes require little fat because they use yogurt or buttermilk. A cobbler is done when a toothpick or cake tester inserted into the crust comes out dry and clean. It's best served warm with frozen yogurt, fruit sauce, or a vanilla-based sauce. Cobblers are great reheated—just place them in a 350°F oven for 10 minutes.

Buttermilk Cranberry-Apple Cobbler

I love cobblers all year round—even if you don't have fresh fruit, you can always use frozen. Just be sure to thaw and drain it well. My favorite apples for baking are Mutsu, Granny Smith, Spy, and Paula Red because of their taste and texture. Serve this cobbler still hot from the oven, with frozen yogurt.

Prep time: 15 minutes • Cook time: 40 minutes • Serves 12

Vegetable cooking spray

Filling

6 cups sliced, peeled apples

1½ cups cranberries

1 cup granulated sugar

¾ tsp. ground cinnamon

⅓ cup apple juice

1½ TB. cornstarch

Topping

¾ cup all-purpose flour

⅓ cup + 1 TB. sugar (divided use)

½ tsp. baking powder

¼ cup buttermilk

1 TB. canola oil

1 large egg

½ tsp. ground cinnamon

Nutrition Watch

Apples provide a good source of dietary fiber and carbohydrate. Cranberries are very high in vitamin C. A cobbler is an easy way to get kids to eat more fruit.

Position a rack in the center of the oven and preheat oven to 375°F. Lightly coat a 9-inch square cake pan with cooking spray.

Make filling: In a large bowl, stir together apples, cranberries, sugar, and cinnamon. In a small bowl, whisk apple juice with cornstarch until smooth; stir the liquid into the fruit mixture. Pour the mixture into the prepared pan.

Make topping: In a bowl, stir together flour, ⅓ cup sugar, and baking powder. In another bowl, mix buttermilk, oil, and egg. With a wooden spoon, add the dry ingredients to the wet and mix until everything is just combined. Drop the batter by spoonfuls on top of the fruit mixture.

Stir together remaining 1 tablespoon sugar and cinnamon; sprinkle the mixture over the batter.

Bake for 40 minutes or until a tester placed in the center comes out dry. Serve warm.

 A Piece of Advice

Feel free to replace the apples with pears for a change. If you're using frozen cranberries, you don't have to thaw them first. If you don't have apple juice, try orange juice. Instead of buttermilk, you can use plain low-fat yogurt or add 1 teaspoon fresh lemon juice to ¼ cup of milk and let stand 5 minutes.

 Nutrition per Serving

Calories: 188
Protein: 1.6 g
Cholesterol: 18 mg

Fat (total): 1.9 g
Fat (saturated): 0.3 g

Carbohydrate: 41 g
Dietary Fiber: 1.9 g

Sour Cream Blueberry Peach Cobbler

Blueberries and peaches make a perfect combination in this warm and delicious cobbler. I like to serve this cobbler hot with a scoop of vanilla frozen yogurt or with Vanilla Cream (see Chapter 16).

Prep time: 15 minutes • Cook time: 35 to 40 minutes • Serves 12

Vegetable cooking spray

Filling

2½ cups blueberries

2½ cups sliced and peeled peaches

1 TB. cornstarch

⅓ cup granulated sugar

¼ tsp. ground cinnamon

Topping

1 cup all-purpose flour

1 tsp. baking powder

⅓ cup granulated sugar

1 large egg

⅓ cup low-fat sour cream

2 TB. margarine or unsalted butter, softened

1 TB. water

Position a rack in the center of the oven and preheat oven to 350°F. Lightly coat an 8-inch square cake pan with cooking spray.

Make filling: In a bowl, stir together blueberries, peaches, and cornstarch. In another bowl, stir together sugar and cinnamon. Set aside 1 tablespoon. Stir remaining cinnamon-sugar mixture into the berry mixture. Pour the mixture into the prepared pan.

Nutrition Watch

Peaches contain both vitamins A and C, as well as potassium. Blueberries are high in vitamin C and are a good source of fiber, potassium, and carbohydrate. Together, they pack a dynamic nutritional punch.

Make topping: In a bowl, stir together flour and baking powder. In another bowl, mix sugar, egg, sour cream, margarine, and water. With a wooden spoon, add the dry ingredients to the wet until everything is combined. Drop by spoonfuls on top of the fruit mixture. Sprinkle the top with reserved cinnamon sugar.

Bake for 35 to 40 minutes or until a tester inserted in the center comes out dry. Serve warm.

Nutrition per Serving

Calories: 154

Protein: 2.3 g

Cholesterol: 20 mg

Fat (total): 3 g

Fat (saturated): 0.8 g

Carbohydrate: 2.9 g

Dietary Fiber: 1.4 g

Crisps

Crisps are similar to cobblers except they have a topping sprinkled over the fruit in place of the dough. Crisps are done when the topping is browned and crisp and the fruit is tender. They are tasty served warm or at room temperature with either frozen yogurt, Vanilla Cream (see Chapter 16), or a pitcher of rich cream.

Rhubarb-Strawberry Granola Crisp

Crisps are especially delicious when fruit is fresh and ripe. Serve this crisp with Vanilla Cream (see Chapter 16). The combination of sweet strawberries, tart rhubarb, and a crunchy sweet topping makes a unique crisp.

Prep time: 15 minutes   •   Cook time: 30 minutes   •   Serves 12

Vegetable cooking spray

Filling

2½ cups sliced strawberries

2 cups sliced rhubarb

¾ cup granulated sugar

1 TB. cornstarch

Topping

¾ cup all-purpose flour

⅔ cup low-fat granola

⅓ cup packed light brown sugar

½ tsp. ground cinnamon

2½ TB. water

2 TB. canola oil

Position a rack in the center of the oven and preheat oven to 350°F. Lightly coat a 9-inch square cake pan with cooking spray.

Make filling: In a bowl, stir together strawberries, rhubarb, sugar, and cornstarch. Pour the mixture into the prepared baking dish.

Make topping: In another bowl, stir together flour, granola, brown sugar, cinnamon, water, and oil until crumbly. Sprinkle it over the fruit mixture.

Bake for 30 minutes or until the topping is browned and crisp. Serve warm.

 A Piece of Advice

Frozen cut-up rhubarb is sold in the supermarket. Measure it when it is still frozen; then thaw it and drain it well before using.

Many different varieties of granola are in the stores; choose your favorite, but be sure that it is low fat.

Nutrition per Serving

Calories: 165
Protein: 1.7 g
Cholesterol: 0 mg

Fat (total): 2.9 g
Fat (saturated): 0.2 g

Carbohydrate: 33 g
Dietary Fiber: 1.8 g

Strawberry-Blueberry Double Crisp

The combination of low-fat granola and oats makes a light and crispy topping, which has a nutty texture without excess fat and calories.

Prep time: 15 minutes • Cook time: 25 minutes • Serves 12

Vegetable cooking spray

1½ cup blueberries

1½ cups sliced strawberries

¼ cup granulated sugar

1 cup + 1 TB. all-purpose flour (divided use)

¾ cup packed light brown sugar

¾ cup quick-cooking oats

½ cup low-fat granola

1 tsp. ground cinnamon

¼ cup canola oil

2 TB. water

Position a rack in the center of the oven and preheat oven to 350°F. Lightly coat an 8-inch square cake pan with cooking spray.

Nutrition Watch _____

Granola cereals might sound healthy, but most are loaded with fat, sugar, and a lot of calories. Low-fat varieties are available that are delicious and contain much less fat and sugar.

In a bowl, stir together blueberries, strawberries, sugar, and 1 tablespoon flour. Set aside.

In another bowl, stir together the remaining 1 cup flour, brown sugar, oats, granola, and cinnamon. Stir in oil and water until the mixture is crumbly. Pat half of it into the prepared pan. Spread the reserved berry mixture evenly over the top. Sprinkle the remaining oat mixture on top.

Bake for 25 minutes or until the crisp is golden. Serve warm.

Nutrition per Serving

Calories: 207
Protein: 2.6 g
Cholesterol: 0 mg

Fat (total): 5.4 g
Fat (saturated): 0.4 g

Carbohydrate: 37 g
Dietary Fiber: 1.9 g

Crumbles

Crumbles are fruit-based desserts topped with a crumbly mixture often made with rolled oats, low-fat granola, or Grape-Nuts, which is a low-fat wheat and toasted barley cereal. A British dessert, crumbles can also be topped with frozen yogurt, Vanilla Cream (see Chapter 16), or a dash of rich cream.

Pear and Plum Crumble

Grape-Nuts cereal makes a wonderfully crunchy topping for a crumble. It is a good substitute for chopped nuts, without excess fat and calories. Ripe pears and plums make this crumble a wonderful summer dessert, especially when teamed with fruit sorbet.

Prep time: 15 minutes • Cook time: 30 to 35 minutes • Serves 12

Vegetable cooking spray

Filling

2 cups sliced, peeled pears

2 cups sliced plums

⅓ cup granulated sugar

¼ tsp. ground cinnamon

¼ cup fresh orange juice

1 TB. cornstarch

Topping

⅔ cup packed light brown sugar

½ cup all-purpose flour

⅓ cup Grape-Nuts cereal

⅓ cup quick-cooking oats

¼ tsp. ground cinnamon

2½ TB. water

2 TB. canola oil

Position a rack in the center of the oven and preheat oven to 350°F. Lightly coat an 8-inch square cake pan with cooking spray.

Make filling: In a bowl, gently stir together pears, plums, sugar, and cinnamon. In a small bowl, whisk orange juice with cornstarch until it is smooth; stir into the fruit mixture. Pour the mixture into a prepared pan.

Make topping: In the bowl, stir together brown sugar, flour, cereal, oats, cinnamon, water, and oil until crumbly. Sprinkle it over the fruit mixture.

Bake for 30 to 35 minutes or until the crumble is golden. Serve warm.

 A Piece of Advice

Be sure that the pears are ripe and sweet. My favorite pears to use in this crisp are Bartlett or Bosc. I think the best plums for this are Italian prune plums, which are small and purple, but any variety of plum will work nicely. Be sure that the plums are ripe—they will ripen to perfection in an ordinary brown paper bag at room temperature.

 Nutrition per Serving

Calories: 168
Protein: 1.5 g
Cholesterol: 0 mg

Fat (total): 2.8 g
Fat (saturated): 0.2 g

Carbohydrate: 34 g
Dietary Fiber: 1.7 g

The Least You Need to Know

- ◆ Fresh fruit and berries are best, but frozen can be used.
- ◆ If using frozen, be sure to measure while still frozen; then thaw and drain well before using.
- ◆ Be sure to position the oven rack in the center of the oven for even baking.
- ◆ Frozen yogurt, ice cream, rich cream, and fruit or vanilla-based sauces can be served on top as a special garnish.

Tarts and Pies

In This Chapter

- ◆ Buttery fruit, chocolate, and pecan tarts
- ◆ Cream pies, chocolate pies, and meringue pies
- ◆ Light mousse pies, tangy with citrus or flavored with peanut butter, chocolate, or spices

Creamy and fancy or simple and down-home, tarts and pies are the perfect desserts and among the simplest to make. They are a combination of French, English, and American cooking traditions, allowing the cook to use all sorts of different ingredients.

How do you reduce the fat in these desserts? Start with the crust. The best low-fat crusts are made with cookie crumbs (crushed graham crackers, chocolate wafers, or vanilla wafers) or with a baked crust made with an egg-white meringue. Crumb crusts are held together with a small amount of oil or butter and water or honey, and they are always patted on the bottom and sides of the pan.

Some recipes have a flaky pie crust made from butter, oil, light cream cheese, and yogurt. Using a food processor to first mix the dough, the dough is then gathered into a ball, flattened slightly, and chilled for 20 minutes. Dust the dough lightly with flour on all sides, brushing off the excess, then place it between two sheets of waxed paper and roll it out. When the dough is rolled to the right thickness, peel off the top sheet of waxed paper and invert the pastry into the pie plate with the second piece of waxed paper still in place. Adjust the position of the dough, if necessary, and then peel off the waxed paper and gently ease the dough into the pan. This delicious crust contains very little fat compared to a regular pie crust. Now you're ready to add any number of delicious fillings and you have a home-made tart or pie that's a hundred times better than any bought at the store.

My tarts are baked in an 8-inch tart pan or 9-inch flan ring, both with removable bottoms. Press the dough against the fluted side of the pan so that when the tart is unmolded it holds the shape of the pan. Turn down the edge about ¼ inch so that it extends only about ⅛ inch above the top of the pan. Using the back edge of a knife blade, held at an angle, make decorative marks all around.

All the pie recipes in this chapter use a standard 9-inch pie plate, either glass or metal. I always spray the plate with vegetable cooking spray. Once the pie dough is in place, trim off the excess, leaving about a ½ inch overhang. Tuck the overhang under the crust border and press down all around the top to seal it. For a rustic look, you can leave the border plain. You can create a decorative edge by crimping the dough or pressing the dough at regular intervals with the tines of a fork. To lower the fat in the fillings, I've used low-fat ricotta cheese in place of regular cream cheese, or low-fat yogurt or sour cream, which takes the place of regular sour cream. Evaporated skim milk and low-fat condensed milk replace heavy cream.

Garnish tarts and pies with confectioners' sugar or cocoa. Make spider or spiral designs on top using melted chocolate or a combination of low-fat sour cream mixed with a little water and sugar. Put the mixture in a small plastic bag, and then cut the very tip of the end off. Draw four concentric circles on top of the pie filling before baking and run a toothpick through the circles at regular intervals. A baked pie is ready when the center is still slightly loose. Let it cool to room temperature and then chill before serving for easy slicing.

If you're one of those people who've never made a pie, you'll find the old saying "as easy as pie" is really true—so let's get started.

Tarts

A tart is quite simply a shallow pastry crust and a filling with no top crust. They are typically baked in a tart pan. Depending on the type of crust you're using, the crust can be baked and then filled or filled and then baked.

Apple Tart

Apples and creamy cheese filling with a shortbread-type crust make a wonderful dessert. The addition of cinnamon and brown sugar to the apples brings out their fresh flavor.

Prep time: 25 minutes • Cook time: 30 minutes • Chill time: at least 1 hour • Serves 12

Vegetable cooking spray

Pastry

⅓ cup granulated sugar

3 TB. canola oil

1½ oz. light cream cheese

1¼ cup all-purpose flour

3 TB. plain low-fat yogurt

Filling

⅓ cup granulated sugar

1 cup smooth 5% ricotta cheese

4 oz. light cream cheese, softened

1 tsp. vanilla extract

Apple Topping

2 tsp. margarine or unsalted butter

4 cups sliced, peeled apples

⅓ cup packed light brown sugar

½ tsp. ground cinnamon

Position a rack in the center of the oven and preheat the oven to 375°F. Lightly coat a 9-inch flan ring with a removable bottom with cooking spray.

Make pastry: In a food processor, purée sugar, oil, and cream cheese until the mixture is smooth. Add the flour and yogurt and process off and on until the mixture is crumbly. Press the mixture into a ball and wrap in plastic wrap. Chill for 20 minutes. Meanwhile, prepare filling.

Make filling: In a food processor, combine sugar, ricotta cheese, cream cheese, and vanilla; purée until smooth. Pour mixture into the cooled crust.

Nutrition Watch

Apples are a good source of vitamins A and C. For baking, I like to use a firm, sweet apple such as a Spy, Royal Gala, Mutsu, or Paula Red.

Roll the pastry between two sheets of floured wax paper into a circle large enough to fit the pan. Fit it into the pan, working the pastry up the side. Place a piece of foil over the pastry. Bake for 20 minutes, uncover, and bake for another 10 minutes or until crust is golden. Let it cool on a wire rack.

Make apple topping: In a nonstick frying pan, melt margarine over medium-high heat; cook apples, brown sugar, and cinnamon for 5 to 7 minutes, stirring occasionally, or until apples are tender. Place the mixture on top of the filling. Chill for 1 hour. Before serving, remove the edge of the flan ring and slide the tart (on the pan bottom) onto a flat serving plate.

 **Nutrition per Serving**

Calories: 228
Protein: 4.9 g
Cholesterol: 12 mg

Fat (total): 7 g
Fat (saturated): 2.6 g

Carbohydrate: 34 g
Dietary Fiber: 1.1 g

Lime Cream Cheese Tart

The combination of limes and a creamy cheese filling makes this tart luscious, and the vanilla wafer cookies add a buttery-flavored crust.

Prep time: 20 minutes   •   Cook time: 35 to 40 minutes   •   Serves 12

Vegetable cooking spray

Crust

1½ cups vanilla wafer crumbs

2 TB. granulated sugar

2 TB. water

1 TB. canola oil

Filling

¼ cup granulated sugar

1 TB. all-purpose flour

⅓ cup fresh lime juice (about 2 limes)

1 TB. finely grated lime zest

¾ cup low-fat sour cream

2 oz. light cream cheese, softened

1 large egg

2 large egg whites

Topping

1 cup low-fat sour cream

3 TB. granulated sugar

A Piece of Advice

Buy whole vanilla wafers and process them in the food processor until they are finely ground. One box contains approximately 2½ cups of crumbs. It takes 2 to 3 limes to obtain ⅓ cup of lime juice.

Nutrition Watch

Traditionally, this tart would be made with cream cheese, whipping cream, and heavy 14 percent sour cream. You can use 1 percent sour cream without any loss of texture or taste.

Position a rack in the center of the oven and preheat the oven to 375°F. Lightly coat a 9-inch pie plate with cooking spray.

Make crust: In a bowl, stir together wafer crumbs, sugar, water, and oil until combined. Pat the mixture over the bottom and up the sides of the prepared plate.

Make filling: In a food processor, purée sugar, flour, lime juice and rind, sour cream, cream cheese, egg, and egg whites until smooth. Pour the mixture into the crust. Bake for 25 to 30 minutes or until the center is just set.

Make topping: In a bowl, stir together sour cream and sugar. Pour the mixture carefully over the hot filling, smoothing it evenly with a knife. Return the plate to the oven and bake for another 10 minutes. Let the plate cool on a wire rack. Chill before serving.

Nutrition per Serving

Calories: 200
Protein: 3.3 g
Cholesterol: 33 mg

Fat (total): 6.0 g
Fat (saturated): 2.4 g

Carbohydrate: 34 g
Dietary Fiber: 0.3 g

Orange Chocolate Cream Cheese Tart

The buttery shortbread crust, with chocolate layer and orange cream cheese filling, makes for a wonderful dessert. Top this tart with strawberries or any fresh fruit that's in season.

Prep time: 20 minutes • Cook time: 20 minutes • Chill time: at least 1 hour • Serves 12

Vegetable cooking spray

Pastry

1 cup + 2 TB. all-purpose flour

⅓ cup granulated sugar

¼ cup margarine or unsalted butter, cold, cut into 8 pieces

3 TB. plain low-fat yogurt

2 TB. water

Chocolate Layer

3 TB. semi-sweet chocolate chips

1 TB. water

Filling

⅓ cup granulated sugar

½ cup smooth 5% ricotta cheese

2 oz. light cream cheese, softened

2 TB. orange juice concentrate

2 tsp. finely grated orange zest

½ tsp. vanilla extract

2 cups sliced fresh strawberries (or other fruit in season)

Position a rack in the center of the oven and preheat the oven to 375°F. Lightly coat an 8-inch tart pan with removable bottom with cooking spray.

Make pastry: In a food processor, add flour, sugar, and margarine. Pulse just until the mixture is crumbly. Add the yogurt and water and pulse just until everything is combined. Press the dough into a ball and wrap it in plastic wrap. Chill for 20 minutes. Meanwhile, prepare filling.

Make chocolate layer: In a small microwavable bowl, combine chocolate chips and water. Microwave on high heat for about 30 seconds. Stir until smooth. Spoon the melted chocolate over the pastry shell and use a knife to spread it thinly.

Between two floured sheets of waxed paper, roll the pastry dough into a circle large enough to fit the pan. Fit the pastry into the pan, working it up the sides. Place a piece of foil over the pastry. Bake for 10 minutes. Remove the foil and bake another 10 minutes or until the crust is golden. Let the pan cool on a wire rack.

Make filling: In a food processor, combine sugar, ricotta cheese, cream cheese, orange juice concentrate, orange zest, and vanilla; purée until smooth. Pour into the pastry shell. Top with fruit. Chill for 1 hour.

Before serving, remove the edge of the tart pan and slide the tart (on the pan bottom) onto a flat serving plate.

Nutrition Watch

Custard tart is usually made with a high-fat crust and a combination of egg yolks and whipping cream for the filling. The calories and fat are greatly reduced in this version.

 **A Piece of Advice**

If you want the berries to shine, melt 2 tablespoons apple jelly or red currant jelly with 1 tablespoon water and brush over the top.

 **Nutrition per Serving**

Calories: 177   Fat (total): 6.5 g   Carbohydrate: 26 g
Protein: 3.5 g   Fat (saturated): 2.2 g   Dietary Fiber: 1.2 g
Cholesterol: 6 mg

Chocolate Mousse Royale Tart

This recipe was a late addition to this book! I had so many wonderful chocolate desserts that I knew one more couldn't hurt, especially a decadent mousse piled into a baked meringue.

Prep time: 20 minutes • Cook time: 75 • Chill time: at least 2 hours • Serves 12

Vegetable cooking spray

Meringue

3 large egg whites

¼ tsp. cream of tartar

½ cup granulated sugar

Mousse

¾ cup + ⅓ cup granulated sugar (divided use)

¾ cup smooth 5% ricotta cheese

2 oz. light cream cheese, softened

¼ cup unsweetened cocoa + additional for garnish

3 TB. semi-sweet chocolate chips

¼ cup water (divided use)

2 tsp. unflavored gelatin

3 TB. cold water

⅔ cup plain low-fat yogurt

2 large egg whites

¼ tsp. cream of tartar

½ TB. confectioners' sugar

Position a rack in the center of the oven and preheat the oven to 275°F. Lightly coat a 9-inch pie plate with cooking spray.

Make meringue: In a bowl, beat egg whites with cream of tartar until foamy. Gradually beat in sugar, beating until stiff peaks form. Spoon the mixture into the prepared plate, spreading it over the bottom and up the sides. Bake for 75 minutes or until meringue is golden and dry. Let the plate cool on a wire rack.

 **A Piece of Advice**

Add the water to the chocolate to make it easier to melt and to add moisture and volume. Be sure to add the melted chocolate to the cheese mixture quickly and process before the chocolate begins to harden.

Make mousse: In a food processor, combine ¾ cup sugar, ricotta cheese, cream cheese, and cocoa; purée until the mixture is smooth. In a small microwavable bowl, melt chocolate with 1 tablespoon water in microwave for 40 seconds on high. Stir it until smooth and add it to the food processor, puréeing until the mixture is smooth.

In a small microwavable bowl, combine gelatin with remaining 3 tablespoons water and let it sit for 2 minutes; microwave on high for 20 seconds. Stir the mixture until gelatin is dissolved.

With the food processor running, add the gelatin mixture through the feed tube. Transfer the mixture to a large bowl and fold in the yogurt.

In another bowl, beat egg whites with the cream of tartar until foamy. Gradually add remaining ⅓ cup sugar, beating until stiff peaks form. Stir one fourth of egg whites into the ricotta mixture. Gently fold in remaining egg whites just until combined. Pour into the crust. Chill for 2 hours or until the filling is firm. Using a fine sieve, dust the top with cocoa and confectioners' sugar.

Nutrition Watch

Traditional chocolate mousse is made with egg yolks, a lot of chocolate, and heavy cream whipped into the mousse. Beaten egg whites, ricotta cheese, cocoa, and a small amount of melted chocolate make this a delicious, yet light-tasting, alternative.

 Nutrition per Serving

Calories: 182
Protein: 5.4 g
Cholesterol: 8.2 mg

Fat (total): 3.6 g
Fat (saturated): 2.2 g

Carbohydrate: 32 g
Dietary Fiber: 0.8 g

Mocha Mousse Chocolate Chip Brownie Tart

When I first created this recipe, I made the crust from cookie crumbs and it tasted fine. But then I thought that a brownie base would raise this dessert to the heavens, and it does!

Prep time: 35 minutes • Cook time: 20 to 25 minutes • Chill time: at least 2 hours • Serves 12

Vegetable cooking spray

Brownie Base

¾ cup granulated sugar

¼ cup canola oil

¼ cup low-fat sour cream

1 large egg

1 tsp. vanilla extract

⅓ cup all-purpose flour

⅓ cup unsweetened cocoa

1 tsp. baking powder

Mousse

¾ cup + ⅓ cup granulated sugar (divided use)

¾ cup smooth 5% ricotta cheese

2 oz. light cream cheese, softened

2 tsp. unflavored gelatin

3 TB. cold water

2 tsp. instant coffee granules

1 TB. hot water

⅔ cup plain low-fat yogurt

2 large egg whites

¼ tsp. cream of tartar

2 TB. semi-sweet chocolate chips

Position a rack in the center of the oven and preheat the oven to 350°F. Lightly coat a 9-inch springform pan with cooking spray.

Make brownie base: In a bowl and using a whisk or electric mixer, beat sugar, oil, sour cream, egg, and vanilla. In another bowl, stir together flour, cocoa, and baking powder. With a wooden spoon, stir the dry ingredients into the sugar mixture just until combined. Spread it into the prepared pan. Bake for 20 to 25 minutes or until a tester inserted in the center comes out clean.

Nutrition Watch

Traditional chocolate mousses are made with egg yolks, a lot of chocolate, and heavy cream. All this makes for an enormous amount of calories, fat, and cholesterol. Beaten egg whites, ricotta cheese, and cocoa in this recipe create a delicious, yet

Make mousse: In a food processor, purée ¾ cup sugar, ricotta cheese, and cream cheese until smooth. In a small bowl, stir gelatin into cold water; let the mixture stand for 2 minutes. Dissolve instant coffee in hot water; stir it into the gelatin mixture. Heat it in the microwave on high for 20 seconds or just until gelatin is dissolved. With the food processor running, add gelatin mixture through the feed tube. Transfer the mixture to a large bowl. Fold in yogurt.

In another bowl, beat egg whites with cream of tartar until they are foamy. Gradually add remaining ⅓ cup sugar, beating until stiff peaks form. Stir one fourth of egg whites into the ricotta mixture. Gently fold in remaining egg whites until blended. Pour the mixture onto the brownie base. Sprinkle with chocolate chips. Chill for 2 hours or until the filling is set firm.

To unmold, loosen the spring and remove the springform sides, leaving the tart on the pan bottom.

 **A Piece of Advice** ___

Although most brownies are baked until they are still slightly loose in the center, this one should be cooked through so it slices easily.

Nutrition per Serving

Calories: 251
Protein: 5.7 g
Cholesterol: 27 mg

Fat (total): 8 g
Fat (saturated): 2.4 g

Carbohydrate: 39 g
Dietary Fiber: 1 g

Pecan Shortbread Tarts

These tarts are buttery and delicious. They taste like an old-fashioned butter pecan pie.

Prep time: 35 minutes   •   Cook time: 20 minutes   •   Serves 12

Pastry

¼ cup granulated sugar

2½ oz. light cream cheese

2 TB. canola oil

1 TB. unsalted butter

1 cup all-purpose flour

1 to 2 TB. ice water

Filling

¼ cup packed dark brown sugar

¼ cup dark corn syrup

⅓ cup chopped pecans, toasted

2 TB. evaporated skim milk

1 TB. margarine or unsalted butter, softened

1 large egg

1 tsp. vanilla extract

Position a rack in the center of the oven and preheat the oven to 375°F. Lightly coat a 12-cup muffin tin with cooking spray.

Make pastry: In a food processor, combine sugar, cream cheese, oil, and butter; purée the mixture until it is smooth. Add the flour and 1 tablespoon water; pulse on and off until the mixture is crumbly, adding more water as needed. Form the dough into a ball and wrap in plastic wrap. Refrigerate for 20 minutes.

Make filling: In a bowl, whisk together brown sugar, corn syrup, pecans, evaporated milk, margarine, egg, and vanilla.

A Piece of Advice ___

To toast the nuts, brown them in a dry skillet over a high heat for approximately 2 to 3 minutes.

Nutrition Watch _____

Pecans, like other nuts, are a good source of protein and can provide a high-energy snack any time of day. Eat them in moderation because they are high in calories and fat, even though the fat is polyunsaturated and considered healthy.

Between two sheets of floured waxed paper, roll the pastry dough out to ⅛-inch thickness. Use a 3½-inch round cutter to cut out circles. Place the circles in the muffin cups, working the pastry up the sides of the cups and reworking the scraps as needed until you have 12 pastry-lined cups. Divide the filling evenly among the pastry cups.

Bake for 20 minutes or until filling is set and pastry is golden.

Serve the tarts warm or at room temperature.

 ### Nutrition per Serving

Calories: 207   Fat (total): 7.6 g   Carbohydrate: 32 g
Protein: 2.7 g   Fat (saturated): 1.9 g   Dietary Fiber: 0.5 g
Cholesterol: 24 mg

Chocolate Cream Tart

I hope you make the sour cream with a spider web design because it truly makes this pie exceptional looking. The filling is especially delicious and so chocolatey.

Prep time: 20 minutes   •   Cook time: 20 to 25 minutes   •   Serves 12

Vegetable cooking spray

Crust

1¼ cups chocolate wafer crumbs

1 TB. granulated sugar

2 TB. water

1 TB. canola oil

Filling

1 can (14 oz.) low-fat sweetened condensed milk

½ cup smooth 5% ricotta cheese

2 oz. light cream cheese, softened

⅓ cup granulated sugar

¼ cup unsweetened cocoa

Topping (optional)

3 TB. low-fat sour cream

1 TB. water

2 tsp. granulated sugar

Position a rack in the center of the oven and preheat the oven to 375°F. Lightly coat a 9-inch tart pan with cooking spray.

Make crust: In a bowl, mix crumbs, sugar, water, and oil just until the crumbs come together. Pat the mixture onto sides and bottom of the prepared pan.

Make filling: In a food processor, combine condensed milk, ricotta cheese, cream cheese, sugar, and cocoa; purée until smooth. Pour it into the crust.

Make topping: In a small bowl, stir together sour cream, water, and sugar. Spoon the mixture into a small plastic bag and cut a tiny hole in one corner. Squeezing topping through hole, draw three concentric circles on the top of the pie. Use a toothpick to draw lines across the circles to create a spider web effect.

 A Piece of Advice

Light condensed milk makes this cake smooth and rich tasting without the addition of egg yolks, butter, and whipping cream. Using a metal tart makes the dessert look fancy, but a glass pie plate works also.

 Nutrition Watch

Condensed milk now comes in a light version that has half the fat of the regular version.

Bake 20 to 25 minutes or until the center is firm. Cool on a wire rack. Before serving, remove the edge of the tart pan and slice the tart (on the pan bottom) onto a flat serving plate.

 Nutrition per Serving

Calories: 288
Protein: 6.7 g
Cholesterol: 13 mg

Fat (total): 7.7 g
Fat (saturated): 2.9 g

Carbohydrate: 48 g
Dietary Fiber: 1.2 g

Pies, Pies, and More Pies

Whether it has a bottom and a top crust, a bottom crust only, or a top crust only (as in deep dish pies), pie means something comforting and delicious to most of us. Here are 11 of my favorite pie recipes to make your mouth water and conjure up memories of lazy summer afternoons.

Pecan Cream Cheese Pie

The combination of cheesecake and pecan is too good for words. I like to serve this pie either at room temperature or chilled.

Prep time: 25 minutes   •   Cook time: 30 to 35 minutes   •   Serves 12

Vegetable cooking spray

Crust

1½ cups vanilla wafer crumbs

2 TB. granulated sugar

2 TB. water

1 TB. canola oil

Cheesecake Filling

¾ cup smooth 5% ricotta cheese

⅓ cup granulated sugar

⅓ cup light cream cheese

¼ cup light sour cream

1 large egg

1 TB. all-purpose flour

1 tsp. vanilla extract

Pecan Filling

⅔ cup packed light brown sugar

½ cup chopped pecans

1 large egg

2 large egg whites

½ cup light corn syrup

1 TB. unsulphured molasses

Nutrition Watch

Pecans are a good source of protein and a healthy polyunsaturated fat. But nuts are high in calories and fat grams, so eat them in moderation or as an alternative source of protein in your diet.

Position a rack in the center of the oven and preheat oven to 375°F. Lightly coat a 9-inch pie plate with cooking spray.

Make crust: Mix crumbs, sugar, water, and oil together until the mixture holds together. Press it into the side and bottom of a pie plate. Bake for 8 minutes.

Make cheesecake filling: In a food processor, purée ricotta cheese, sugar, cream cheese, sour cream, egg, flour, and vanilla until the mixture is smooth. Pour it into the pie crust.

Make pecan filling: In a bowl, whisk together brown sugar, pecans, egg, egg whites, corn syrup, and molasses. Pour the mixture carefully over the cheesecake layer.

Bake for approximately 30 to 35 minutes, or until the filling is almost set. It might rise up around the edges or even through the middle of the pecan filling. Let the pie cool in its pie plate on a wire rack.

 **A Piece of Advice**

Be sure to process the cheesecake batter well to make it as smooth as possible. Pay attention when pouring the pecan layer on top of the cheesecake so that they don't mix.

 Nutrition per Serving

Calories: 290
Protein: 5.1 g
Cholesterol: 48 mg

Fat (total): 10 g
Fat (saturated): 2.9 g

Carbohydrate: 46 g
Dietary Fiber: 0.7 g

Banana Cream Pie

Luscious banana mousse with a chocolate crust and layered sautéed bananas are the best combination possible! You'd never believe that this pie was low-fat.

Prep time: 20 minutes • Chill time: at least 2 hours • Serves 12

Vegetable cooking spray

Crust

1¾ cups chocolate wafer crumbs

2 TB. granulated sugar

2½ TB. water

1 TB. canola oil

Filling

2 tsp. margarine or unsalted butter

¼ cup packed light brown sugar

2 ripe (¾ cup) medium bananas, sliced

⅔ cup smooth 5% ricotta cheese

2 oz. light cream cheese, softened

½ cup + ¼ cup granulated sugar (divided use)

⅔ cup low-fat yogurt

1½ tsp. vanilla extract

⅛ tsp. salt

2 tsp. unflavored gelatin

3 TB. cold water

2 large egg whites

¼ tsp. cream of tartar

Lightly coat a 9-inch pie plate with cooking spray.

Make crust: In a bowl, stir together wafer crumbs, sugar, water, and oil. Set aside 1 tablespoon of the mixture. Pat the remaining mixture onto the bottom and up the sides of the prepared pan.

 Nutrition Watch

Bananas are high in carbohydrates, as well as rich in potassium and vitamin C.

Make filling: In a frying pan, melt margarine over medium heat. Stir in brown sugar and bananas; cook for 2 minutes. Spoon the mixture evenly into the crust.

In a food processor, combine ricotta cheese, cream cheese, ½ cup sugar, yogurt, vanilla, and salt; purée until smooth. In a small microwavable bowl, combine gelatin and water and let it sit for 2 minutes; microwave on high for 20 seconds. Stir the mixture until it is dissolved. With the food processor running, add gelatin through the feed tube. Transfer the mixture to a large bowl.

In another bowl, beat egg whites with cream of tartar until foamy. Gradually add remaining ¼ cup sugar, beating until stiff peaks form. Stir one fourth of egg whites into the ricotta mixture. Gently fold in remaining egg whites just until blended. Pour the mixture into the crust. Sprinkle with reserved crumb mixture. Chill for 2 hours or until set.

 **Nutrition per Serving**

Calories: 239   Fat (total): 6.9 g   Carbohydrate: 39 g
Protein: 5.2 g   Fat (saturated): 2.1 g   Dietary Fiber: 1.1 g
Cholesterol: 7.7 mg

Coconut Cream Pie

People looking for lighter desserts usually avoid coconut cream pie because coconut milk contains highly saturated fat. Not here! The newest addition to the grocery store is light coconut milk, which is 75 percent reduced in fat and calories.

Prep time: 20 minutes   •   Bake (crust) time: 10 minutes   •   Chill time: at least 2 hours   •
Serves 12

Vegetable cooking spray

Crust

1½ cups graham crumbs

¼ cup granulated sugar

1 TB. unsweetened coconut, toasted

3 TB. water

1 TB. canola oil

Filling

½ cup + ¼ cup granulated sugar (divided use)

½ cup smooth 5% ricotta cheese

⅔ cup light coconut milk

2 oz. light cream cheese, softened

2 tsp. vanilla extract

2 tsp. unflavored gelatin

2 TB. cold water

¼ cup unsweetened coconut, toasted (divided use)

2 large egg whites

¼ tsp. cream of tartar

Position a rack in the center of the oven and preheat oven to 400°F. Lightly coat a 9-inch pie plate with cooking spray.

Make crust: In a bowl, stir together crumbs, sugar, coconut, water, and oil until mixed. Pat the mixture onto the bottom and up the sides of the prepared pan. Bake for 10 minutes or until the crust is slightly browned. Let the pan cool on a wire rack.

Make filling: In a food processor, combine ½ cup sugar, ricotta cheese, coconut milk, cream cheese, and vanilla; purée until smooth. In a small microwavable bowl, combine gelatin and water and let it sit for 2 minutes; microwave on high for 20 seconds. Stir until it is dissolved. With the food processor running, add gelatin through the feed tube. Transfer the mixture to a large bowl and stir in 3 tablespoons toasted coconut.

Nutrition Watch

Coconut is high in potassium, but also high in saturated fat. I only use it for appearance in small amounts and stick to light coconut milk for the coconut flavor.

A Piece of Advice

To toast coconut, put it in a dry skillet over medium heat and toast until it is lightly browned, approximately 2 minutes. Be careful not to burn it!

In another bowl, beat egg whites with cream of tartar until foamy. Gradually add remaining ¼ cup sugar, beating until stiff peaks form. Gently fold the mixture into the ricotta mixture just until combined and pour it into the crust. Sprinkle remaining toasted coconut over top. Chill for 2 hours or until the filling is set firm.

 **Nutrition per Serving**

Calories: 193   Fat (total): 6.2 g   Carbohydrate: 30 g
Protein: 4.2 g   Fat (saturated): 3 g   Dietary Fiber: 0.9 g
Cholesterol: 6.1 mg

Key Lime Pie

Key lime refers to a small, yellow-tinged lime that comes from Florida. Outside of Florida, Key limes are only found in specialty produce markets and larger supermarkets that carry gourmet produce. The most commonly available lime is actually a Persian lime. But you might not recognize the dessert if I called it Persian Lime Pie! With either type of lime, this is a creamy tart pie.

Prep time: 15 minutes   •   Cook time: 20 minutes   •   Serves 12

Vegetable cooking spray

Crust

1½ cups graham crumbs

3 TB. granulated sugar

2 TB. water

1 TB. canola oil

Filling

1 can (14 oz.) low-fat sweetened condensed milk

½ cup smooth 5% ricotta cheese

4 oz. light cream cheese, softened

⅓ cup fresh lime juice (approximately 2 limes)

2 tsp. finely grated lime zest

¼ cup granulated sugar

Position a rack in the center of the oven and preheat oven to 375°F. Lightly coat a 9-inch pie plate with cooking spray.

 **A Piece of Advice**

To get the most juice from limes, first be sure that they are ripe. Roll them firmly on the kitchen counter, which helps to release the juices, or microwave them for approximately 20 seconds.

Make crust: In a bowl, stir together graham crumbs, sugar, water, and oil until mixed. Pat the mixture onto the bottom and up the sides of the prepared pan.

Make filling: In a food processor, combine condensed milk, ricotta cheese, cream cheese, lemon juice and zest, and sugar; purée until smooth. Pour it into the crust.

Bake for about 20 minutes or just until the filling is set. Let the pie cool in its pan on a wire rack. Chill before serving.

 **Nutrition per Serving**

Calories: 277   Fat (total): 6.9 g   Carbohydrate: 47 g
Protein: 6.8 g   Fat (saturated): 3 g   Dietary Fiber: 0.5 g
Cholesterol: 16 mg

Chocolate Mud Pie

This mud pie tastes so rich that you'll think it has a pound of chocolate in it. I like to serve this with a raspberry or chocolate sauce (see Chapter 16).

Prep time: 15 minutes   •   Cook time: 25 to 30 minutes   •   Chill time: 1 hour   •   Serves 12

Vegetable cooking spray

Crust

1½ cups chocolate wafer crumbs

2 TB. packed light brown sugar

2 TB. water

1 TB. canola oil

Filling

2 TB. semi-sweet chocolate chips

1 TB. water

1 tsp. instant coffee granules

1 TB. hot water

1¼ cups packed light brown sugar

½ cup unsweetened cocoa

1 TB. all-purpose flour

2½ oz. light cream cheese, softened

1 large egg

2 large egg whites

¼ cup low-fat sour cream

3 TB. light corn syrup

1 tsp. vanilla extract

Position a rack in the center of the oven and preheat oven to 350°F. Lightly coat a 9-inch pie plate with cooking spray.

Make crust: In a bowl, stir together wafer crumbs, brown sugar, water, and oil until mixed. Pat the mixture onto the bottom and up the sides of the prepared pan.

Make filling: In a small microwavable bowl, combine chocolate chips and water. Microwave on high for about 30 seconds or just until chips begin to melt. Stir the mixture until smooth. Cool.

Dissolve the instant coffee granules in hot water. Cool.

In a food processor, combine brown sugar, cocoa, flour, cream cheese, egg, egg whites, sour cream, corn syrup, vanilla, chocolate, and coffee; purée until smooth. Pour it into the crust.

Bake for 25 to 30 minutes or until the center is just set. Let the pie cool in its pan on a wire rack. Chill for 1 hour.

Nutrition Watch

Chocolate and cocoa differ greatly in fat and calories. Each ounce of chocolate contains 14 grams of fat and 140 calories. For each ounce of cocoa, there are 40 calories and 1 gram of fat!

A Piece of Advice

Be careful not to burn the chocolate in the microwave. It's safest to use the defrost cycle, although it takes longer. Always use less time to be certain.

Nutrition per Serving

Calories: 244   Fat (total): 6.2 g   Carbohydrate: 45 g
Protein: 3.8 g   Fat (saturated): 2.1 g   Dietary Fiber: 1.8 g

Orange Chocolate Marble Pie

Orange and chocolate are wonderful flavors together. The swirled marble top makes this pie look as good as it tastes.

Prep time: 15 minutes • Cook time: 25 to 30 minutes • Serves 12

Vegetable cooking spray

Crust

1¾ cups chocolate wafer crumbs

2 TB. granulated sugar

2½ TB. water

1 TB. canola oil

Filling

¾ cup granulated sugar

2 TB. all-purpose flour

½ cup evaporated skim milk

½ cup low-fat sour cream

¼ cup orange juice concentrate

2 tsp. finely grated orange zest

1 large egg

2 large egg whites

Marble

1 TB. semi-sweet chocolate chips

1½ tsp. water

 Nutrition Watch

The small amount of chocolate used here does not add much to the calorie and fat count of each serving. One tablespoon of chocolate chips has approximately 80 calories and 8 grams of fat.

 A Piece of Advice

Be sure to use orange juice concentrate—not just orange juice—for the most intense flavor. Keep a can in the freezer just for baking and cooking purposes.

Position a rack in the center of the oven and preheat oven to 375°F. Lightly coat a 9-inch pie plate with cooking spray.

Make crust: In a bowl, stir together wafer crumbs, sugar, water, and oil until combined. Pat the mixture onto the bottom and up the sides of the prepared pan.

Make filling: In a bowl, whisk together sugar, flour, evaporated milk, sour cream, orange juice concentrate, orange zest, egg, and egg whites until mixture is smooth. Pour it into crust.

Make marble: In a small microwavable bowl, combine chocolate chips and water. On high, microwave for about 30 seconds or until chocolate begins to melt. Stir until smooth. Spoon it on top of the filling; using a knife, swirl chocolate through the orange filling to give it a marbled effect.

Bake for 25 to 30 minutes or until the center is set. Let the pie cool in its pan on a wire rack.

Nutrition per Serving

Calories: 204
Protein: 3.7 g
Cholesterol: 21 mg

Fat (total): 5.5 g
Fat (saturated): 1.5 g

Carbohydrate: 35 g
Dietary Fiber: 0.8 g

Orange Mousse in Meringue Shell

A pastry shell made with whipped egg whites is very dramatic. Any mousse filling could fill this meringue, but my orange mousse makes for a truly remarkable dessert. The longer the meringue stays in the oven, the crisper it becomes.

Prep time: 20 minutes   •   Bake (meringue) time: 1 hour   •   Chill time: at least 1 hour   •
Serves 12

Vegetable cooking spray

Meringue

3 large egg whites

¼ tsp. cream of tartar

¾ cup granulated sugar

Mousse

1 cup smooth 5% ricotta cheese

2 oz. light cream cheese, softened

½ cup + ⅓ cup granulated sugar (divided use)

¼ cup orange juice concentrate

4 tsp. finely grated orange zest

2 tsp. unflavored gelatin

2 TB. cold water

½ cup plain low-fat yogurt

2 large egg whites

Pinch cream of tartar

Grated orange zest

Position a rack in the center of the oven and preheat oven to 275°F. Lightly coat a 9-inch glass pie plate with cooking spray.

In a bowl, beat egg whites with cream of tartar until foamy. Gradually beat in sugar until stiff peaks form. Spoon the mixture evenly into the prepared pie plate, forming a shell across the bottom and up the sides. Bake for 1 hour, and then cool on a wire rack while you prepare the mousse.

Make mousse: In a food processor, combine ricotta cheese, cream cheese, ½ cup sugar, orange juice concentrate, and orange rind; purée the mixture until it is smooth. In a small microwavable bowl, combine gelatin and water; let sit for 2 minutes. Microwave on high for 20 seconds. Stir until smooth. With the motor running, add gelatin and yogurt though the feed tube. Transfer the mixture to a large bowl.

In another bowl and using an electric mixer, beat egg whites with cream of tartar until foamy. Gradually add remaining ⅓ cup sugar, beating until stiff peaks form. Stir one-fourth of egg whites into the ricotta-gelatin mixture. Gently fold in remaining egg whites just until combined. Pour the mixture into the pie shell and chill for at least 1 hour. Garnish with orange zest.

 A Piece of Advice

When you're beating egg whites, have the egg whites at room temperature and make sure that the bowl and beaters are dry and clean. If the egg whites don't form still peaks, there is probably foreign matter in the bowl. Adding 1 teaspoon of lemon juice for every 3 egg whites might help.

Nutrition Watch

Most mousse recipes contain whipping cream, which has 35 percent milkfat. This is a highly saturated fat with a lot of calories and cholesterol. By comparison, the ricotta and cream cheeses in this recipe contain little fat: Ricotta has only 5 percent milkfat, and light cream cheese is reduced by 25 percent fat from regular cream cheese.

 **Nutrition per Serving**

Calories: 170   Fat (total): 2.6 g   Carbohydrate: 31 g
Protein: 5.4 g   Fat (saturated): 1.6 g   Dietary Fiber: 0.1 g
Cholesterol: 9.3 mg

Lemon Sour Cream Meringue Pie

This version of lemon meringue pie is so unique because the filling is made creamy by the addition of low-fat sour cream, not butter.

Prep time: 25 minutes   •   Cook time: 23 to 25 minutes, then 5 to 7 minutes   •   Serves 12

Vegetable cooking spray

Pastry

⅓ cup granulated sugar

3 TB. canola oil

3 TB. plain low-fat yogurt

1½ oz. light cream cheese

1¼ cup all-purpose flour

Filling

1 cup granulated sugar

3½ TB. cornstarch

1 cup low-fat milk

2 large egg yolks

2 tsp. finely grated lemon zest

¼ cup fresh lemon juice

⅓ cup low-fat sour cream

Meringue Topping

3 large egg whites

¼ tsp. cream of tartar

⅓ cup granulated sugar

Position a rack in the center of the oven and preheat oven to 425°F. Lightly coat a 9-inch pie plate with cooking spray.

Make pastry: In a food processor, purée sugar, oil, yogurt, and cream cheese until mixture is smooth. Add flour and process on and off until mixture is crumbly. Roll it into a smooth ball and wrap in plastic wrap. Chill for 20 minutes.

Make filling: In a saucepan off the heat, whisk together sugar, cornstarch, and milk until mixture is smooth. Bring it to a boil over medium heat, whisking constantly until it thickens, about 2 to 3 minutes. Remove pan from heat. In a bowl, beat egg yolks; pour half the hot milk mixture into eggs and mix well. Return the mixture to the saucepan and cook over low heat for 1 minute, stirring, or until the mixture is thickened and bubbling. Remove from heat and stir in lemon zest and lemon juice. Pour the mixture into a bowl and cool for 10 minutes. Whisk in the sour cream. Pour the mixture into the crust.

 A Piece of Advice

When cooking the lemon filling, after you've added the eggs, keep the temperature low or the filling will cook too quickly and curdle. Keep whisking!

Roll the pastry into a circle large enough to fit the pie plate. Fit it into the plate, working it up the sides. Place a piece of foil over top. Bake for 15 minutes. Remove the foil and bake for another 8 to 10 minutes or until crust is golden. Let the plate cool on a wire rack. Reduce oven heat to 400°F.

Make meringue topping: In a clean bowl, beat egg whites with cream of tartar until foamy. Gradually add sugar, beating until stiff peaks form. Spoon the mixture over the warm filling, spreading it all the way to the pastry. Bake for 5 to 7 minutes or until meringue is golden. Let the pie cool on a wire rack.

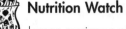 **Nutrition Watch**

Lemon meringue pie is traditionally loaded with calories, not so much from the filling, even though it usually contains butter, but from the buttery pie crust. Traditional pie crusts are high in fat. My version is lower in fat, but very flaky and easy to handle.

 Nutrition per Serving

Calories: 243 calories
Protein: 4 g
Cholesterol: 41 mg

Fat (total): 5.1 g
Fat (saturated): 1.6 g

Carbohydrate: 43 g
Dietary Fiber: 0.4 g

Mousse Pies

Mousse is a French term for "foam" or "froth," but to most of us, it means an airy dessert that tastes rich and so delicious. Traditionally made with whipped heavy cream, my lower-fat mousse recipes are made with stiffly beaten egg whites with excellent results. Since the egg whites are not cooked, you might want to read Chapter 1 where I discuss the safety of using uncooked egg whites and your options.

Gelatin is used in several of the mousse pie recipes to further stabilize the mixture. One package of unflavored gelatin contains about 1 tablespoon powdered gelatin. Add 2 to 3 tablespoons cold water and let it sit for 2 minutes to allow the gelatin to soften. Then either add 1 tablespoon additional hot water or microwave the mixture just until the gelatin dissolves, about 20 seconds. Stir until it is well mixed.

Lemon Mousse Pie

A light, creamy lemon filling over a chocolate cookie crust is to die for! This pie is sensational and begs to be part of your next dinner party.

Prep time: 20 minutes   •   Chill time: at least 2 hours   •   Serves 12

Vegetable cooking spray

Crust

1¼ cups chocolate wafer crumbs

1 TB. granulated sugar

1 TB. canola oil

2 TB. water

Mousse

¾ cup + ½ cup granulated sugar (divided use)

½ cup smooth 5% ricotta cheese

2 oz. light cream cheese, softened

1 TB. finely grated lemon zest + additional grated zest for garnish (optional)

⅓ cup fresh lemon juice

2 tsp. unflavored gelatin

3 TB. cold water

3 large egg whites

¼ tsp. cream of tartar

Lightly coat a 9-inch pie plate with cooking spray.

Make crust: In a bowl, mix crumbs, sugar, oil, and water just until crumbs come together. Pat the mixture onto the sides and bottom of the prepared pie plate.

Make mousse: In a food processor, combine ¾ cup sugar, ricotta cheese, cream cheese, lemon zest, and lemon juice; purée until smooth. In a small microwavable bowl, combine gelatin and water and let it sit for 2 minutes; microwave on high for 20 seconds. Stir the mixture until gelatin is dissolved. With the food processor running, add the gelatin mixture through the feed tube. Transfer the mixture to a large bowl.

In another bowl, beat egg whites with the cream of tartar until they are foamy. Gradually add remaining ½ cup sugar, beating until stiff peaks form. Stir one fourth of egg whites into the ricotta mixture. Gently fold in remaining egg whites just until blended. Spoon the mixture into the crust. Chill for 2 hours or until the filling is set firm. Serve garnished with additional lemon zest, if using.

 A Piece of Advice ___

Ricotta cheese, cream cheese, and egg whites make this mousse so light that you won't miss the cream. Be sure to process the filling well.

 Nutrition Watch ___

Whipping cream is traditionally used in mousses—and contains 35 percent milkfat. One tablespoon has 50 calories and 5 grams of fat. In a traditional mousse, you'd use 1 to 2 cups of cream. That's a lot of calories!

 Nutrition per Serving

Calories: 200   Fat (total): 5.7 g   Carbohydrate: 33 g
Protein: 4.2 g   Fat (saturated): 1.7 g   Dietary Fiber: 0.7 g
Cholesterol: 5.8 mg

Peanut Butter Mousse Pie

I never thought I could have a peanut butter mousse with a chocolate wafer crust and still call it low-fat. You must try this dessert—it's sensational!

Prep time: 20 minutes • Chill time: at least 2 hours • Serves 12

Vegetable cooking spray

Crust

1¾ cups chocolate wafer crumbs

2 TB. granulated sugar

2 TB. water

1 TB. canola oil

Mousse

¾ cup smooth 5% ricotta cheese

2 oz. light cream cheese, softened

⅔ cup + ⅓ cup granulated sugar (divided use)

⅓ cup smooth peanut butter

½ cup plain low-fat yogurt

2 tsp. unflavored gelatin

3 TB. cold water

3 large egg whites

¼ tsp. cream of tartar

Lightly coat a 9-inch pie plate with cooking spray.

Make crust: In a bowl, stir together wafer crumbs, sugar, water, and oil until combined. Set aside 1 tablespoon crumb mixture and pat the remainder onto the bottom and up the sides of the prepared pie plate.

Nutrition Watch _____

Peanuts contain a monounsaturated fat, which has proven to be a healthy fat in terms of lowering blood cholesterol. But they should be eaten in moderation because they have a high number of calories and grams of fat. When buying peanut butter, choose a natural, smooth one. The commercial brands are often filled with sugar and are hydrogenated, making them a source of saturated fat.

Make filling: In a food processor, combine ricotta cheese, cream cheese, ⅔ cup sugar, peanut butter, and yogurt; purée until smooth. In a small microwavable bowl, combine gelatin and water and let it sit for 2 minutes; microwave on high for 20 seconds. Stir until gelatin is dissolved. With the food processor running, add gelatin through the feed tube. Transfer the mixture to a large bowl.

In another bowl, beat egg whites with cream of tartar until foamy. Gradually add remaining ⅓ cup sugar, beating until stiff peaks form. Stir one fourth of egg whites into the ricotta mixture. Gently fold in remaining egg whites just until blended. Pour the mixture into the crust. Sprinkle the remaining 1 tablespoon crumb mixture over top. Chill for 2 hours or until the filling is set firm.

Nutrition per Serving

Calories: 174
Protein: 5.9 g
Cholesterol: 8.0 mg

Fat (total): 6.9 g
Fat (saturated): 2 g

Carbohydrate: 22 g
Dietary Fiber: 0.5 g

Gingerbread Mousse Pie

Gingerbread flavor relies on dark molasses and ground ginger for its distinctive taste. It is the perfect flavor for a cookie, cake, or mousse.

Prep time: 20 minutes • Chill time: at least 2 hours • Serves 12

Vegetable cooking spray

Crust

1½ cups graham cracker crumbs

¼ cup packed light brown sugar

¼ tsp. ground cinnamon

3 TB. water

1 TB. canola oil

Mousse

½ cup smooth 5% ricotta cheese

2 oz. light cream cheese, softened

⅓ cup packed light brown sugar

¼ cup dark molasses

½ tsp. ground cinnamon

¼ tsp. ground ginger

2 tsp. unflavored gelatin

3 TB. cold water

½ cup plain low-fat yogurt

3 large egg whites

½ tsp. cream of tartar

½ cup granulated sugar

Lightly coat a 9-inch pie plate with cooking spray.

Make crust: In a bowl, stir together graham crumbs, brown sugar, cinnamon, water, and oil until mixed. Set aside 1 tablespoon crumb mixture and pat the remainder onto the bottom and up the sides of the prepared pan.

Make mousse: In a food processor, combine ricotta cheese, cream cheese, brown sugar, molasses, cinnamon, and ginger. In a small microwavable bowl, combine gelatin and water and let it sit for 2 minutes; microwave on high for 20 seconds. Stir the mixture until it is dissolved. With the food processor running, add gelatin through the feed tube. Transfer it to a large bowl. Fold in yogurt.

In another bowl, beat egg whites with cream of tartar until they are foamy. Gradually add sugar, beating until stiff peaks form. Stir one fourth of egg whites into the ricotta mixture. Gently fold in remaining egg whites just until blended. Pour the mixture into the crust. Sprinkle remaining 1 tablespoon crumb mixture over top. Chill for 2 hours or until the filling is set firm.

Nutrition Watch

Molasses contains iron, calcium, and phosphorus. Blackstrap molasses is only fractionally richer in these nutrients; besides, it has a bitter flavor, so only buy dark molasses.

 Nutrition per Serving

Calories: 207

Protein: 4.6 g

Cholesterol: 6.4 mg

Fat (total): 4.6 g

Fat (saturated): 1.5 g

Carbohydrate: 37 g

Dietary Fiber: 0.5 g

The Least You Need to Know

◆ Luscious doesn't have to mean high in fat and cholesterol. With my precise use of low-fat cheeses and yogurt, excess eggs, heavy cream, and butter are not needed—and there's no loss of flavor or texture.

◆ Chocolate is high in saturated fat, but I get the intense taste of chocolate flavor with only a trace of saturated fat by using cocoa powder. Because you're counting on it for flavor, use the best cocoa powder that you can afford.

◆ Coconut is also high in saturated fat, but light coconut milk is not and it adds wonderful coconut flavor to my baking. Once you've tried this wonderful product, you're likely to find yourself adding it to recipes when it's not called for—just for its lovely coconut flavor.

Chapter 8

Soufflés, Caramels, and Brûlées

In This Chapter

- Light and airy soufflés, flavored with chocolate, liqueurs, mocha, or lemon
- Rich custard baked in a caramel-coated mold
- Brûlées—Stirred custard with a crackling caramelized sugar topping

These are show-stopper desserts, suitable for your fanciest occasion, yet so easy to prepare there's no need to wait for a special occasion to make them. When ordered in a restaurant, you can almost feel the fat grams adding up. I've used lower-fat substitutes so these divine indulgences can be enjoyed every day. It's amazing that a basic combination of milk, sugar, and eggs can be transformed into entirely different desserts with a subtle addition of an ingredient or two or a change in the cooking method.

If you're serving these desserts to company or for a formal family dinner, you might want to serve them with a restaurant-style presentation by lining the plate underneath the soufflé dish or ramekin with an artfully folded linen napkin.

Soufflés

A delight to behold and sublime to taste, a soufflé has a light and airy texture. It has a flavored base and egg whites beaten in to increase the volume, and is baked in a water bath (bain-marie) to ensure even baking and a perfect texture.

The key to a perfect soufflé is beating the egg whites properly. Egg whites beat best if they are at room temperature. Always use clean and dry beaters and bowls—if any foreign substance is in the bowl, the whites will not beat properly. Adding cream of tartar helps to stabilize the whites. Beat them until they are foamy and then gradually add the sugar while beating constantly until stiff peaks form. Fold the whites into the base mixture quickly and gently. Do not overfold, or the whites will deflate.

Because soufflés begin to collapse in minutes, they must be served straight out of the oven. They are delicious when served with a sauce (see Chapter 16).

Chocolate Soufflé

A classic soufflé is a light, airy mixture that begins with a thick egg yolk–based sauce lightened by beaten egg whites; whipped cream or rich chocolate sauce is usually added when it is served. This version has no egg yolks and is thickened with egg whites and cornstarch. Serve these heavenly soufflés with Chocolate Sauce or Crème Anglaise (see Chapter 16).

Prep time: 15 minutes • Cook time: 20 to 25 minutes • Serves 8

Vegetable cooking spray

½ cup + ½ cup granulated sugar (divided use) + extra sugar for dusting

½ cup unsweetened cocoa

1 TB. cornstarch

1 cup low-fat milk

6 large egg whites

½ tsp. cream of tartar

> **Nutrition Watch**
>
> Egg whites are a complete source of protein and contain no fat, which means that you can enjoy an egg-white omelet with sautéed vegetables and low-fat cheese for a nutritious breakfast.

Position a rack in the center of the oven and preheat the oven to 350°F. Lightly coat eight ½-cup ramekins or individual soufflé dishes with cooking spray and dust them lightly with sugar.

In a saucepan off the heat, whisk together ½ cup sugar, cocoa, cornstarch, and milk until smooth. Cook the mixture over medium-low heat for 4 minutes or until thickened, stirring constantly. Remove the pan from the heat. Cool.

In a bowl, beat egg whites with cream of tartar until foamy. Gradually add ½ cup sugar, beating until stiff peaks form. Stir one fourth of egg whites into the cocoa mixture. Gently fold in remaining egg whites just until blended. Divide the mixture among the prepared ramekins.

Set the ramekins in a large baking dish. Pour in enough hot water to come halfway up the sides of the ramekins. Bake for 20 to 25 minutes or until the soufflés are puffed. Serve them immediately.

 A Piece of Advice

When whipping egg whites, take great care that the bowl and beaters are clean and dry. The egg whites will beat faster at room temperature. For even baking, cook the soufflés in a water bath (bain-marie).

 Nutrition per Serving

Calories: 153
Protein: 4.7 g
Cholesterol: 1.2 mg

Fat (total): 1.1 g
Fat (saturated): 0.6 g

Carbohydrate: 31 g
Dietary Fiber: 1.8 g

Orange Grand Marnier Soufflé

The marmalade, orange juice concentrate, and Grand Marnier give this soufflé an intense orange flavor. It's extra special when served with Mango Coulis or Chocolate Sauce (see Chapter 16).

Prep time: 15 minutes • Cook time: 20 minutes • Serves 8

Vegetable cooking spray

½ cup + ⅓ cup granulated sugar (divided use) + extra sugar for dusting

2 TB. cornstarch

½ cup water

¼ cup orange juice concentrate

¼ cup orange marmalade

2 TB. Grand Marnier or other orange-flavored liqueur

4 large egg whites

¼ tsp. cream of tartar

Position a rack in the center of the oven and preheat the oven to 350°F. Lightly coat eight ½-cup ramekins or individual soufflé dishes with cooking spray and dust them with sugar.

 A Piece of Advice

This recipe works well with apricot or peach jam, too. You can use an additional 2 tablespoons of orange juice concentrate instead of the orange liqueur.

Nutrition Watch

If you're going to order dessert in a restaurant, soufflés are probably your best choice, as long as you skip the whipped cream and any cream-based sauces.

In a saucepan off the heat, whisk together ½ cup sugar, cornstarch, water, orange juice concentrate, and marmalade until smooth. Cook the mixture over medium-low heat for 4 to 5 minutes or until it is thickened, stirring constantly. Remove the pan from the heat. Stir in the Grand Marnier. Cool.

In a bowl, beat egg whites with cream of tartar until foamy. Gradually add ⅓ cup sugar, beating until stiff peaks form. Stir one fourth of egg whites into the cooled orange mixture. Gently fold in remaining egg whites just until blended. Divide the mixture among the prepared ramekins.

Set the ramekins in a large baking dish. Pour in enough hot water to come halfway up the sides of the ramekins. Bake for 20 minutes or until the soufflés are puffed. Serve them immediately.

 Nutrition per Serving

Calories: 144
Protein: 2 g
Cholesterol: 0 mg

Fat (total): 0 g
Fat (saturated): 0 g

Carbohydrate: 34 g
Dietary Fiber: 0.1 g

Mocha Irish Cream Soufflé

Setting the ramekins in a pan of hot water allows the soufflés to bake evenly. This is called a bain-marie, or water bath. The texture results in a much creamier consistency. Serve this coffee-based soufflé with Chocolate Sauce (see Chapter 16).

Prep time: 15 minutes   •   Cook time: 20 minutes   •   Serves 8

Vegetable cooking spray

½ cup + ⅓ granulated sugar (divided use) + extra sugar for dusting

2 TB. cornstarch

½ cup low-fat milk

1 TB. Bailey's Irish Cream or other coffee cream liqueur

1 TB. brewed strong coffee

4 large egg whites

¼ tsp. cream of tartar

Position a rack in the center of the oven and preheat the oven to 350°F. Lightly coat eight ½-cup ramekins or individual soufflé dishes with cooking spray and dust them with sugar.

In a saucepan off the heat, whisk together ½ cup sugar, cornstarch, milk, liqueur, and coffee until smooth. Cook the mixture over medium-low heat for 7 minutes or until it is thickened, stirring constantly. Remove the pan from the heat. Cool.

In a bowl, beat egg whites with cream of tartar until foamy. Gradually add ⅓ cup sugar, beating until stiff peaks form. Stir one fourth of egg whites into the coffee mixture. Gently fold in remaining egg whites just until blended. Divide among the prepared ramekins.

Set the ramekins in a large baking dish. Pour in enough hot water to come halfway up the sides of the ramekins. Bake for 20 minutes or until the soufflés are puffed and lightly browned. Serve them immediately.

 Nutrition Watch

You can use 2 percent milkfat for a creamier texture. One cup of 1 percent milkfat contains 100 calories and 2.5 grams of fat, and 2 percent milkfat contains 120 calories and 4.5 grams of fat. When you divide this among eight servings, it doesn't make a big difference.

 A Piece of Advice

A chocolate- or coffee-based liqueur is a wonderful addition. If you want to omit the alcohol, add another tablespoon of brewed coffee to the mixture.

 Nutrition per Serving

Calories: 110
Protein: 2.3 g
Cholesterol: 0.9 mg

Fat (total): 0.5 g
Fat (saturated): 0.3 g

Carbohydrate: 24 g
Dietary Fiber: 0 g

Lemon Soufflé

This is such a fluffy, cloud-light soufflé with a subtle lemon flavor. If you want more lemon taste, serve with Lemon Sauce (see Chapter 16).

Prep time: 15 minutes • Cook time: 20 to 25 minutes • Serves 6

Vegetable cooking spray

½ cup + ½ cup granulated sugar (divided use) + extra sugar for dusting

1½ TB. cornstarch

⅓ cup water

2 tsp. finely grated lemon zest

⅓ cup fresh lemon juice

4 large egg whites

¼ tsp. cream of tartar

Position a rack in the center of the oven and preheat the oven to 350°F. Lightly coat six ½-cup ramekins or individual soufflé dishes with cooking spray and dust them with sugar.

Nutrition Watch

Lemons are an excellent source of vitamin C, but they begin to lose potency as soon as they are squeezed.

A Piece of Advice

Only use freshly squeezed lemon juice. The bottled version is not suitable for a dessert whose flavor depends on lemon.

In a saucepan off the heat, whisk together ½ cup sugar, cornstarch, water, lemon zest, and lemon juice until smooth. Cook over medium-low heat for 3 to 4 minutes or until it is thickened, stirring constantly. Remove the pan from the heat. Cool.

In a bowl, beat egg whites with cream of tartar until foamy. Gradually add ½ cup sugar, beating until stiff peaks form. Stir one fourth of egg whites into the cooled lemon mixture. Gently fold in remaining egg whites just until blended. Divide among the prepared ramekins.

Set the ramekins in a large baking dish. Pour in enough hot water to come halfway up the sides of the ramekins. Bake in the center of the oven for 20 to 25 minutes or until the soufflés are puffed. Serve them immediately.

Nutrition per Serving

Calories: 158
Protein: 2.4 g
Cholesterol: 0 mg

Fat (total): 0 g
Fat (saturated): 0 g

Carbohydrate: 37 g
Dietary Fiber: 0.1 g

Caramels and Brûlées

Crème caramel, also known as flan, is a rich custard that has been baked in a caramel-coated mold. When the chilled custard is turned out onto a dish, it is already glazed and sauced with the caramel. When making the caramel sauce for crème caramel, allow the sugar and water to boil without being stirred. It reaches the perfect consistency when the sauce is medium brown. If it cooks to the dark brown stage, the caramel will become brittle and cannot be used. If it is too light, the syrup won't caramelize and will be too runny.

A crème brûlée is a chilled, stirred custard that is sprinkled with brown or granulated sugar. The sugar is quickly caramelized under either a broiler or torch-like instrument called a salamander. The topping becomes brittle and creates a wonderful texture (you should literally hear a crackle when you take your first spoonful) and taste, along with the rich, smooth custard.

For creamier results, use 2 percent milk products. The calories and fat will not differ considerably, considering that these recipes make between six and eight desserts.

To tell if a caramel or brûlée is ready, the center should just appear set—not too loose and not too dry. It sets further upon cooling.

Orange Crème Caramel

I love the silky, velvety texture of this caramel. The orange zest gives it a kiss of sunshine. This is a wonderful dessert to serve in the dead of winter.

Prep time: 20 minutes   •   Cook time: 30 to 35 minutes   •   Serves 8

Caramel

⅔ cup granulated sugar

⅓ cup water

Custard

1 cup low-fat milk

1 cup evaporated skim milk

¾ cup granulated sugar

2 large eggs

1 large egg white

2 tsp. finely grated orange zest

1 tsp. vanilla extract

Position a rack in the center of the oven and preheat the oven to 350°F. Use eight ungreased ½-cup ramekins or custard cups.

Make caramel: In a small saucepan, stir together ⅔ cup sugar and water. Bring the mixture to a boil, and cook for 6 to 8 minutes without stirring or until it becomes medium brown. Remove the pan from the heat. Pour the mixture into the ramekins. Pick each one up and swirl caramel over the bottom and up the sides.

Nutrition Watch

Crème caramel is traditionally made with whipping cream, which contains 35 percent milkfat, and several egg yolks, which also contain a lot of cholesterol and fat. I have reduced the calories and fat by using 2 percent milk and 2 percent evaporated milk, fewer egg yolks, and more egg whites.

Make custard: In a saucepan, heat milk with evaporated milk. In a bowl, whisk together ¾ cup sugar, eggs, egg white, orange zest, and vanilla. Gradually whisk in the hot milk mixture. Pour the custard evenly into the ramekins.

Set the ramekins into a large baking dish. Pour in enough hot water to come halfway up the sides of the ramekins. Bake 30 to 35 minutes or until the caramels are almost set.

Remove the ramekins from the water bath. Let them cool on a wire rack. Chill.

To serve, run a sharp knife around the inside edge of each ramekin and quickly invert it onto a dessert plate.

 Nutrition per Serving

Calories: 200
Protein: 5.4 g
Cholesterol: 56 mg

Fat (total): 1.6 g
Fat (saturated): 0.6 g

Carbohydrate: 41 g
Dietary Fiber: 0.1 g

Fudge Crème Custard

Cocoa, chocolate chips, and a hint of chocolate liqueur make this an ultimate creamy custard.

Prep time: 10 minutes   •   Cook time: 30 to 35 minutes   •   Serves 8

Vegetable cooking spray

2 cups low-fat milk

1 cup granulated sugar

⅓ cup unsweetened cocoa powder

2 large eggs

1 large egg white

1 TB. chocolate liqueur

2 TB. semi-sweet chocolate chips

1 tsp. vanilla extract

Position a rack in the center of the oven and preheat the oven to 350°F. Lightly coat eight ½-cup ramekins or custard cups with cooking spray.

In a saucepan, heat milk.

In a bowl, whisk together sugar, cocoa, eggs, egg white, liqueur, chocolate chips, and vanilla. Gradually whisk in hot milk and pour the mixture into the ramekins.

Set the ramekins in a large baking dish. Pour in enough hot water to come halfway up the sides of the ramekins. Bake for 30 to 35 minutes or until the custards are set.

Remove the ramekins from the water bath. Let them cool on a wire rack. Chill.

 **A Piece of Advice**

You can use a creamy chocolate liqueur, such as Bailey's Irish Cream, or a mocha or nut-based chocolate liqueur. If you don't want a liqueur, add 1 tablespoon chocolate syrup or strong coffee.

 **Nutrition per Serving**

Calories: 183
Protein: 4.9 g
Cholesterol: 56 mg

Fat (total): 3.5 g
Fat (saturated): 1.7 g

Carbohydrate: 33 g
Dietary Fiber: 1.4 g

Mocha Crème Brûlée

Brûlée is the French word for "burned." The crackly and delicious topping of this custard is set under a broiler or torch to caramelize the sugar. Watch carefully so that the sugar is only caramelized with a dark golden color, not really burned. Serve within 15 minutes or the sugar will start to weep.

Prep time: 15 minutes • Cook time: 45 to 60 minutes • Serves 6

1½ cups low-fat milk

½ cup evaporated skim milk

1 TB. instant espresso powder or instant coffee granules

2 large eggs

2 large egg whites

½ cup granulated sugar

3 TB. chocolate-flavored liqueur

2 TB. packed light brown sugar

Position a rack in the center of the oven and preheat the oven to 350°F. Use six ungreased ½-cup ramekins or custard cups.

In a saucepan, heat the milk, evaporated milk, and espresso powder.

In a bowl, beat eggs, egg whites, and sugar; gradually whisk in the hot milk mixture. Beat in the liqueur and pour the mixture into the ramekins.

 **A Piece of Advice**

Instant espresso is usually available where ground coffee is sold. It is strong and gives a wonderful mocha flavor when combined with chocolate. Alternatively, use regular instant coffee—taste for flavoring and increase to 1½ tablespoons if necessary.

Set the ramekins into a large baking dish. Pour in enough hot water to come halfway up the sides of the ramekins. Cover the dish loosely with foil. Bake 45 to 60 minutes or until the custards are set.

Remove the ramekins from the water bath. Let them cool on a wire rack. Chill.

Preheat the oven to broil. Set the top rack as close to the element as possible. Sprinkle brown sugar over the custards. Broil them until sugar melts and caramelizes, about 1 to 2 minutes. Serve immediately.

 Nutrition per Serving

Calories: 174

Protein: 7 g

Cholesterol: 74 mg

Fat (total): 2.4 g

Fat (saturated): 1 g

Carbohydrate: 31 g

Dietary Fiber: 0 g

The Least You Need to Know

◆ The key to making soufflés is to properly beat the egg whites until they form stiff peaks.

◆ Take care when boiling the sugar and water to make the caramel sauce—the mixture should be boiled until it's medium brown in color. If you cook it too long to the dark brown stage, the caramel will be brittle and can't be used. If it is too light, the syrup won't caramelize and will be too runny.

◆ The caramelized sugar topping of a brûlée should crackle when it's cut into with a spoon.

◆ For creamier results, use 2 percent milk products when making these desserts.

Chapter 9

Puddings, Bread Puddings, and Pudding Cakes

In This Chapter

- Comforting, deeply satisfying stirred puddings
- Old-fashioned baked bread puddings
- Delight cakes baked over a layer of creamy pudding

There's something quintessentially wonderful about these desserts—maybe it's because they are so easy to make—just a few minutes of mixing some simple ingredients to cook on the stove or bake in the oven, and you have a treat that's welcome anytime. Perhaps, it's just that they look and taste so good. Or, could it be because they are a perfect example of pure basic comfort food, soothing to the senses and palate? Who can't remember their mother or grandmother making them some type of pudding for dessert?

Whatever the reason, you're going to be making these desserts time and time again. I've taken poetic license with some of my family's favorite recipes and have both lightened and updated them in this chapter. Get started making some memories of your own.

Pudding

The secret to low-fat puddings is to use lower-fat milk, either 2% milkfat or less, instead of heavy cream, half and half, or whole milk. Cornstarch and an egg thicken the puddings. Combine the ingredients in the saucepan before putting it on the stove so that the cornstarch dissolves. If you heat the mixture before the cornstarch is dissolved, the mixture will not thicken properly and will have lumps. Always use medium-low heat when making pudding to avoid burning or scalding the milk. Keep whisking until the mixture begins to thicken. If an egg is called for, whisk a few tablespoons of the hot pudding into the egg to temper (warm without scrambling) the egg. Then add the egg mixture to the pudding in the pan and continue whisking over low heat until the pudding is thickened, about 1 to 2 minutes.

You can then pour the pudding into individual custard cups or pretty dessert dishes, cover with plastic warp, and chill. I think pudding is best eaten the same day, but I will confess to occasionally eating leftover pudding the next morning for a marvelous breakfast treat.

Coconut Rum Raisin Pudding

Since I discovered light coconut milk, which has 75 percent less fat than regular, all those recipes I never made because they were too high in fat are now possible. I'm in heaven! Coconut milk adds a silky texture and subtle flavor to desserts.

Prep time: 10 minutes • Cook time: 5 minutes • Serves 6

1¼ cups low-fat milk	2 TB. cornstarch
½ cup light coconut milk	1 large egg
2 TB. dark rum	¼ cup unsweetened coconut, toasted
½ cup granulated sugar	¼ cup dark raisins

 **A Piece of Advice**

Instead of rum, use 2 teaspoons vanilla extract and an additional 1½ tablespoons coconut milk. To toast coconut, heat it in a dry skillet on high for 1 to 2 minutes or just until it is lightly browned.

In a heavy-bottomed saucepan off the heat, whisk together milk, coconut milk, rum, sugar, and cornstarch until smooth. Bring the mixture to a boil over medium-high heat, whisking constantly. Remove the pan from the heat.

In a bowl, whisk egg. Whisk ½ cup of the hot mixture into egg. Whisk the egg mixture back into the saucepan. Cook the mixture over medium-low heat for 1 minute, stirring, or until it is thickened and bubbling. Remove the pan from the heat.

Stir in coconut and raisins. Divide the pudding between 6 dessert dishes, cover, and chill.

 **Nutrition per Serving**

Calories: 165   Fat (total): 4.5 g   Carbohydrate: 28 g
Protein: 3.2 g   Fat (saturated): 3.4 g   Dietary Fiber: 1 g
Cholesterol: 37 mg

Jamoca Pecan Pudding

One of my favorite ice creams is Jamoca Almond Fudge. This pudding is just as good, but much, much lower in calories and fat.

Prep time: 10 minutes • Cook time: 5 minutes • Serves 6

2 cups low-fat milk

¾ cup packed light brown sugar

¼ cup unsweetened cocoa

2 TB. cornstarch

4 tsp. instant coffee granules

1 large egg

3 TB. chopped pecans, toasted

2 TB. semi-sweet chocolate chips

In a heavy-bottomed saucepan off the heat, whisk together milk, brown sugar, cocoa, cornstarch, and coffee until smooth. Bring the mixture to a boil over medium-high heat, whisking constantly. Remove the pan from the heat.

In a bowl, whisk egg. Whisk ½ cup of the hot mixture into egg. Whisk the egg mixture back into the saucepan. Cook the mixture over medium-low heat for 1 minute, stirring, or until it is thickened and bubbling. Remove the pan from the heat.

Stir in pecans and chocolate chips. Divide the pudding between 6 dessert dishes, cover, and chill.

 A Piece of Advice

To toast nuts, place in a small dry skillet over high heat for approximately 3 minutes, until they are browned. I often do a large batch and freeze them for easier use.

 Nutrition Watch

Puddings are a great way to increase calcium and vitamin A in one's diet, thanks to their milk content.

 **Nutrition per Serving**

Calories: 226   Fat (total): 5.9 g   Carbohydrate: 38 g
Protein: 5.1 g   Fat (saturated): 1.9 g   Dietary Fiber: 1.8 g
Cholesterol: 39 mg

Apricot Date Orange Pudding

The combination of dried fruits and orange makes this a tropical, sweet, citrus-flavored pudding.

Prep time: 10 minutes • Cook time: 5 minutes • Serves 6

1¼ cups low-fat milk

½ cup evaporated skim milk

3 TB. orange juice concentrate

½ cup granulated sugar

2 TB. cornstarch

2 tsp. finely grated orange zest

1 large egg

¼ cup chopped dried apricots

¼ cup chopped dried dates

 A Piece of Advice

I like to use orange juice concentrate for its intensity of flavor—always keep a can in the freezer for cooking. Store dried fruits in the freezer and use them as needed; to chop, cut them with kitchen sheers.

 Nutrition Watch

Dried fruits are an excellent source of carbohydrate. Use them for an energy boost any time of day.

In a heavy-bottomed saucepan off the heat, whisk together milk, evaporated milk, orange juice concentrate, sugar, cornstarch, and orange zest until smooth. Bring the mixture to a boil over medium-high heat, whisking constantly. Remove the pan from the heat.

In a bowl, whisk egg. Whisk ½ cup of the hot mixture into egg. Whisk the egg mixture back into saucepan. Cook the mixture over medium-low heat for 1 minute, stirring, or until it is thickened and bubbling. Remove the pan from the heat.

Stir in apricots and dates. Divide the pudding between 6 dessert dishes, cover, and chill.

Nutrition per Serving

Calories: 181   Fat (total): 1.5 g   Carbohydrate: 37 g
Protein: 4.9 g   Fat (saturated): 0.6 g   Dietary Fiber: 1.1 g
Cholesterol: 38 mg

Maple-Walnut Pudding

We all know that maple syrup is good over pancakes, but try it in cooking as a substitute for honey or as an additional sweetener for heavenly results.

Prep time: 10 minutes • Cook time: 5 minutes • Serves 6

1½ cups low-fat milk

½ cup pure maple syrup

⅓ cup packed light brown sugar

3 TB. cornstarch

1 large egg

¼ cup chopped walnuts, toasted

In a heavy-bottomed saucepan off the heat, whisk together milk, maple syrup, brown sugar, and cornstarch until smooth. Bring the mixture to a boil over medium-high heat, whisking constantly. Remove the pan from the heat.

In a bowl, whisk egg. Whisk ½ cup of the hot mixture into egg. Whisk the egg mixture back into the saucepan. Cook the mixture over medium-low heat for 1 minute, stirring, or until it is thickened and bubbling. Remove the pan from the heat.

Stir in the walnuts. Divide the pudding between six dessert dishes, cover, and chill.

 Nutrition Watch

Walnuts are a good source of protein and are an unsaturated fat. But, they also contain a lot of calories and fat, so eat them in moderation.

 A Piece of Advice

Be sure to buy pure maple syrup, AA or Fancy Grade. The imitation syrups are nothing more than corn syrup with maple extract.

 Nutrition per Serving

Calories: 206

Protein: 3.8 g

Cholesterol: 38 mg

Fat (total): 4.8 g

Fat (saturated): 1 g

Carbohydrate: 37 g

Dietary Fiber: 0.4 g

Bread Pudding

Bread puddings are an old-fashioned dessert made from cubes (or slices) of bread that are saturated with a mixture of milk, eggs, sugar, and flavorings. I like to use a large Italian loaf that's at least a day or two old. I remove the crusts and cut the bread into small cubes. My recipes for bread puddings use lower-fat milk and fewer eggs than the traditional recipes. Dried fruits, coffee, cocoa, and other low-fat ingredients enhance their flavor. These bread puddings need to be baked just until they're set, and they're tastiest served warm with Crème Anglaise or Vanilla Cream (see Chapter 16).

Chocolate Cappuccino Bread Pudding

Bread puddings are simple, old-fashioned baked desserts made with cubes of leftover or stale bread and milk. This combination of day-old bread, chocolate, and coffee is unique. Serve it with Chocolate Sauce or Crème Anglaise (see Chapter 16).

Prep time: 10 minutes • Cook time: 30 minutes • Serves 12

Vegetable cooking spray

3 cups crustless day-old Italian bread, cubed

2 large eggs

1⅓ cups evaporated skim milk

⅔ cup brewed coffee

⅔ cup granulated sugar

¼ cup unsweetened cocoa

¼ cup semi-sweet chocolate chips

⅛ tsp. salt

 A Piece of Advice

Use the wide Italian bread, not the long, thin baguette, which has too much crust. Freeze any leftover bread for another use. If brewed coffee is unavailable, dissolve 1 tablespoon instant coffee in ⅔ cup hot water.

Position a rack in the center of the oven and preheat the oven to 375°F. Lightly coat an 8-inch square baking dish with cooking spray.

Place the cubed bread in a large bowl.

In another bowl, whisk together eggs, evaporated milk, coffee, sugar, cocoa, chocolate chips, and salt. Pour the mixture over bread and cover with plastic wrap. Let stand for 15 minutes.

Pour the mixture into the prepared baking dish and bake for 30 minutes or until pudding is set. Serve warm.

 Nutrition per Serving

Calories: 144
Protein: 4.9 g
Cholesterol: 36 mg

Fat (total): 2.7 g
Fat (saturated): 1.2 g

Carbohydrate: 25 g
Dietary Fiber: 1.2 g

Buttermilk Bread Pudding with Dried Fruits

Dried cranberries are the newest addition to my pantry. I love cooking and baking with these tangy, chewy morsels, often merely replacing raisins in an old recipe to come up with an entirely different tasting dish. Try serving this bread pudding with Mango Coulis (see Chapter 16).

Prep time: 20 minutes • Cook time: 30 minutes • Serves 12

Vegetable cooking spray	¾ cup granulated sugar
3 cups crustless day-old Italian bread, cubed	½ cup chopped dried apricots or dates
2 large eggs	⅓ cup dried cranberries or golden raisins
2 cups buttermilk	⅛ tsp. salt
2 tsp. vanilla extract	

Position a rack in the center of the oven and preheat the oven to 375°F. Lightly coat an 8-inch square baking dish with cooking spray.

Place the cubed bread in a large bowl.

In another bowl, whisk together eggs, buttermilk, vanilla, sugar, apricots, cranberries, and salt. Pour the mixture over bread and cover with plastic wrap. Let stand for 15 minutes.

Pour the mixture into the prepared baking dish and bake for 30 minutes or until pudding is set. Serve warm.

 **A Piece of Advice**

If you don't have buttermilk, substitute plain low-fat yogurt or make your own buttermilk by stirring 1 tablespoon lemon juice into 1 cup milk and letting it sit 5 minutes. You can also buy canisters of dry buttermilk powder, which reconstitutes readily with water.

 Nutrition per Serving

Calories: 148
Protein: 3.9 g
Cholesterol: 37 mg

Fat (total): 1.8 g
Fat (saturated): 0.6 g

Carbohydrate: 29 g
Dietary Fiber: 1 g

Upside-Down Apple Bread Pudding

Upside-down cakes are so attractive that I decided to try the technique on a bread pudding. It's fabulous. Serve this homey dessert with Vanilla Cream or Crème Anglaise (see Chapter 16).

Prep time: 25 minutes • Cook time: 35 minutes • Serves 12

Vegetable cooking spray

3½ cups crustless day-old Italian bread, cubed

2 large eggs

1 cup low-fat milk

1 cup low-fat sour cream

2 tsp. vanilla extract

½ cup packed light brown sugar

½ tsp. ground cinnamon

2 tsp. margarine or unsalted butter

2 TB. light corn syrup

2½ cups peeled, thinly sliced apples (about 3 medium apples)

3 TB. granulated sugar

½ tsp. ground cinnamon

Position a rack in the center of the oven and preheat the oven to 375°F. Lightly coat an 8-inch square baking dish with cooking spray.

Place the cubed bread in a large bowl.

Nutrition Watch

An apple a day keeps the doctor away! Apples are a good source of vitamins A and C, as well as fiber and carbohydrate. Choose a firm apple, such as Spy, Mutsu, Granny Smith, or Paula Red when baking. McIntosh and Golden Delicious lack flavor and texture when baked.

In another bowl, whisk together eggs, milk, sour cream, vanilla, brown sugar, and cinnamon. Pour the mixture over bread and cover with plastic wrap. Let stand for 15 minutes.

In a large nonstick skillet, melt margarine with corn syrup over medium-high heat, stirring. Add apples, sugar, and cinnamon; cook for 4 minutes, stirring occasionally, or until apples are tender. Pour the mixture into the prepared dish.

Pour soaked bread on top of the apple mixture and bake for 35 minutes or until pudding is set. Let the dish cool slightly on a wire rack, and then invert it onto a large rimmed platter. Serve warm.

Nutrition per Serving

Calories: 169
Protein: 3.9 g
Cholesterol: 43 mg

Fat (total): 3.7 g
Fat (saturated): 1.7 g

Carbohydrate: 30 g
Dietary Fiber: 1.2 g

Pudding Cakes

Pudding cakes are a delightful marriage of cake and creamy pudding. As the batter bakes, it magically layers into a cake-like top with pudding beneath so that when the dessert is served, each spoonful of cake is laced with pudding. Bake pudding cakes in a water bath (bain-marie) to allow the cake to bake evenly and remain moist. The cake is set when the center is no longer loose. Pudding cakes are best served straight from the oven.

Orange Apricot Pudding Cake

Pudding cakes are best eaten just out of the oven. They fall after they have cooled and lose their fluffy texture but are still quite delicious. Orange and dried apricots are a great flavor combination in this cake.

Prep time: 15 minutes • Cook time: 25 to 30 minutes • Serves 12

Vegetable cooking spray	2 tsp. finely grated orange zest
2 large eggs, separated	⅓ cup all-purpose flour
¾ cup + 3 TB. granulated sugar (divided use)	⅛ tsp. salt
1 cup plain low-fat yogurt	¼ cup dried apricots, diced
¼ cup apricot jam	¼ tsp. cream of tartar
2 TB. orange juice concentrate	

Position a rack in the center of the oven and preheat the oven to 350°F. Lightly coat a 8-inch square baking dish with cooking spray.

In a large bowl and using a whisk or electric mixer, beat egg yolks with ¾ cup sugar until the mixture is thick and pale yellow. With a wooden spoon, stir in yogurt, jam, orange juice concentrate, orange zest, flour, salt, and apricots.

In another bowl and using clean beaters, beat egg whites with cream of tartar until foamy. Gradually add 3 tablespoons sugar, continuing to beat until stiff peaks form. Fold the mixture into the batter just until blended. Pour it into the prepared baking dish.

Set the baking dish into a larger baking pan. Pour enough hot water into the pan to reach halfway up the side of the dish. Bake for 25 to 30 minutes or until the cake is golden and the top is firm to the touch. Serve immediately.

Nutrition Watch

Apricots are rich in vitamin A and are a valuable source of iron and calcium.

Nutrition per Serving

Calories: 130	Fat (total): 1.2 g	Carbohydrate: 27 g
Protein: 2.7 g	Fat (saturated): 0.5 g	Dietary Fiber: 0.3 g
Cholesterol: 37 mg		

Lemon Pudding Cake

Any lemon dessert makes me weak at the knees. This dream of a cake has the texture of a soufflé but it's slightly denser. Serve it right out of the oven, with Vanilla Cream (see Chapter 16).

Prep time: 15 minutes • Cook time: 25 to 30 minutes • Serves 12

Vegetable cooking spray

2 large eggs, separated

⅔ cup + 3 TB. granulated sugar (divided use)

1 cup plain low-fat yogurt

1 TB. finely grated lemon zest

¼ cup fresh lemon juice

¼ cup all-purpose flour

¼ tsp. cream of tartar

 A Piece of Advice

I always use fresh lemon juice, rather than bottled, when the recipe depends on lemon for its taste. Bottled lemon juice has a bitter aftertaste. I often squeeze a few lemons and freeze the juice in ice cube trays for later use.

Nutrition Watch

Lemons are an excellent source of vitamin C—they provide between 40 and 70 percent of the minimum daily requirements, but they start to lose their nutritional potency as soon as they're squeezed.

Position a rack in the center of the oven and preheat the oven to 350°F. Lightly coat an 8-inch square baking dish with cooking spray.

In a large bowl and using a whisk or electric mixer, beat egg yolks with ⅔ cup sugar until the mixture is thick and pale yellow. With a wooden spoon, stir in yogurt, lemon zest, lemon juice, and flour.

In another bowl and using clean beaters, beat egg whites with cream of tartar until foamy. Gradually add 3 tablespoons sugar, continuing to beat until stiff peaks form. Fold the mixture into the batter just until blended. Pour it into the prepared baking dish.

Set the baking dish into a larger baking pan. Pour enough hot water into the pan to reach halfway up the side of the dish. Bake for 25 to 30 minutes or until the cake is golden and the top is firm to the touch. Serve immediately.

 Nutrition per Serving

Calories: 93

Protein: 2.4 g

Cholesterol: 37 mg

Fat (total): 1.2 g

Fat (saturated): 0.5 g

Carbohydrate: 18 g

Dietary Fiber: 0.1 g

Coconut-Cranberry Pudding Cake

Dried cranberries are replacing raisins in many recipes today. They have a wonderfully tart taste that adds flavor to your baking. Light coconut milk, also used in this delightful cake, is another great find for lower-fat cooking.

Prep time: 15 minutes • Cook time: 25 to 30 minutes • Serves 12

Vegetable cooking spray

2 large eggs, separated

⅔ cup + 3 TB. granulated sugar (divided use)

½ cup light coconut milk

½ cup plain low-fat yogurt

⅓ cup dried cranberries

¼ cup all-purpose flour

¼ cup unsweetened coconut, toasted (divided use)

1½ tsp. vanilla extract

⅛ tsp. salt

¼ tsp. cream of tartar

Position a rack in the center of the oven and preheat the oven to 350°F. Lightly coat an 8-inch square baking dish with cooking spray.

In a large bowl and using a whisk or electric mixer, beat egg yolks with ⅔ cup sugar until the mixture is thick and pale yellow. With a wooden spoon, stir in coconut milk, yogurt, cranberries, flour, 3 tablespoons coconut, vanilla, and salt.

In another bowl and using clean beaters, beat egg whites with cream of tartar until foamy. Gradually add 3 tablespoons sugar, continuing to beat until stiff peaks form. Fold the mixture into the batter just until blended. Pour it into the prepared baking dish.

Set the baking dish into a larger baking pan. Pour enough hot water into the pan to reach halfway up the side of the dish. Bake for 25 to 30 minutes or until the cake is golden and the top is firm to the touch. Sprinkle with remaining 1 tablespoon coconut. Serve immediately.

Nutrition Watch

One-fourth cup regular coconut milk has 110 calories and 11 grams of fat. The light version has 36 calories and 3 grams of fat.

 **Nutrition per Serving**

Calories: 115
Protein: 2 g
Cholesterol: 36 mg

Fat (total): 2.6 g
Fat (saturated): 1.8 g

Carbohydrate: 21 g
Dietary Fiber: 0.7 g

Four Spice Pudding Cake

The combination of four spices and molasses makes an unbelievably tasty cake. Pudding cakes are an unusual combination of pudding and cake: You get a flavorful, creamy pudding underneath a layer of cake.

Prep time: 15 minutes   •   Cook time: 25 to 30 minutes   •   Serves 12

Vegetable cooking spray

2 large eggs, separated

1 cup packed dark brown sugar

3 TB. dark molasses

1 cup plain low-fat yogurt

⅓ cup all-purpose flour

½ tsp. ground cinnamon

¼ tsp. ground ginger

⅛ tsp. allspice

⅛ tsp. nutmeg

¼ tsp. cream of tartar

3 TB. granulated sugar

Nutrition Watch

A pudding cake is a great low-fat dessert because there is no added fat. The sauce-like pudding texture combined with the cake texture makes a deceptively smooth, velvety taste and appearance.

A Piece of Advice

You can use only two or three of the four spices, keeping in mind that allspice and nutmeg are stronger than cinnamon and ginger.

Position a rack in the center of the oven and preheat the oven to 350°F. Lightly coat an 8-inch square baking dish with cooking spray.

In a large bowl and using a whisk or electric mixer, combine egg yolks, brown sugar, and molasses. With a wooden spoon, stir in yogurt, flour, cinnamon, ginger, allspice, and nutmeg.

In another bowl and using clean beaters, beat egg whites with cream of tartar until foamy. Gradually add granulated sugar, continuing to beat until stiff peaks form. Fold the mixture into the batter just until blended and pour it into the prepared baking dish.

Set the baking dish into a larger baking pan. Pour enough hot water into the pan to reach halfway up the side of the dish. Bake for 25 to 30 minutes or until the cake no longer moves when you shake the dish. Serve immediately.

Nutrition per Serving

Calories: 137
Protein: 2.5 g
Cholesterol: 37 mg

Fat (total): 1.2 g
Fat (saturated): 0.5 g

Carbohydrate: 29 g
Dietary Fiber: 0.2 g

Mocha Fudge Pudding Cake

Try a flavored yogurt, such as vanilla or coffee, to enhance this pudding cake. Coffee and chocolate are a perfect flavor combination. Try serving it with Chocolate Sauce (see Chapter 16).

Prep time: 10 minutes • Cook time: 25 to 30 minutes • Serves 12

2 large eggs, separated

1 cup + 3 TB. granulated sugar (divided use)

2 TB. strong brewed coffee

1 cup low-fat yogurt

¼ cup all-purpose flour

3 TB. unsweetened cocoa

⅛ tsp. salt

¼ tsp. cream of tartar

2 TB. semi-sweet chocolate chips

Position a rack in the center of the oven and preheat the oven to 350°F. Lightly coat an 8-inch square baking dish with cooking spray.

In a large bowl and using a whisk or electric mixer, beat egg yolks, 1 cup sugar, and coffee. With a wooden spoon, stir in yogurt, flour, cocoa, and salt.

In another bowl and using clean beaters, beat egg whites with cream of tartar until foamy. Gradually add 3 tablespoons sugar, continuing to beat until stiff peaks form. Fold the mixture into the batter just until blended. Pour it into the prepared baking dish.

Set the baking dish into a larger baking pan. Pour enough water into the pan to reach halfway up the side of the dish. Bake for 15 minutes. Scatter chocolate chips on top. Bake 10 to 15 minutes longer or until the top is firm to the touch. Serve immediately.

Nutrition Watch

Most flavored yogurts are available in 1 percent milkfat, which is low in calories and cholesterol. I often use them in baking, especially because they are a good source of protein and calcium.

Nutrition per Serving

Calories: 139

Protein: 2.7 g

Cholesterol: 36 mg

Fat (total): 1.8 g

Fat (saturated): 0.9 g

Carbohydrate: 27 g

Dietary Fiber: 0.6 g

The Least You Need to Know

♦ You should first start stirred puddings off the stove, mixing until the cornstarch is dissolved, then cook over medium-high heat, whisking constantly.

♦ When adding an egg, temper the egg (heat without scrambling) first by adding some of the hot mixture before stirring the whisked egg into the pudding.

♦ Use day or two-day old bread when making bread pudding.

♦ Bake pudding cakes in a water bath (bain-marie) for even baking and a moister cake.

Squares, Bars, and Brownies

In This Chapter

- ◆ Fruit, cheese, and all kinds of filled squares
- ◆ Fantastic oatmeal, granola, and cheesecake bars
- ◆ Outrageous brownies

I admit it … I love squares, bars, and especially brownies, each more outrageously delicious than the one before. These are excellent at lunch, delicious as an afternoon snack, satisfying after dinner, and fantastic as a midnight snack with a cold glass of low-fat milk.

I'm always amazed how adding a little bit more of this or a little less of that can produce an entirely different product. Change a spice or add lemon zest in place of vanilla and you're on your way to developing a new recipe. So feel free to tinker with the recipes in this chapter, once you've given it a try and understand it. That's part of the fun of baking.

Most of my recipes call for an 8-inch square pan. Either glass or metal can be used. Glass will cook slightly quicker, so check it 5 minutes before the baking time is done. Always spray the pan well with vegetable cooking spray.

As with other baked desserts, preheat the oven and have the ingredients at room temperature before mixing. Choose a whisk, electric mixer, or food processor according to the filling. Just be sure that the ingredients are well incorporated.

Although it's tempting to dig right into the pan, let this type of cookie cool completely before cutting. Squares, bars, and brownies can be kept at room temperature for a couple of days. They can be frozen if they are well wrapped in plastic wrap or foil, and placed in freezer bags for six weeks. Cheesecake bars must be refrigerated and can also be frozen.

Sumptuous Squares

Squares are made with a soft dough and a filling or topping that are baked, then cooled, and cut into squares. Some of my recipes call for a shortbread crust. Shortbread crusts are traditionally made with butter and contain a lot of calories, fat, and cholesterol. In my version, I use only a small amount of oil. Other squares call for a cake-like dough with a topping.

Oatmeal squares have a crust made of oatmeal, flour, sugar, and some oil. You don't have to worry about the mixing of these crusts—just combine the ingredients until everything comes together. Bake the crust until golden and crisp. If you're using dried fruit, be sure that it is pitted.

Cheesecake Shortbread Squares

This shortbread cookie crust with a layer of creamy cheesecake filling is irresistible. I like to decorate each square with a piece of fresh fruit.

Prep time: 10 minutes • Bake time: 20 to 25 minutes • Chill time: at least 1 hour • Serves 16

Vegetable cooking spray

Crust

½ cup granulated sugar

1 large egg

1 TB. canola oil

½ tsp. vanilla extract

¾ cup all-purpose flour

Filling

½ cup granulated sugar

1 TB. all-purpose flour

¾ cup smooth 5% ricotta cheese

¼ cup light cream cheese, softened

2 TB. low-fat sour cream

1 large egg white

½ tsp. vanilla extract

Position a rack in the center of the oven and preheat the oven to 350°F. Lightly coat an 8-inch square cake pan with cooking spray.

Make crust: In a bowl, stir together sugar, egg, oil, and vanilla. Stir in flour until combined. Pat crust onto the bottom and slightly up the sides of the prepared pan.

Make filling: In a food processor, combine sugar, flour, ricotta cheese, cream cheese, sour cream, egg white, and vanilla; purée the mixture until smooth. Pour the mixture into the pan.

Bake for 20 to 25 minutes or until it is just slightly loose in the center. Let the pan cool on a wire rack. Chill at least 1 hour before cutting into 2-inch squares.

 Nutrition Watch _____

Traditional cheesecake is made with 35 percent milkfat cream cheese and eggs.

These squares use a combination of ricotta cheese and cream cheese with egg white, so the fat and calories are greatly reduced.

 Nutrition per Serving

Calories: 114   Fat (total): 2.9 g   Carbohydrate: 19 g
Protein: 3 g   Fat (saturated): 1.2 g   Dietary Fiber: 0.2 g
Cholesterol: 19 mg

Chocolate Sour Cream Cheesecake Squares

In my thinking, chocolate cheesecake in any way, shape, or form is not to be refused. These luscious squares have a brownie type of crust that is simply mouthwatering.

Prep time: 10 minutes • Bake time: 20 to 25 minutes • Chill time: at least 1 hour •
Serves 16

Vegetable cooking spray

Crust

½ cup granulated sugar

3 TB. unsweetened cocoa

2 TB. canola oil

1 large egg

½ tsp. vanilla extract

⅔ cup all-purpose flour

Filling

⅔ cup granulated sugar

2 TB. unsweetened cocoa

1 TB. all-purpose flour

⅔ cup 5% smooth ricotta cheese

¼ cup light cream cheese, softened

2 TB. low-fat sour cream

1 large egg white

½ tsp. vanilla extract

1 oz. white or semi-sweet chocolate chunks or 2 TB. chocolate chips

Nutrition Watch

For my chocolate desserts, I depend on cocoa and highlight the dessert with a small amount of chocolate chips. Cocoa only has 3 grams of fat per ounce, whereas chocolate has 9 grams per ounce.

A Piece of Advice

To get chocolate chunks, use a block of chocolate and shave off chunks with a sharp knife.

Position a rack in the center of the oven and preheat the oven to 350°F. Lightly coat an 8-inch square baking dish with cooking spray.

Make crust: In a bowl, stir together sugar, cocoa, oil, egg, and vanilla. Stir in flour just until combined. Pat the mixture into the bottom of the dish.

Make filling: In a food processor, combine sugar, cocoa, flour, ricotta cheese, cream cheese, sour cream, egg white, and vanilla; purée until the mixture is smooth. Spread it over the crust. Sprinkle with chocolate.

Bake for 20 to 25 minutes or until the center is still slightly loose in the middle. Let the dish cool on a wire rack. Chill at least 1 hour before cutting into 2-inch squares.

Nutrition per Serving

Calories: 138
Protein: 3.2 g
Cholesterol: 18 mg

Fat (total): 4.2 g
Fat (saturated): 1.5 g

Carbohydrate: 21 g
Dietary Fiber: 0.6 g

Brownie Cream Cheese Squares with Sliced Berries

These brownie squares with a cream cheese topping and sliced berries are downright decadent and are incredibly moist.

Prep time: 20 minutes   •   Bake time: 20 to 25 minutes   •   Serves 16

Vegetable cooking spray	1 tsp. baking powder
Cake	2 large egg whites
2 tsp. instant coffee granules	¼ tsp. cream of tartar
3 TB. hot water	**Topping**
¾ cup + 3 TB. granulated sugar (divided use)	⅔ cup smooth 5% ricotta cheese
3 TB. canola oil	1½ oz. light cream cheese, softened
1 large egg yolk	⅓ cup confectioners' sugar
1 tsp. vanilla extract	1½ tsp. water
½ cup all-purpose flour	½ tsp. vanilla extract
3 TB. unsweetened cocoa	1 cup sliced strawberries

Position a rack in the center of the oven and preheat the oven to 350°F. Lightly coat a 9-inch square metal cake pan with cooking spray.

Make cake: In a large bowl, dissolve instant coffee in hot water. With a whisk or electric mixer, add ¾ cup sugar, oil, egg yolk, and vanilla; mix until everything is combined.

In another bowl, stir together flour, cocoa, and baking powder. With a wooden spoon, stir the flour mixture into the coffee mixture until combined.

In a separate bowl and using clean beaters, beat egg whites with cream of tartar until foamy. Gradually add 3 tablespoons sugar, beating until stiff peaks form. Fold egg whites into the batter just until blended. Pour the mixture into the prepared pan.

Bake for 20 to 25 minutes, until the center is just set. Let the dish cool on a wire rack.

Make topping: In a food processor, combine ricotta cheese, cream cheese, confectioners' sugar, water, and vanilla; purée until smooth. Spread the mixture over the cake. Arrange strawberries over top.

Nutrition Watch

The sliced berries on top of these brownies provide an excellent source of vitamin C and also supply some potassium and iron.

Nutrition per Serving

Calories: 127	Fat (total): 4.4 g	Carbohydrate: 19 g
Protein: 2.8 g	Fat (saturated): 1.2 g	Dietary Fiber: 0.7 g
Cholesterol: 18 mg		

Orange Chocolate Squares with Cream Cheese Icing

Orange and chocolate have always been a wonderful combination. The orange juice concentrate is what gives this cake its intense orange flavor.

Prep time: 15 minutes • Bake time: 25 to 30 minutes • Serves 16

Vegetable cooking spray

Cake

¾ cup granulated sugar

2 tsp. finely grated orange zest

¼ cup orange juice concentrate

3 TB. Chocolate Sauce (see Chapter 16) or store-bought chocolate sauce

3 TB. canola oil

1 large egg

¼ cup plain low-fat yogurt

¾ cup all-purpose flour

3 TB. unsweetened cocoa

1 tsp. baking powder

½ tsp. baking soda

Icing

2 oz. light cream cheese, softened

½ cup confectioners' sugar

1 TB. orange juice concentrate

Position a rack in the center of the oven and preheat the oven to 350°F. Lightly coat an 8-inch square baking dish with cooking spray.

Make cake: In a bowl and using a whisk or electric mixer, beat sugar, orange rind, orange juice concentrate, chocolate sauce, oil, egg, and yogurt.

Nutrition Watch

Icings are usually made with butter, lard, or vegetable shortening. Using a little light cream cheese makes them lower in fat, calories, and cholesterol, and they're delicious with any cake.

In another bowl, stir together flour, cocoa, baking powder, and baking soda. With a wooden spoon, stir the flour mixture into the orange mixture until mixed. Spread it into the prepared dish.

Bake for 25 to 30 minutes or until a tester inserted into the center comes out dry. Let the dish cool on a wire rack.

Make icing: In a food processor, combine cream cheese, confectioners' sugar, and orange juice concentrate; purée until smooth. Spread it over the cake.

Nutrition per Serving

Calories: 127
Protein: 1.8 g
Cholesterol: 15 mg

Fat (total): 3.7 g
Fat (saturated): 0.8 g

Carbohydrate: 21 g
Dietary Fiber: 0.6 g

Date Pecan Oatmeal Squares

Date squares, often known as matrimonial squares, have been a classic for decades. The oatmeal crust often contains a cup or more of butter or vegetable shortening. My version only uses ⅓ cup oil mixed with some water, and it's incredibly delicious and rich tasting.

Prep time: 25 minutes   •   Bake time: 25 minutes   •   Serves 16

Vegetable cooking spray	¾ cup packed light brown sugar
1½ cups (8 oz.) chopped pitted dates	¼ cup chopped pecans, toasted
¼ cup granulated sugar	½ tsp. ground cinnamon
1 cup orange juice	⅓ cup canola oil
1¼ cups quick-cooking oats	¼ cup water
1 cup all-purpose flour	

Position a rack in the center of the oven and preheat the oven to 350°F. Lightly coat an 8-inch square baking dish with cooking spray.

In a saucepan, combine dates, sugar, and orange juice. Bring to a boil, and then simmer over medium heat for 15 minutes or until dates are soft and liquid is absorbed. Mash the mixture and let it cool.

In a bowl, stir together oats, flour, brown sugar, pecans, cinnamon, oil, and water until combined. Pat half of the mixture onto the bottom of the prepared dish. Spread the date mixture over top. Sprinkle the remaining oat mixture on top of the dates.

Bake for 25 minutes or until the squares are golden. Let the dish cool on a wire rack.

 A Piece of Advice

I buy my dried fruit at a bulk food store and keep it in the freezer. To chop dried fruit, I use kitchen shears, which is easier than a knife.

Toast pecans in a dry skillet over a high heat until they are lightly browned.

 Nutrition per Serving

Calories: 211
Protein: 2.4 g
Cholesterol: 0

Fat (total): 6.4 g
Fat (saturated): 0.5 g

Carbohydrate: 36 g
Dietary Fiber: 2.1 g

Apricot Oatmeal Squares

In my original cookbook on light cooking, *Rose Reisman Brings Home Light Cooking*, I had a traditional yet low-fat version of date squares. I still make them, but this version calls for apricots instead of dates. They're great.

Prep time: 25 minutes • Bake time: 20 minutes • Serves 16

Vegetable cooking spray

Purée

8 oz. dried apricots

¼ cup granulated sugar

1 cup water

Crust

1 cup quick-cooking oats

¾ cup all-purpose flour

⅔ cup packed light brown sugar

½ cup Grape-Nuts cereal

½ tsp. baking powder

½ tsp. baking soda

½ tsp. ground cinnamon

⅓ cup canola oil

3 TB. water

Position a rack in the center of the oven and preheat the oven to 350°F. Lightly coat an 8-inch baking dish with cooking spray.

Make purée: In a saucepan, combine apricots, sugar, and water. Bring the mixture to a boil; reduce the heat to medium-low and simmer for 15 to 20 minutes, uncovered, or until the apricots are very soft. Transfer the mixture to a food processor and purée.

Nutrition Watch

Apricots, rich in vitamin A and a source of iron and calcium, are a great concentrated source of energy.

Meanwhile, make crust: In a bowl, stir together oats, flour, brown sugar, cereal, baking powder, baking soda, cinnamon, oil, and water until crumbly. Divide the mixture in half. Pat one half into the bottom of the prepared dish. Spread the apricot purée on top. Sprinkle the crust mixture over the top.

Bake for 20 minutes or until the squares are golden. Let the dish cool on a wire rack.

Nutrition per Serving

Calories: 180
Protein: 2.3 g
Cholesterol: 0

Fat (total): 5 g
Fat (saturated): 0.3 g

Carbohydrate: 31 g
Dietary Fiber: 2.3 g

Orange-Cranberry Squares

Dried cranberries and orange go well together in these squares. You can always use another dried fruit of your choice, such as dried cherries, raisins, dates, or apricots.

Prep time: 15 minutes • Bake time: 15 to 20 minutes • Serves 12

Vegetable cooking spray

Squares

⅓ cup packed light brown sugar

⅓ cup granulated sugar

2 tsp. finely grated orange rind

¼ cup fresh orange juice

3 TB. canola oil

1 large egg

1 tsp. vanilla extract

1 cup all-purpose flour

½ cup dried cranberries

½ tsp. baking powder

½ tsp. ground cinnamon

Topping

1 TB. granulated sugar

⅛ tsp. ground cinnamon

Position a rack in the center of the oven and preheat the oven to 350°F. Lightly coat an 8-inch square baking dish with cooking spray.

Make squares: In a bowl and using a whisk or electric mixer, beat brown sugar, sugar, orange rind, orange juice, oil, egg, and vanilla.

In another bowl, stir together flour, cranberries, baking powder, and cinnamon. With a wooden spoon, stir the mixture into the orange mixture until mixed. Spread into the prepared dish.

Make topping: In a small bowl, stir together sugar and cinnamon. Sprinkle the mixture over the squares.

Bake for 15 to 20 minutes or until a tester inserted into the center comes out dry. Let the dish cool on a wire rack.

 A Piece of Advice

These squares freeze well. I like to include them in my children's lunch boxes. In fact, I like them as an afternoon snack, too, when I'm picking up the kids!

 Nutrition Watch

Dried cranberries are very high in vitamin C and can be a high-energy snack any time. You only need a small amount because their nutrients and calories are concentrated.

 Nutrition per Serving

Calories: 143
Protein: 1.7 g
Cholesterol: 18 mg

Fat (total): 4 g
Fat (saturated): 0.4 g

Carbohydrate: 25 g
Dietary Fiber: 0.8 g

Cinnamon Pumpkin Oatmeal Squares

The pumpkin, oatmeal, and dates make these squares chewy and moist. Great for a lunch-time snack or a breakfast nibble.

Prep time: 10 minutes • Bake time: 25 to 30 minutes • Serves 16

Vegetable cooking spray

1 cup packed light brown sugar

½ cup canned pumpkin purée

⅓ cup low-fat milk

¼ cup canola oil

1 large egg

1 tsp. vanilla extract

¾ cup all-purpose flour

⅔ cup quick-cooking oats

½ cup chopped pitted dates or golden raisins

1 tsp. baking powder

1 tsp. ground cinnamon

¼ tsp. ground ginger

⅛ tsp. allspice

A Piece of Advice

Don't buy pumpkin pie filling, which contains sugar and other ingredients. Buy pure, puréed pumpkin, with nothing added. Freeze any

Nutrition Watch

These squares are loaded with nutrition. Pumpkin is a good source of vitamin A, oats are high in vitamin B1, and dates are a good source of protein and iron.

Position a rack in the center of the oven and preheat the oven to 350°F. Lightly coat an 8-inch square baking dish with cooking spray.

In a bowl and using a whisk or electric mixer, beat brown sugar, pumpkin, milk, oil, egg, and vanilla.

In another bowl, stir together flour, oats, dates, baking powder, cinnamon, ginger, and allspice. With a wooden spoon, stir the mixture into the pumpkin mixture just until everything is combined. Pour the batter into the prepared dish.

Bake for 25 to 30 minutes or until a tester inserted into the center comes out dry. Let the dish cool on a wire rack.

Nutrition per Serving

Calories: 146
Protein: 1.9 g
Cholesterol: 13.5 mg

Fat (total): 4 g
Fat (saturated): 0.4 g

Carbohydrate: 25 g
Dietary Fiber: 1.3 g

Quick Snack Bars

Bars are another type of soft cookie where the dough is spread evenly in the pan, baked, cooled, and cut into bars. Sometimes I've added a filling and a topping for a more complex flavor. These bars are not particularly good keepers so plan to eat them within a day or so or freeze them for longer storage. Cheesecake bars have a pastry crust that will be tough and dry if it is over mixed, so mix the batter just until everything is well incorporated. Pat the crust into the pan along the bottom and slightly up the sides. The filling for cheesecake bars must be processed well so that the batter is smooth. They are baked like a cheesecake, just until the center is slightly loose. Let them cool on a wire rack until they are room temperature, and then chill them before serving.

Maple Syrup Dried Cherry Oatmeal Bars

These bars are a great snack for midday or in your little angels' school lunches. The maple syrup and oatmeal give the bars a chewy, moist texture.

Prep time: 10 minutes   •   Bake time: 15 to 18 minutes   •   Serves 12

Vegetable cooking spray

½ cup packed light brown sugar

⅓ cup pure maple syrup

1 large egg

3 TB. canola oil

1½ tsp. vanilla extract

¾ cup quick-cooking oats

⅔ cup all-purpose flour

⅓ cup dried cherries

1 tsp. baking powder

Position a rack in the center of the oven and preheat the oven to 350°F. Lightly coat an 8-inch square baking dish with cooking spray.

In a bowl and using a whisk or electric mixer, beat brown sugar, maple syrup, egg, oil, and vanilla.

In another bowl, stir together oats, flour, cherries, and baking powder. With a wooden spoon, stir the mixture into the maple mixture until combined. Spread it into the prepared dish.

Bake for 15 to 18 minutes or until a tester inserted into the center comes out dry. Let the dish cool on a wire rack.

 A Piece of Advice

Always buy pure maple syrup for the best flavor. The imitation brands are mostly corn syrup with the addition of artificial maple extract.

 Nutrition Watch

Rolled oats are high in vitamin B1 and contain a good amount of vitamins B2 and E.

Nutrition per Serving

Calories: 150   Fat (total): 4.2 g   Carbohydrate: 26 g
Protein: 2.1 g   Fat (saturated): 0.4 g   Dietary Fiber: 0.9 g
Cholesterol: 18 mg

Molasses Oatmeal Bars

Molasses, oatmeal, and gingerbread spices make a wonderful tasting bar. It's my version of a granola bar.

Prep time: 10 minutes   •   Bake time: 15 to 18 minutes   •   Serves 12

Vegetable cooking spray

½ cup packed brown sugar

½ tsp. ground cinnamon

¼ tsp. ground ginger

⅛ tsp. allspice

⅓ cup dark molasses

3 TB. canola oil

1 large egg

¾ cup all-purpose flour

½ cup quick-cooking oats

1 tsp. baking powder

A Piece of Advice

When buying rolled oats, use either regular old fashioned or quick cooking. Avoid the instant because it gives a sticky texture to your baking. Molasses comes from the process of refining sugar cane and sugar beets. The juice is squeezed from the plants and boiled into a syrupy mixture. Each subsequent boiling produces light, dark, and then blackstrap molasses. For baking, dark is the best choice.

Position a rack in the center of the oven and preheat the oven to 350°F. Lightly coat an 8-inch square baking dish with cooking spray.

In a bowl and using a whisk or electric mixer, beat brown sugar, cinnamon, ginger, allspice, molasses, oil, and egg.

In another bowl, stir together flour, oats, and baking powder. With a wooden spoon, stir the mixture into the molasses mixture until blended. Spread it into the prepared dish.

Bake for 15 to 18 minutes or until a tester inserted into the center comes out dry. Let the dish cool on a wire rack.

Nutrition per Serving

Calories: 141   Fat (total): 4.1 g   Carbohydrate: 24 g
Protein: 1.9 g   Fat (saturated): 0.4 g   Dietary Fiber: 0.6 g
Cholesterol: 18 mg

Chewy Peanut Oatmeal Bars

The peanut butter, oatmeal, and peanut butter chips make this an outstanding bar for a quick snack. I pack them in the kids' lunches and offer them as an after-school treat.

Prep time: 10 minutes • Bake time: 25 minutes • Serves 16

Vegetable cooking spray

½ cup packed light brown sugar

½ cup granulated sugar

¼ cup smooth peanut butter

¼ cup low-fat milk

2 TB. canola oil

1 large egg

1 tsp. vanilla extract

¾ cup all-purpose flour

⅔ cup quick-cooking oats

3 TB. peanut butter chips or semi-sweet chocolate chips

½ tsp. baking soda

Position a rack in the center of the oven and preheat the oven to 350°F. Lightly coat an 8-inch square baking dish with cooking spray.

In a bowl and using a whisk or electric mixer, beat brown sugar, sugar, peanut butter, milk, oil, egg, and vanilla.

In another bowl, stir together flour, oats, peanut butter chips, and baking soda. With a wooden spoon, stir the mixture into the peanut butter mixture until everything is well combined. Pat it into the prepared dish.

Bake for 25 minutes or until a tester inserted into the center comes out dry. Let the dish cool on a wire rack.

 A Piece of Advice

Peanut butter chips are available in most grocery stores. You can also use semi-sweet chocolate chips or, for a different flavor altogether, try mint-flavored chocolate chips.

 Nutrition Watch

Oatmeal is still a great way to start your day. This food is classified as a low-glycemic food, which means that it raises your blood sugar slowly. (This keeps you full longer.)

 Nutrition per Serving

Calories: 144

Protein: 3 g

Cholesterol: 13 mg

Fat (total): 4.8 g

Fat (saturated): 0.7 g

Carbohydrate: 21 g

Dietary Fiber: 0.9 g

Pumpkin Cream Cheese Bars

I love pumpkin pie and I love cheesecake. Because I can't have both at once, I decided to create this unusual and delicious recipe. The combination is great.

Prep time: 20 minutes • Bake time: 30 to 35 minutes • Chill time: at least 2 hours • Serves 16

Vegetable cooking spray

Base

¾ cup packed light brown sugar

¼ cup granulated sugar

½ tsp. ground cinnamon

¼ tsp. ground ginger

⅓ cup canned pumpkin purée

3 TB. canola oil

1 large egg

2 TB. plain low-fat yogurt

1 cup all-purpose flour

1 tsp. baking powder

Cheesecake Layer

½ cup smooth 5% ricotta cheese

2 oz. light cream cheese, softened

⅓ cup granulated sugar

1 large egg white

½ tsp. vanilla extract

Topping

⅓ cup packed light brown sugar

¼ cup all-purpose flour

½ tsp. ground cinnamon

2 tsp. water

1½ tsp. canola oil

Position a rack in the center of the oven and preheat the oven to 350°F. Lightly coat an 8-inch square baking dish with cooking spray.

Make base: In a bowl and using a whisk or electric mixer, beat brown sugar, sugar, cinnamon, ginger, pumpkin, oil, egg, and yogurt.

In another bowl, stir together flour and baking powder. With a wooden spoon, stir the mixture into the pumpkin mixture until combined. Pour it into the prepared dish.

Make cheesecake layer: In a food processor, combine ricotta cheese, cream cheese, sugar, egg white, and vanilla; purée until the mixture is smooth. Pour it over the base.

Make topping: In a bowl, stir together brown sugar, flour, cinnamon, water, and oil until combined. Sprinkle it over the cheesecake.

Bake for 30 to 35 minutes or until the cheesecake center has just set and a tester inserted into the pumpkin filling comes out dry. Let the dish cool on a wire rack. Chill for 2 hours. Serve at room temperature or chilled.

 **Nutrition per Serving**

Calories: 177
Protein: 3.1 g
Cholesterol: 18 mg

Fat (total): 4.6 g
Fat (saturated): 1.1 g

Carbohydrate: 30 g
Dietary Fiber: 0.5 g

Orange Poppy Seed Cheesecake Bars

This crust tastes like a moist shortbread cookie crust, even though it has less fat than regular shortbread. The orange-flavored cheesecake filling is thick and creamy.

Prep time: 15 minutes • Bake time: 10 minutes plus 20 minutes • Chill time: at least 1 hour • Serves 16

Vegetable cooking spray

Crust

½ cup granulated sugar

1 TB. margarine or unsalted butter

1 large egg

1 TB. orange juice concentrate

1 tsp. finely grated orange zest

¾ cup all-purpose flour

Filling

½ cup granulated sugar

1 TB. all-purpose flour

1 tsp. poppy seeds

1 tsp. finely grated orange zest

¾ cup smooth 5% ricotta cheese

¼ cup light cream cheese, softened

1 large egg white

1 TB. orange juice concentrate

Position a rack in the center of the oven and preheat the oven to 350°F. Lightly coat an 8-inch square baking dish with cooking spray.

Make crust: In a bowl, combine sugar, margarine, egg, orange juice concentrate, and orange rind. Mix in flour until combined. Pat the mixture into the bottom of the prepared dish. Bake in the center of the oven for 10 minutes.

Make filling: In a food processor, combine sugar, flour, poppy seeds, orange rind, ricotta cheese, cream cheese, egg white, and orange juice concentrate; purée until the mixture is smooth. Pour it over the crust. Bake for 20 minutes or until the center is slightly loose. Let the dish cool on a wire rack. Chill for at least 1 hour.

 A Piece of Advice

When grating zest, be careful not to grate the white pith underneath the skin. It is bitter and will ruin your dessert.

 Nutrition Watch

Oranges are a great nutritious snack during the day. They are an excellent source of vitamin C and contain some vitamin A.

 Nutrition per Serving

Calories: 114
Protein: 3 g
Cholesterol: 26 mg

Fat (total): 2.7 g
Fat (saturated): 1.2 g

Carbohydrate: 19 g
Dietary Fiber: 0.2 g

Pear-Raisin Streusel Bars

The crust is a tender yet crisp base for this tasty fruit bar. It requires little fat because of the added water.

Prep time: 20 minutes • Bake time: 10 minutes plus 25 minutes • Serves 12

Vegetable cooking spray

Crust

¼ cup all-purpose flour

⅔ cup quick-cooking oats

⅓ cup granulated sugar

¾ tsp. ground cinnamon

3 TB. canola oil

3 TB. water

Filling

2 large pears, peeled, cored, and diced (about 2 cups)

⅓ cup golden raisins

2 TB. granulated sugar

1 TB. fresh lemon juice

Topping

⅓ cup packed light brown sugar

⅓ cup all-purpose flour

½ tsp. ground cinnamon

1 TB. margarine or unsalted butter

2 tsp. water

 A Piece of Advice

When buying pears, always look for those that are fragrant and free from blemishes. Don't use overly ripe ones for cooking because they'll get too soft in the baking. I like the Bosc and Bartlett varieties for these bars.

 Nutrition Watch

Pears contain small amounts of phosphorous and vitamin A; raisins are especially rich in iron.

Position a rack in the center of the oven and preheat the oven to 350°F. Lightly coat an 8-inch square baking dish with cooking spray.

Make crust: In a bowl, stir together flour, oats, sugar, cinnamon, oil, and water until combined. Pat the mixture into the prepared dish. Bake for 10 minutes.

Make filling: In a bowl, stir together pears, raisins, sugar, and lemon juice. Spread the mixture over the crust.

Make topping: In a bowl, stir together brown sugar, flour, cinnamon, margarine, and water. Sprinkle the mixture over the filling. Bake for another 25 minutes or until the pears are tender. Let the dish cool on a wire rack.

 Nutrition per Serving

Calories: 185
Protein: 2.2 g
Cholesterol: 0

Fat (total): 4.9 g
Fat (saturated): 0.5 g

Carbohydrate: 33 g
Dietary Fiber: 1.7 g

Peanut Butter and Chocolate Chip Granola Bars

Peanut butter and chocolate make a delicious combination. These granola bars are better and healthier than any commercial ones. They make a great lunch snack for the kids.

Prep time: 10 minutes • Bake time: 20 to 25 minutes • Serves 16

Vegetable cooking spray

1¼ cups quick-cooking oats

½ cup packed light brown sugar

¼ cup unsweetened coconut, toasted

2 TB. semi-sweet chocolate chips

2 TB. peanut butter chips

3 TB. light corn syrup

2 TB. honey

3 TB. smooth peanut butter

3 TB. canola oil

3 TB. water

2 tsp. vanilla extract

Position a rack in the center of the oven and preheat the oven to 350°F. Lightly coat an 8-inch square cake pan with cooking spray.

In large bowl, stir together oats, brown sugar, coconut, chocolate chips, peanut butter chips, corn syrup, honey, peanut butter, oil, water, and vanilla until combined. Pat the mixture into the prepared pan.

Bake for 20 to 25 minutes or until the top is golden and the bars seem firm. Let the pan cool on a wire rack.

 **A Piece of Advice**

Always choose natural peanut butter. The commercial brands are loaded with sugar and are often hydrogenated, which makes them a saturated fat.

Toast the coconut in a dry non-stick skillet on a high heat, just until it is lightly browned, to give the flavor more intensity.

 Nutrition per Serving

Calories: 134
Protein: 2.1 g
Cholesterol: 0

Fat (total): 6 g
Fat (saturated): 1.6 g

Carbohydrate: 18 g
Dietary Fiber: 1.3 g

Chewy Cocoa Granola Bars

By adding some cocoa to these granola bars I created a delicious chocolate version of this popular snack. They have a chewy and moist texture.

Prep time: 15 minutes • Bake time: 20 to 25 minutes • Serves 12

Vegetable cooking spray

⅔ cup packed light brown sugar

2 TB. light corn syrup

2 TB. canola oil

1 large egg

1 tsp. vanilla extract

¾ cup low-fat granola

½ cup all-purpose flour

3 TB. semi-sweet chocolate chips

2 TB. unsweetened cocoa

½ tsp. baking powder

Nutrition Watch

Regular granola has approximately double the fat and calories of low-fat brands, thanks to the addition of sugar and oil. Also, beware of commercial granola bars—these are usually not a healthy low-fat snack. The homemade version is always the best choice.

Position a rack in the center of the oven and preheat the oven to 350°F. Lightly coat an 8-inch square baking dish with cooking spray.

In large bowl with whisk or electric mixer, beat brown sugar, corn syrup, oil, egg, and vanilla.

In another bowl, stir together granola, flour, chocolate chips, cocoa, and baking powder. With a wooden spoon, stir the mixture into the brown sugar mixture until combined. Spread the mixture into the prepared dish.

Bake for 20 to 25 minutes or until the bars have set. Let the dish cool on a wire rack.

Nutrition per Serving

Calories: 142
Protein: 1.8 g
Cholesterol: 18 mg

Fat (total): 3.9 g
Fat (saturated): 0.9 g

Carbohydrate: 25 g
Dietary Fiber: 0.9 g

Brownies You Won't Forget

I am addicted to brownies. I'm not alone; whole books have been devoted to the subject. Brownies are the quintessential chocolate fix. On luxury cruise lines that offer a Decadent Chocolate Tea, no less than a dozen different kinds of brownies are offered.

Brownies are simple and quick to make. For best results, prepare pans as directed in each recipe, using the specified pan size. Always mix the wet ingredients first and then add the dry ingredients just until they are incorporated. Do not over mix, or the brownies will be dry. For the best texture, bake them just until the center is slightly loose. Let them cool in the pan on a wire rack and serve them right from the pan.

Whether you make these brownies for your family for dessert, decide to bake them only for yourself, or whip up a batch to lavish on friends as gifts, you're sure to find a brownie or two for everyone.

Cream Cheese–Filled Brownies

These brownies were featured in *Rose Reisman's Light Vegetarian Cooking* and were rated the number-one brownie recipe. The layer of cream cheese combined with the chocolate brownies makes them simply decadent.

Prep time: 15 minutes • Bake time: 20 to 25 minutes • Serves 16

Vegetable cooking spray	⅓ cup low-fat sour cream
Filling	¼ cup canola oil
4 oz. light cream cheese, softened	1 large egg
2 TB. granulated sugar	1 large egg white
2 TB. low-fat milk	¾ cup all-purpose flour
1 tsp. vanilla extract	½ cup unsweetened cocoa
Cake	1 tsp. baking powder
1 cup packed brown sugar	

Position a rack in the center of the oven and preheat the oven to 350°F. Lightly coat an 8-inch square baking dish with cooking spray.

Make filling: In a food processor or bowl with an electric mixer, beat together cream cheese, sugar, milk, and vanilla until the mixture is smooth. Set aside.

 **A Piece of Advice**

Double the recipe and bake it in a 9-inch square baking dish for 10 minutes longer or until it is slightly loose in the center. When pouring the batter, don't worry if there's a swirling pattern—the result will be attractive.

Nutrition Watch

Brownies are traditionally extremely high in calories and fat because they usually contain a lot of butter or other shortening, eggs, and often sour cream. These are much lower in fat and calories because the cocoa replaces the high-fat chocolate.

Make the cake: In a large bowl, whisk together brown sugar, sour cream, oil, whole egg, and egg white. In a separate bowl, stir together flour, cocoa, and baking powder. Add the liquid ingredients to the dry ingredients, blending just until everything is mixed.

Pour half the cake batter into the prepared dish. Spoon the filling on top; spread it with a wet knife. Pour the remaining batter into the pan. Bake for 20 to 25 minutes or until it is just barely loose in the center. Let cool in the pan on a wire rack.

Nutrition per Serving

Calories: 133
Protein: 3 g
Cholesterol: 19 mg

Fat (total): 5 g
Fat (saturated): 2 g

Carbohydrate: 20 g
Dietary Fiber: 1 g

Chocolate Banana Pecan Brownies

Brownies are already a top favorite in my family. By adding bananas, I gave this classic dessert a whole new twist. The bananas give moisture and texture.

Prep time: 15 minutes   •   Bake time: 25 to 30 minutes   •   Serves 16

Vegetable cooking spray

¾ cup granulated sugar

2 medium mashed ripe bananas (⅔ cup)

3 TB. canola oil

1 large egg

1 tsp. vanilla extract

1 cup all-purpose flour

⅓ cup unsweetened cocoa

⅓ cup chopped pecans

1 tsp. baking powder

⅓ cup low-fat yogurt

A Piece of Advice

To enhance the flavor of bananas in your baking, toss overripe ones in the freezer; then thaw and use. The flavor will be much more intense.

Position a rack in the center of the oven and preheat the oven to 350°F. Lightly coat an 8-inch square baking dish with cooking spray.

In a bowl and using a whisk or electric mixer, beat sugar, bananas, oil, egg, and vanilla.

In another bowl, stir together flour, cocoa, pecans, baking powder, and yogurt. With a wooden spoon, stir the mixture into the banana mixture just until everything is moistened. Pour the batter into the prepared pan.

Bake for 25 to 30 minutes or until a tester inserted in the center comes out with just a few crumbs clinging to it. Do not over bake. Let the dish cool on a wire rack.

Nutrition Watch

Bananas are high in carbohydrate, potassium, and vitamin C—a great nutritious low-fat snack when you're running out the door.

 Nutrition per Serving

Calories: 127
Protein: 1.8 g
Cholesterol: 13.5 mg

Fat (total): 5 g
Fat (saturated): 0.6 g

Carbohydrate: 18 g
Dietary Fiber: 1.3 g

Rocky Mountain Brownies

When I first developed a recipe for low-fat brownies, my whole family said that they loved me forever! Now I've taken my next most favorite flavor—Rocky Mountain—and added it to this already delicious recipe.

Prep time: 15 minutes   •   Bake time: 30 minutes   •   Serves 16

Vegetable cooking spray

1 cup granulated sugar

⅓ cup unsweetened cocoa

⅓ cup unsweetened applesauce

¼ cup canola oil

1 large egg

1 tsp. vanilla extract

¼ cup plain low-fat yogurt

¾ cup all-purpose flour

½ tsp. baking powder

¾ cup miniature marshmallows

¼ cup semi-sweet chocolate chips

Position a rack in the center of the oven and preheat the oven to 350°F. Lightly coat an 8-inch square baking dish with cooking spray.

In a bowl and using a whisk or electric mixer, beat sugar, cocoa, applesauce, oil, egg, vanilla, and yogurt.

 Nutrition Watch

Be sure to buy unsweetened applesauce. Sugar is added to some brands, which adds unnecessarily to the calories.

A Piece of Advice

The addition of apple-sauce adds volume without fat to these brownies. Using any puréed fruit, such as bananas, cooked dates, or prunes, will do the same.

In another bowl, stir together flour and baking powder. Stir the mixture into the applesauce mixture just until everything is combined. Pour the batter into the prepared dish.

Bake for 20 minutes. Sprinkle with marshmallows and chocolate chips. Bake another 10 minutes. Let the dish cool on a wire rack.

Nutrition per Serving

Calories: 136
Protein: 1.2 g
Cholesterol: 13.5 mg

Fat (total): 5.2 g
Fat (saturated): 0.9 g

Carbohydrate: 22 g
Dietary Fiber: 0.8 g

Mint Chocolate Cream Cheese Brownies

Brownies with a cream cheese swirl and a mint flavor are so unusual. I may never go back to regular brownies again.

Prep time: 15 minutes • Bake time: 20 to 25 minutes • Serves 16

Vegetable cooking spray

Brownies

¾ cup granulated sugar

3 TB. canola oil

1 large egg

½ tsp. peppermint extract

½ cup plain low-fat yogurt

⅔ cup all-purpose flour

⅓ cup unsweetened cocoa

1 tsp. baking powder

¼ cup mint chocolate chips

Cream Cheese Mixture

2 oz. light cream cheese

4 tsp. granulated sugar

1 TB. water

Position a rack in the center of the oven and preheat the oven to 350°F. Lightly coat an 8-inch square baking dish with cooking spray.

A Piece of Advice

Be careful when using mint extract. It's quite intense, so if you use too much you'll ruin your baked goods.

Make brownies: In a bowl, whisk together sugar, oil, egg, peppermint extract, and yogurt.

In another bowl, stir together flour, cocoa, baking powder, and chocolate chips. Stir the mixture into the sugar mixture just until everything is combined. Pour it into the prepared dish.

Make cream cheese mixture: In a food processor or using an electric hand mixer, combine cream cheese, sugar, and water; purée until the mixture is smooth. Pour the mixture over the top of the brownie batter. Using a knife, swirl the cream cheese mixture through the batter.

Bake for 20 to 25 minutes or until the center is slightly loose. Let the dish cool on a wire rack.

Nutrition Watch

Yogurt is now available in 1 percent milkfat or less, including the fruit-flavored varieties. I avoid the artificially sweetened ones. In fact, sometimes I use a plain yogurt and add fruit and a little honey to sweeten it.

 ### Nutrition per Serving

Calories: 123
Protein: 2.1 g
Cholesterol: 15 mg

Fat (total): 4.7 g
Fat (saturated): 1.3 g

Carbohydrate: 18 g
Dietary Fiber: 0.9 g

Peanut Butter Chip Brownies

Chocolate and peanut butter are a natural combination. This brownie recipe, with its morsels of peanut butter chips, hits the spot.

Prep time: 15 minutes • Bake time: 25 minutes • Serves 16

Vegetable cooking spray

¾ cup granulated sugar

¼ cup smooth peanut butter

2 TB. canola oil

1 large egg

1 tsp. vanilla extract

⅔ cup plain low-fat yogurt

⅔ cup all-purpose flour

⅓ cup unsweetened cocoa

1 tsp. baking powder

¼ cup peanut butter chips

Position a rack in the center and preheat the oven to 350°F. Lightly coat an 8-inch square baking dish with cooking spray.

In a bowl and using a whisk or electric mixer, beat together sugar, peanut butter, oil, egg, vanilla, and yogurt.

In another bowl, stir together flour, cocoa, baking powder, and peanut butter chips. With a wooden spoon, stir the mixture into the peanut butter mixture just until everything is combined. Pour the batter into the prepared dish.

Bake for 25 minutes or until a tester inserted in the center comes out with a few crumbs attached to it. Let the dish cool on a wire rack.

A Piece of Advice

Always buy pure, natural peanut butter. The commercial brands are often loaded with sugar and can also be hydrogenated, turning peanut butter into a saturated fat. Store natural peanut butter in the refrigerator after opening; it'll keep for up to 6 months.

 **Nutrition per Serving**

Calories: 141   Fat (total): 5.1 g   Carbohydrate: 17 g
Protein: 3.1 g   Fat (saturated): 1 g   Dietary Fiber: 1.2 g
Cholesterol: 13.5 mg

The Least You Need to Know

◆ Glass or metal baking pans and dishes can be used. Adjust baking time accordingly.

◆ Take care to not over mix the pastry crust for cheesecake bars; process the filling well so the filling's smooth.

◆ Bake oatmeal squares until the crust is golden and crisp. Make sure any dried fruit used is pitted.

◆ Do not over mix brownies; bake until center is slightly loose—they'll continue to bake further as they cool.

◆ None of these cookies are good keepers so plan to eat them within a day or so or freeze for up to 6 weeks.

Chapter 11

Soy Sweets

In This Chapter

- ◆ Light, moist cakes and cake rolls
- ◆ Spectacular pies and tarts
- ◆ Old-fashioned puddings made extra nutritious with soy products
- ◆ Special treats made with soy

We've all read about the power of soy. The United States Department of Food and Drug Administration has stated that products containing soy protein may lower cholesterol levels, which can lead to a reduced risk of heart disease and strokes.

In addition, soy and tofu desserts are perfect for those who are lactose intolerant, those who want to increase the soy in their diet, and those who are vegetarian and do not eat any animal products. It is also good for kosher dietary reasons, specifically not mixing meat with dairy.

Soy is easy to digest, and it's low in calories, cholesterol, and sodium. High in protein, soy can also be a good source of calcium when coagulated with calcium chloride or calcium sulphate. Some soy products can be high in fat, so check the labels.

Soy milk is the liquid squeezed from soaked soy beans. It is rich in protein and iron, cholesterol free, lactose free, and low in saturated fat. It comes in three flavors: plain, vanilla, or chocolate. Soy milk acts like cow's milk in cooking and baking. You can even make buttermilk out of soy milk by stirring 1 table-spoon lemon juice into 1 cup soy milk and letting it stand for 5 minutes before using.

When most of us think of soy products, tofu immediately comes to mind. Tofu, also called soybean curd, is the vegetarian equivalent of cottage cheese in the dairy world. It's marvelous for desserts as it quite literally absorbs the other flavors from the recipe, while adding an excellent source of protein.

Although it comes in soft, firm, or extra firm, I usually use firm tofu when making jelly roll–type cakes. Be sure to process it well. I also use silken tofu, which is made from extra thick soy milk and is strained through silk, hence the name. The result is a creamy custard-like consistency, ideal for cheesecakes because it purées well.

Tofu can be kept, in water, in the refrigerator for up to one week. You can freeze tofu if wrapped tightly for up to six months. The texture will change slightly but will still be fine for desserts.

I add salt and a lot of flavoring to my soy recipes because on its own soy has a bland, flat flavor and tends to absorb the flavors from foods. The salt allows the other flavors to emerge.

Using tofu and other soy products may be a sneaky way to add good nutrition to your desserts, but I won't tell. These desserts are so good it's likely no one will ever suspect that they are good for them. After all, you, your family, and your friends deserve to eat well and stay healthy.

A Piece of Advice

Using salt is necessary when baking with soy products because the soy seems to prevent the taste of other foods from coming through. Even a small amount of salt brings out those flavors.

Soy Cakes, Pies, and Tarts

These are wonderfully delicious desserts for a sweet finish to a meal or a special treat with coffee or tea. If you're not used to baking with soy products, be sure to read the recipe from start to finish and carefully follow my directions. Now even those people who are lactose intolerant can have their cake, pie, or tart and eat it, too.

Lemon Cheesecake

Lemon adds a refreshing flavor, and silken tofu provides a creamy texture in this cheesecake that's perfect after a heavy meal. Serve it with Raspberry Coulis (see Chapter 16).

Prep time: 15 minutes • Bake time: 45 minutes • Chill time: at least 2 hours • Serves 12

Vegetable cooking spray

Crust

1½ cups graham cracker crumbs

2 tsp. granulated sugar

2 TB. water

1 TB. canola oil

Filling

1 lb. soft silken tofu, drained

⅓ cup light soy milk

1 large egg

1 cup granulated sugar

1 TB. finely grated lemon zest

¼ cup fresh lemon juice

3 TB. all-purpose flour

¼ tsp. salt

Position a rack in the center of the oven and preheat the oven to 350°F. Lightly coat a 9-inch springform pan with cooking spray.

Make crust: In a bowl, stir together graham cracker crumbs, sugar, water, and oil until combined. Pat the mixture onto the bottom and up the sides of the pre-pared pan.

Make filling: In a food processor, combine tofu, soy milk, egg, sugar, lemon zest and juice, flour, and salt; purée until smooth. Pour it into the crust. Set the pan on a large baking sheet.

Place a pan of hot water on the bottom rack of the oven. Bake for 45 minutes or until it is just slightly loose at the center. Run a knife around the edge of the cake. Let the pan cool on a wire rack until the cake is room temperature. Chill at least 2 hours.

To unmold the cake, loosen the spring and lift off the sides, leaving the cake on the bottom of the pan.

 A Piece of Advice

Be sure to buy silken, not firm, tofu. Only silken tofu will give the creamy texture required by this cheesecake.

 Nutrition Watch

Tofu is an excellent source of protein, and it is a good source of calcium when coagulated with calcium chloride or calcium sulphate.

 Nutrition per Serving

Calories: 181
Protein: 3.8 g
Cholesterol: 18 mg

Fat (total): 4.2 g
Fat (saturated): 0.6 g

Carbohydrate: 32 g
Dietary Fiber: 0.6 g

Banana Marble Coffeecake

I featured this "anytime-of-day" cake in my first cookbook on light cooking, *Rose Reisman Brings Home Light Cooking*. The use of soy milk now makes it available to anyone.

Prep time: 15 minutes • Bake time: 35 to 40 minutes • Serves 12

Vegetable cooking spray	¾ cup light soy milk
1⅓ cups all-purpose flour	2 large eggs
1 tsp. baking powder	¼ cup canola oil
½ tsp. baking soda	1 tsp. vanilla extract
¼ tsp. salt	1 cup + 2 TB. granulated sugar (divided use)
2 small ripe bananas, mashed (⅔ cup)	1 TB. unsweetened cocoa

Position a rack in the center of the oven and preheat the oven to 350°F. Lightly coat a 9-inch square baking dish with cooking spray.

Nutrition Watch

Soy milk comes in different levels of milkfat. I like to use the low-fat variety, which is usually labeled "light."

A Piece of Advice

Be sure to keep over-ripe bananas in the freezer to get the most intense flavor. Just defrost and mash them.

In a bowl, stir together flour, baking powder, baking soda, and salt.

In a food processor, combine bananas, soy milk, eggs, oil, vanilla, and 1 cup sugar; purée the mixture until smooth. Pour it over the dry ingredients; with a wooden spoon, stir until everything is combined. Set aside ⅓ cup of the batter. Pour the remaining batter into the prepared baking dish.

Stir remaining 2 tablespoons sugar and cocoa into the reserved batter. Drizzle the mixture over the top of the cake batter. Using a knife, swirl the dark batter into the light batter.

Bake for 35 to 40 minutes or until a tester inserted in the center comes out clean. Let the pan cool on a wire rack.

Nutrition per Serving

Calories: 175
Protein: 2.9 g
Cholesterol: 36 mg

Fat (total): 5.7 g
Fat (saturated): 0.7 g

Carbohydrate: 28 g
Dietary Fiber: 1 g

Glazed Mocha Cake

This cake was such a hit in my first light cookbook, *Rose Reisman Brings Home Light Cooking*, that I have adapted it to soy milk.

Prep time: 20 minutes • Bake time: 30 to 35 minutes • Serves 12

Vegetable cooking spray

Cake

1 TB. instant coffee granules

⅓ cup hot water

¾ cup granulated sugar

¼ cup canola oil

2 large eggs

¼ cup unsweetened cocoa

1 cup all-purpose flour

1 tsp. baking powder

1 tsp. baking soda

⅛ tsp. salt

½ cup light soy milk

Glaze

1 tsp. instant coffee granules

1½ TB. hot water

⅔ cup confectioners' sugar

Position a rack in the center of the oven and preheat the oven to 350°F. Lightly coat a 9-inch springform pan with cooking spray.

Dissolve instant coffee in hot water. In a bowl and using a whisk or electric mixer, beat together sugar, oil, and eggs. Add the cocoa and beat until everything is blended.

In another bowl, stir together flour, baking powder, baking soda, and salt. Pour the cocoa mixture, soy milk, and coffee over the dry ingredients; with a wooden spoon, stir just until everything is combined. Pour the mixture into the prepared pan.

Bake for 30 to 35 minutes or until a tester inserted in the center comes out clean. Let the pan cool on a wire rack. Loosen the spring and remove the springform sides, leaving the cake on the pan bottom.

Make glaze: Dissolve instant coffee in hot water. In small bowl, mix confectioners' sugar with coffee until the mixture is smooth. Spread it over the top of the cake, smoothing with a knife.

 A Piece of Advice

For a real coffee zing, try using ⅓ cup strong brewed coffee or espresso instead of instant coffee.

 Nutrition Watch

Normally, icings for cakes are made from butter, cream cheese, or vegetable oil—all loaded with fat, calories, and cholesterol. This icing is free of fat and cholesterol.

Nutrition per Serving

Calories: 180
Protein: 2.9 g
Cholesterol: 35 mg

Fat (total): 5.8 g
Fat (saturated): 0.8 g

Carbohydrate: 29 g
Dietary Fiber: 1 g

Banana Chocolate Meringue Pie

This was another classic dessert from my earlier book, *Rose Reisman's Light Vegetarian Cooking*. The soy milk makes this delicious and caters to those who are lactose intolerant.

Prep time: 20 minutes • Bake time: 8 to 10 minutes • Serves 12

Vegetable cooking spray

Crust

1½ cups chocolate wafer crumbs

2 TB. water

1 TB. canola oil

Filling

1⅓ cups light soy milk

¾ cup granulated sugar

3 TB. unsweetened cocoa

2 TB. cornstarch

⅛ tsp. salt

2 large egg yolks

3 TB. semi-sweet chocolate chips

1 tsp. vanilla extract

2 medium ripe bananas

Meringue Topping

3 large egg whites

¼ tsp. cream of tartar

½ cup granulated sugar

Position a rack in the center of the oven and preheat the oven to 425°F. Lightly coat a 9-inch springform pan with cooking spray.

Make crust: In a bowl, stir together wafer crumbs, water, and oil until mixed. Pat the mixture onto the bottom and up the sides of the prepared pan. Let it chill while you make the filling.

Make filling: In a saucepan, heat ⅔ cup soy milk until it is hot. In a bowl, whisk remaining soy milk, sugar, cocoa, cornstarch, salt, and egg yolks until they are smooth. Whisk the hot soy milk into the cold mixture. Return the mixture to the saucepan and cook it over medium heat, whisking, for 4 minutes or until thickened. Remove from the heat. Stir in chocolate chips and vanilla until chips melt. Slice bananas and arrange them over the bottom of the crust. Pour the hot filling over the top.

Make meringue topping: In a bowl, beat egg whites with cream of tartar until foamy. Gradually add sugar, beating until stiff peaks form. Spoon the mixture over the hot filling, spreading it to the sides of the pan.

Bake for 8 to 10 minutes or until the meringue is golden. Let the pan cool on a wire rack.

Nutrition Watch

Bananas are high in carbohydrate and low in fat. They're rich in potassium and vitamin C. I love them as an energizing snack.

 Nutrition per Serving

Calories: 237

Protein: 3.8 g

Cholesterol: 35 mg

Fat (total): 5.7 g

Fat (saturated): 1.4 g

Carbohydrate: 42 g

Dietary Fiber: 1.8 g

Sour Cream Apple Pie

The cooked apples, puréed tofu, and a crunchy topping make this an exceptional dessert.

Prep time: 20 minutes • Bake time: 30 minutes • Serves 16

Vegetable cooking spray

Crust

1½ cups graham cracker crumbs

2 TB. packed light brown sugar

3 TB. water

1 TB. canola oil

Filling

4 cups sliced peeled apples, about 4 medium

½ cup granulated sugar

¼ cup golden raisins

3 TB. all-purpose flour

1 tsp. ground cinnamon

¾ cup silken tofu, drained

1 large egg, beaten

1 tsp. vanilla extract

Topping

⅓ cup packed light brown sugar

¼ cup all-purpose flour

¼ cup quick-cooking oats

½ tsp. ground cinnamon

2 tsp. canola oil

1 tsp. water

Position a rack in the center of the oven and preheat the oven to 350°F. Lightly coat a 9-inch springform pan with cooking spray.

Make crust: In a bowl, stir together graham cracker crumbs, brown sugar, water, and oil until mixed. Pat the mixture onto the bottom and up the sides of the prepared pan.

Make filling: In a bowl, stir together apples, sugar, raisins, flour, and cinnamon. With a food processor, purée tofu, egg, and vanilla. Add to the apple mixture and pour it into the crust.

Make topping: In a small bowl, stir together brown sugar, flour, oats, cinnamon, oil, and water until crumbly. Sprinkle it over the filling.

Bake for 30 minutes or until the topping is golden and apples are tender. Let the pan cool on a wire rack.

 A Piece of Advice

I like to use a delicious tasting apple for this dessert. My preferences are Mutsu, Royal Gala, Spy, or Paula Red. I avoid the Golden Delicious and the McIntosh, which I think are too soft and not as flavorful in baking.

 Nutrition per Serving

Calories: 164   Fat (total): 3.4 g   Carbohydrate: 31 g
Protein: 2.4 g   Fat (saturated): 0.4 g Dietary Fiber: 1.3 g
Cholesterol: 13 mg

Creamy Orange Tart

The texture of the silken tofu is perfect for this creamy orange tart. Be sure to process the filling until it's very smooth.

Prep time: 15 minutes • Bake time: 25 to 30 minutes • Chill time: at least 2 hours • Serves 12

Vegetable cooking spray

Crust

1½ cups vanilla wafer crumbs

1 TB. granulated sugar

2 TB. water

1 TB. canola oil

Filling

8 oz. silken tofu, drained

¾ cup light soy milk

1¼ cups granulated sugar

3 TB. cornstarch

¼ tsp. salt

¼ cup orange juice concentrate

2 tsp. finely grated orange zest + additional zest for garnish

Position a rack in the center of the oven and preheat the oven to 350°F. Lightly coat a 9-inch flan pan with removable bottom with cooking spray.

 A Piece of Advice

Vanilla wafers usually come as whole cookies in a box. I place the wafers in the food processor and puree until they are finely ground. One box makes approximately 2½ cups of ground crumbs.

Make crust: In a bowl, stir together wafer crumbs, sugar, water, and oil until combined. Pat the mixture onto the bottom and up the sides of the prepared pan.

Make filling: In a food processor, combine tofu, soy milk, sugar, cornstarch, salt, orange juice concentrate, and orange zest; purée the mixture until smooth. Pour it into the crust.

Bake for 25 to 30 minutes or until filling is set. Let the pan cool on a wire rack. Garnish with grated orange rind and chill for at least 2 hours.

 Nutrition per Serving

Calories: 215
Protein: 2.5 g
Cholesterol: 1.4 mg

Fat (total): 5 g
Fat (saturated): 0.8 g

Carbohydrate: 40 g
Dietary Fiber: 0.4 g

Soy Puddings

Think of the smile on your lactose-intolerant child or loved one's face when you place a bowl of luscious pudding at their place at the table. Pudding is a right of passage through childhood; a right that doesn't stop when we no longer eat nursery food. Pudding is pure comfort food.

Bailey's Irish Cream Chocolate Pudding

After a filling meal, I enjoy a light flavorful pudding. This one does the trick.

Prep time: 10 minutes • Cook time: 10 minutes • Chill time: at least 1 hour • Serves 8

Vegetable cooking spray

About 3 tablespoons granulated sugar

¼ cup unsweetened cocoa

¾ cup packed light brown sugar

2½ TB. cornstarch

2 tsp. instant coffee granules

2 cups light soy milk

1 large egg

1 TB. Bailey's Irish Cream liqueur

2 TB. semi-sweet chocolate chips

Lightly coat eight ½-cup ramekins or custard cups with cooking spray and dust them with sugar.

In a heavy-bottom saucepan off the heat, whisk in cocoa, brown sugar, cornstarch, instant coffee, and soy milk until the mixture is smooth. Bring it to a boil over medium-high heat, whisking constantly. Remove the pan from the heat.

In a bowl, whisk egg. Whisk ½ cup hot mixture into egg. Whisk the egg mixture back into the saucepan, and then cook over medium-low heat for 1 minute, stirring, or until the mixture is thickened and bubbling. Remove the pan from the heat. Stir in liqueur. Divide the pudding among the prepared dessert dishes and chill at least 1 hour. Serve sprinkled with chocolate chips.

A Piece of Advice

If you don't have Bailey's Irish Cream, use another chocolate or coffee liqueur. Even chocolate syrup will work. I've tried this recipe with chocolate and vanilla soy milk, and it is delicious.

Nutrition Watch

Soy milk is rich in protein and iron. It is cholesterol free and

 Nutrition per Serving

Calories: 158	Fat (total): 2.6 g	Carbohydrate: 30 g
Protein: 3.7 g	Fat (saturated): 1.1 g	Dietary Fiber: 1.6 g
Cholesterol: 27 mg		

Peanut Butter Pudding

Puddings are real comfort food. The use of soy milk makes this available to anyone. The use of peanut butter and chips is decadent.

Prep time: 5 minutes • Cook time: 10 minutes • Chill time: at least 1 hour • Serves 8

¾ cup granulated sugar

3 TB. cornstarch

2 cups light soy milk

¼ cup smooth peanut butter

2 TB. peanut butter chips

Nutrition Watch _____

Peanut butter is high in calories and fat, but keep in mind that it's rich in protein and the fat is monounsaturated, which has been known to lower the bad cholesterol in your blood. But eat it in moderation.

In a heavy-bottom saucepan off the heat, whisk together sugar, cornstarch, and soy milk until the mixture is smooth. Whisk in peanut butter. Bring the mixture to a boil over medium-high heat, whisking constantly. Reduce the heat to medium-low and simmer for 4 minutes, whisking occasionally, or until the mixture is thickened and smooth.

Divide the mixture among 8 dessert dishes, cover, and chill. Serve sprinkled with peanut butter chips.

 Nutrition per Serving

Calories: 179
Protein: 4.5 g
Cholesterol: 0

Fat (total): 5.2 g
Fat (saturated): 0.9 g

Carbohydrate: 28 g
Dietary Fiber: 1.2 g

Chocolate Rice Pudding

When I first served this pudding to my family, no one guessed that soy milk was in it. The texture is light and creamy, and the flavor is intensely rich.

Prep time: 5 minutes • Cook time: 60 minutes • Serves 8

3 ⅔ cups light soy milk

1 cup packed light brown sugar

½ cup Arborio rice

¼ cup unsweetened cocoa

2 TB. semi-sweet chocolate chips

In a heavy-bottom medium saucepan, combine soy milk, brown sugar, rice, and cocoa. Bring the mixture to a simmer over medium heat, stirring often. Reduce the heat to low; cook, partially covered and stirring occasionally, for 50 minutes or until the rice is tender and the mixture is thickened.

Remove the pan from the heat. Let it cool slightly. Stir in chocolate chips. Pour into 8 dessert dishes. Serve the pudding warm or at room temperature.

Nutrition Watch

Rice is gluten free and an excellent source of complex

 Nutrition per Serving

Calories: 235
Protein: 5.5 g
Cholesterol: 0

Fat (total): 2 g
Fat (saturated): 0.8 g

Carbohydrate: 48 g
Dietary Fiber: 2.2 g

Rice Pudding with Dates and Apricots

This is a sure way to get my children to have soy in their diet, especially because they don't love tofu. No one will know the difference.

Prep time: 5 minutes • Cook time: 60 minutes • Serves 8

3 ¾ cups light soy milk

½ cup Arborio rice

⅓ cup granulated sugar

½ tsp. ground cinnamon

1 tsp. vanilla extract

⅓ cup chopped dried apricots

⅓ cup chopped dried dates

 A Piece of Advice

Although I call for short grain Arborio rice, you can also use medium grain rice. Brown rice provides more fiber, but you need to increase the soy milk to 4 or 4½ cups and cook the pudding 15 minutes longer, or until the rice is tender.

In a heavy-bottom saucepan, combine soy milk, rice, sugar, and cinnamon. Bring the mixture to a simmer over medium heat, stirring often. Reduce the heat to medium-low; cook, partially covered and stirring occasionally, for 45 to 50 minutes or until the rice is tender and the mixture is thickened.

Stir in vanilla, apricots, and dates. Serve it warm or at room temperature.

 Nutrition per Serving

Calories: 180
Protein: 5.4 g
Cholesterol: 0

Fat (total): 0.5 g
Fat (saturated): 0.1 g

Carbohydrate: 37 g
Dietary Fiber: 2.1 g

Apple Cinnamon Noodle Pudding Cake

I featured this recipe using dairy products in *Sensationally Light Pasta and Grains*. The substitution of silken tofu makes a wonderful and creamy pudding cake.

Prep time: 25 minutes • Cook time: 35 minutes • Serves 12

Vegetable cooking spray

Pudding

8 oz. wide egg noodles

1 lb. silken tofu, drained

1 large egg

1 large egg white

1 TB. finely grated orange rind

¼ cup fresh orange juice

¾ cup + 1 TB. granulated sugar (divided use)

½ tsp. + ½ tsp. ground cinnamon (divided use)

¼ tsp. salt

⅛ tsp. ground nutmeg

1 cup sliced peeled apples

⅓ cup golden raisins or dried cranberries

Topping

⅓ cup packed light brown sugar

¼ cup all-purpose flour

3 TB. quick-cooking oats

2 tsp. margarine or unsalted butter

¼ tsp. ground cinnamon

Position a rack in the center of the oven and preheat the oven to 350°F. Lightly coat a 9-inch springform pan with cooking spray.

In a large pot of boiling water, cook noodles for 8 minutes or until they are tender, but firm. Drain. Rinse them under cold running water; drain.

In a food processor, combine tofu, egg, egg white, orange rind and juice, ¾ cup sugar, ½ teaspoon cinnamon, salt, and nutmeg; purée the mixture until it is smooth.

In a large bowl, stir together apples, raisins, 1 tablespoon sugar, and ½ teaspoon cinnamon. Stir in the tofu mixture and noodles. Pour everything into a prepared pan.

Make topping: In a small bowl, stir together brown sugar, flour, oats, margarine, and cinnamon until crumbly. Sprinkle the mixture over noodle mixture.

Bake for 35 minutes or until it is set. Serve warm, at room temperature, or chilled.

A Piece of Advice

Only use egg noodles for this dessert. They differ from regular pasta because they contain eggs or egg yolks. I use the dried version and cook them according to the package directions.

Nutrition Watch

Keep in mind that egg noodles contain egg yolks, thus making them slightly higher in fat and cholesterol. Eating them occasionally is fine.

Nutrition per Serving

Calories: 220

Protein: 6 g

Cholesterol: 36 mg

Fat (total): 3.1 g

Fat (saturated): 0.6 g

Carbohydrate: 42 g

Dietary Fiber: 1.3 g

Miscellaneous Soy Treats

Sometimes a recipe doesn't really fit into any category so like these gems, I tuck them under "miscellaneous." Most of these contain a cake-like batter in some part of the recipe; the tiramisu calls for purchased lady fingers, which are a cake-like cookie. I can almost guarantee that unless you tell them, or they watch you while you're cooking, no one will know that these desserts contain soy.

Mocha Brownies with Creamy Icing

These brownies are wonderfully moist and delicious, with the addition of soy milk.

Prep time: 15 minutes • Cook time: 18 to 20 minutes • Serves 16

Vegetable cooking spray

Brownies

2 tsp. instant coffee granules

1 TB. hot water

3 TB. canola oil

1 large egg

¾ cup granulated sugar

½ cup all-purpose flour

⅓ cup unsweetened cocoa

1 tsp. baking powder

⅓ cup light soy milk

Icing

½ cup confectioners' sugar

2 TB. unsweetened cocoa

1½ TB. light soy milk

Position a rack in the center of the oven and preheat the oven to 350°F. Lightly coat a 9-inch square cake pan with cooking spray.

Nutrition Watch

Light soy milk is slightly higher in protein than cow's milk. It's a nondairy product rich in iron, and it's cholesterol free and low in fat and sodium.

A Piece of Advice

If you don't have instant coffee, use 1½ tablespoons brewed strong coffee.

Make brownies: In a large bowl, dissolve instant coffee in hot water. Add oil, egg, and sugar; using a whisk or electric mixer, beat until the mixture is smooth.

In another bowl, stir together flour, cocoa, and baking powder. Add the dry ingredients to the coffee mixture alternately with soy milk, in two batches, stirring with a wooden spoon just until everything is blended. Pour the mixture into a prepared baking pan.

Bake for 18 to 20 minutes or until the edges begin to pull away from the pan. (The center will still be slightly soft.) Let the pan cool on a wire rack.

Make icing: In a small bowl, beat together confectioners' sugar, cocoa, and soy milk until the mixture is smooth. Spread it over the brownies.

 **Nutrition per Serving**

Calories: 108   Fat (total): 3.3 g   Carbohydrate: 18 g
Protein: 1.5 g   Fat (saturated): 0.5 g   Dietary Fiber: 1 g
Cholesterol: 13 mg

Chocolate Coffee Tiramisu

I developed a wonderful chocolate tiramisu in *Enlightened Home Cooking*, which used ricotta cheese and beaten egg whites. I find that this tofu version has its own character and is delicious.

Prep time: 30 minutes • Chill time: at least 3 hours • Serves 16

1 lb. firm tofu, drained	3 large egg whites
¾ cup + ½ cup granulated sugar (divided use)	¼ tsp. cream of tartar
3 TB. unsweetened cocoa	½ cup granulated sugar
1 large egg yolk	½ cup brewed strong coffee
1 tsp. vanilla	1 TB. chocolate liqueur
⅛ tsp. salt	20 3-inch ladyfinger cookies

Use an ungreased 9-inch square baking dish. In a food processor, combine tofu, ¾ cup sugar, cocoa, egg yolk, vanilla, and salt; purée the mixture until smooth. Transfer it to a large bowl.

In another bowl, beat egg whites with cream of tartar until foamy. Gradually add remaining ½ cup sugar, beating until stiff peaks form. Stir one fourth of egg whites into the tofu mixture. Gently fold in remaining egg whites just until blended.

In a small bowl, stir together coffee and liqueur. One at a time, dip half of each ladyfinger in the mixture and place it in the bottom of the baking dish. Spoon half of the cocoa-tofu mixture over the ladyfingers. Repeat layers. Chill for at least 3 hours.

 A Piece of Advice

Ladyfingers come in all sizes and in either a hard or soft texture. Either will work. If using large ones, you need only 10 to 12, and you can break them to fit the pan.

 Nutrition Watch

Firm tofu is an excellent source of protein and contains no

 **Nutrition per Serving**

Calories: 180   Fat (total): 4.4 g   Carbohydrate: 27 g
Protein: 7.2 g   Fat (saturated): 1.1 g   Dietary Fiber: 1.1 g
Cholesterol: 73 mg

Apricot Roll

This apricot- and orange-flavored roll is light and delicious with a creamy apricot filling. Serve it with Mango Coulis (see Chapter 16).

Prep time: 30 minutes • Bake time: 12 minutes • Serves 8

Vegetable cooking spray

Filling

8 oz. firm tofu, drained

½ cup granulated sugar

⅓ cup apricot jam

1 tsp. finely grated orange zest

1 tsp. vanilla

⅛ tsp. salt

2 TB. confectioners' sugar

⅓ cup diced dried apricots

Cake

1 large egg

⅓ cup + ¼ cup granulated sugar (divided use)

2 tsp. finely grated orange zest

¼ cup fresh orange juice

⅔ cup all-purpose flour

½ tsp. baking powder

3 large egg whites

¼ tsp. cream of tartar

Confectioners' sugar

Position a rack in the center of the oven and preheat the oven to 350°F. Line a 15-inch by 10-inch jelly roll pan with parchment paper and lightly coat the paper with cooking spray.

Make filling: In a food processor, combine tofu, sugar, jam, orange zest, vanilla, and salt; purée the mixture until smooth. Chill it while you make the cake.

Make cake: In a bowl and using a whisk or electric mixer, beat egg with ⅓ cup sugar until the mixture is thickened and pale yellow. Beat in orange zest and juice. In a separate bowl, sift flour with baking powder; gently fold the mixture into the egg mixture.

Nutrition Watch

Dried apricots are rich in vitamin A and are a valuable source of iron, calcium, potassium, and fiber.

A Piece of Advice

Buy dried apricots in a bulk food store and keep them in the freezer. Use kitchen sheers to cut dried fruit into pieces.

In another bowl and using clean beaters, beat egg whites with cream of tartar until foamy. Gradually beat in remaining ¼ cup sugar, beating until stiff peaks form. Stir one fourth of egg whites into the cake batter. Gently fold in remaining egg whites just until blended. Spread the mixture into the prepared pan.

Bake for 12 minutes or until a tester comes out dry. Let the pan cool on a wire rack. Dust the cake with confectioners' sugar. Invert it onto a clean tea towel. Remove the pan and peel off parchment paper. Spread the filling over the surface. Sprinkle it with apricots. Starting from the short end, gently roll up the cake with the help of the tea towel. Transfer the roll to a serving platter, seam side down. Sprinkle it with extra confectioners' sugar to garnish.

 **Nutrition per Serving**

Calories: 269   Fat (total): 3.2 g   Carbohydrate: 52 g
Protein: 8 g   Fat (saturated): 0.6 g   Dietary Fiber: 1.4 g
Cholesterol: 27 mg

Mocha Roll

This coffee-flavored roll is moist and delicious, without added fat, and the tofu filling is creamy and smooth. Serve it with Chocolate Sauce (see Chapter 16).

Prep time: 30 minutes   •   Cook time: 15 minutes   •   Serves 8

Vegetable cooking spray

Cake

2 large egg yolks

⅓ cup + ½ cup granulated sugar

3 TB. brewed strong coffee

⅓ cup all-purpose flour

¼ cup unsweetened cocoa

4 large egg whites

¼ tsp. cream of tartar

Filling

8 oz. firm tofu, drained

½ cup granulated sugar

2 TB. unsweetened cocoa

1 TB. brewed strong coffee

⅛ tsp. salt

2 TB. confectioners' sugar + additional for sprinkling

Position a rack in the center of the oven and preheat the oven to 350°F. Line a 15-inch by 10-inch jelly roll pan with parchment paper and lightly coat the paper with cooking spray.

Make cake: In a bowl and using a whisk or electric mixer, beat egg yolks with ⅓ cup sugar until they are thickened and pale yellow. Beat in coffee. In a separate bowl, sift flour with cocoa; gently fold the dry ingredients into the yolk mixture just until mixed.

In another bowl and using clean beaters, beat egg whites with cream of tartar until foamy. Gradually beat in remaining ½ cup sugar, beating until stiff peaks form. Stir one fourth of egg whites into the cake batter. Gently fold in remaining egg whites just until blended. Spread the mixture into the prepared pan.

Bake for 15 minutes or until a tester inserted in the center comes out clean. Let the pan cool on a wire rack.

 Nutrition Watch

Tofu is easy to digest, is low in calories, cholesterol, and sodium, and is high in protein. Some tofu can be higher in fat. Check the label on the partic-

Make filling: In a food processor, combine tofu, sugar, cocoa, coffee, and salt; purée the mixture until it is smooth. Dust the cake with confectioners' sugar. Invert it onto a clean tea towel. Remove the pan and peel off the parchment paper. Spread the filling over the cake. Starting from the short end, gently roll up the cake with the help of the tea towel. Sprinkle the cake with extra confectioners' sugar to garnish.

 **Nutrition per Serving**

Calories: 245
Protein: 8.3 g
Cholesterol: 53 mg

Fat (total): 4.4 g
Fat (saturated): 1.1 g

Carbohydrate: 43 g
Dietary Fiber: 2.1 g

Lemon Poppy Seed Loaf

This was one of my most delicious desserts in my first cookbook on light cooking, *Rose Reisman Brings Home Light Cooking*. The silken tofu gives the loaf a light and creamy texture. I often make one and eat it the same day or make a couple and freeze them.

Prep time: 15 minutes • Cook time: 25 to 30 minutes • Serves 12

Vegetable cooking spray

Loaf

¾ cup granulated sugar

¾ cup silken tofu, drained

2 tsp. finely grated lemon zest

¼ cup fresh lemon juice

¼ cup canola oil

1 large egg

1¼ cups all-purpose flour

2 tsp. poppy seeds

1 tsp. baking powder

½ tsp. baking soda

¼ tsp. salt

Glaze

¼ cup confectioners' sugar

2 TB. fresh lemon juice

Position a rack in the center of the oven and preheat the oven to 350°F. Lightly coat a 9-inch by 5-inch loaf pan with cooking spray.

Make loaf: In a food processor, combine sugar, tofu, lemon zest and juice, oil, and egg; purée the mixture until it is smooth. Add flour, poppy seeds, baking powder, baking soda, and salt; pulse on and off just until everything is combined. Pour the mixture into the prepared pan.

Bake for 25 to 30 minutes or until a tester comes out dry. Let the pan cool on a wire rack.

Make glaze: In a bowl, beat confectioners' sugar with lemon juice until the mixture is smooth. Poke holes in the cake while it is still in the pan. Pour the glaze over the cake. Let the cake cool completely before serving.

A Piece of Advice

As with any dish that relies on lemon for its taste, use only fresh lemon juice for this dessert. Use it as soon as it's squeezed.

 Nutrition per Serving

Calories: 166
Protein: 2.7 g
Cholesterol: 18 mg

Fat (total): 5.7 g
Fat (saturated): 0.6 g

Carbohydrate: 26 g
Dietary Fiber: 0.5 g

The Least You Need to Know

- Be sure to buy the type of tofu that the recipe calls for—it comes soft, firm, or extra firm. Silken tofu is made from extra thick soy milk and is strained through silk.
- Soy milk is used in place of cow's milk, making these desserts perfect for people who are lactose intolerant.
- A small of amount of salt and a lot of other flavorings are added to desserts made with tofu because tofu is bland by itself. Tofu does readily absorb flavoring from other ingredients in the recipe.

Chapter 12

Passover Desserts

In This Chapter

- ◆ Ingredients used in making desserts for the eight-day festival of Passover
- ◆ Wonderful celebratory layer cakes and fruit crisp
- ◆ Special cheesecakes and cheese pies
- ◆ Light sponge cakes and cake rolls
- ◆ Exceptional brownies and mandelbrot

When you are baking for Passover, of course you must observe the religious requirements for cooking during the holiday, but at the same time, you want to ensure that your desserts are in keeping with the festiveness of the occasion. My Passover dessert recipes in this chapter fill both requirements.

Religious Requirements You Don't Want to Forget

Here's a quick list of what to avoid and what to look for when you're shopping for Passover baking and dessert making supplies:

- ◆ Avoid wheat flour (except for matzo), and any foods containing flour, such as ladyfingers and cookie crumbs.

- Don't use any leavening agents such as yeast and baking powder. Your Passover cakes will not rise like traditional cakes. They will be smaller and denser, with an intense flavor and texture.

- Avoid cornstarch and corn syrup, which are derivatives of corn, and cream of tartar because it is made during alcohol distillation.

- These baking products require a Passover label: vanilla and other extracts (regular extracts are made with grain alcohol); yogurt; powdered sugar (must be made without cornstarch); dried fruits; matzo and matzo products; oils, of which only peanut oil is permissible; and vinegar.

- These products require a label *if* purchased during Passover: salt (must not be iodized), spices, frozen fruits and juices, milk, butter, baking soda, nuts, cocoa, cottage cheese, coffee, sugar, and honey.

- For chocolate, use pareve Passover chocolate or chocolate chips (pareve means acceptable for kosher use). Don't buy chocolate that does not contain cocoa butter because it doesn't taste like chocolate and doesn't melt well.

- Coconut products are not usually made specifically for Passover, but people who are more lenient in their dietary restrictions can include it in the recipes.

- None of my Passover recipes require gelatin. If you have a Passover recipe requiring gelatin, you must use kosher gelatin. Whisk the gelatin into cold liquid and then quickly bring it to a boil. It begins to set immediately, so add it to the remaining ingredients at once.

- You can use jams or jellies—just make sure that they don't contain corn syrup.

- Matzo cake meal is a very finely ground, mild-tasting product perfect for baking. But don't substitute it for matzo meal, which is just coarsely ground matzo. Potato starch is used in smaller quantities in baking along with matzo cake meal. The balance of both produces a better texture and taste.

- The use of peanut butter is acceptable for Conservative congregations.

Layer Cakes and Fruit Crisp

Layer cakes are party cakes, perfect when they are lovingly produced for a Passover meal. Most layer cake recipes derived from English pound cakes, but once here in America they became softer and less formal in appearance. Even though Passover cakes do not contain any leavening, they are still light and delicious. The trick is to beat as much air as possible into the egg whites and to take great care when folding the beaten whites into the cake batter.

Banana Layer Cake with Chocolate Icing

Banana and chocolate are a great combination, especially with a delicious icing at a special meal.

Prep time: 25 minutes • Cook time: 15 to 20 minutes • Serves 12

Vegetable cooking spray

Cake

1 cup + ½ cup granulated sugar (divided use)

2 ripe small bananas, mashed (⅔ cup)

2 large eggs

⅓ cup Passover vegetable oil

1½ tsp. vanilla extract

¾ cup matzo cake meal

⅓ cup potato starch

4 large egg whites

Icing

2½ oz. light cream cheese, softened

⅔ cup Passover confectioners' sugar

3 TB. unsweetened cocoa

⅓ cup low-fat sour cream

1 ripe medium banana

Position a rack in the center of the oven and preheat the oven to 350°F. Lightly coat three 8-inch round cake pans with cooking spray.

Make cake: In a large bowl and using a whisk or electric mixer, beat 1 cup sugar, bananas, eggs, oil, and vanilla. With a wooden spoon, stir in the cake meal and potato starch until combined.

In another bowl, beat egg whites until they are foamy. Gradually add ½ cup sugar, beating until stiff peaks form. Stir one fourth of egg whites into the batter. Gently fold in remaining egg whites just until combined. Divide the mixture between the prepared cake pans.

Bake for 15 to 20 minutes or until a tester inserted in the center comes out clean. Let the pans cool on a wire rack.

Make icing: In a food processor, combine cream cheese, confectioners' sugar, cocoa, and sour cream; purée the mixture until smooth.

Place one cake layer on a cake platter. Spread some of the icing over top. Slice banana; place half on the cake layer. Place the second cake layer on top of the first. Spread some of the icing over top. Place remaining banana slices on top. Place the third cake layer on top of the second. Ice the top and sides.

Nutrition Watch

Bananas provide a high source of potassium, as well as some vitamin A and fiber.

A Piece of Advice

I always keep ripe bananas in the freezer so that I have them on hand for baking. Nothing tastes better. To ripen bananas, place them in a perforated brown paper bag for a few days.

Nutrition per Serving

Calories: 284

Protein: 4.2 g

Cholesterol: 41 mg

Fat (total): 8.8 g

Fat (saturated): 1.8 g

Carbohydrate: 47 g

Dietary Fiber: 1.3 g

Chocolate Layer Cake with Italian Meringue

Passover desserts are usually terribly high in fat and calories, due to the excessive use of eggs and oil. Not this one! I adore this cake all year round, but it's a special treat at Passover, with its fluffy and creamy meringue topping.

Prep time: 15 minutes • Cook time: 15 to 20 minutes • Serves 12

Vegetable cooking spray

Cake

2 large egg yolks

⅔ cup + ⅓ cup granulated sugar (divided use)

⅓ cup Passover vegetable oil

⅔ cup plain low-fat yogurt

⅓ cup unsweetened cocoa

⅓ cup matzo cake meal

2 TB. potato starch

4 large egg whites

Icing

3 large egg whites

¾ cup granulated sugar

¼ cup water

2 TB. unsweetened cocoa

Position a rack in the center of the oven and preheat the oven to 350°F. Lightly coat two 8-inch round cake pans with cooking spray.

Make cake: In a large bowl and using a whisk or electric mixer, beat egg yolks, ⅔ cup sugar, and oil. With a wooden spoon, stir in yogurt, cocoa, cake meal, and potato starch until combined.

 A Piece of Advice

Don't confuse matzo cake meal with matzo meal. Cake meal is finer and produces a more tender cake. The light and fluffy meringue icing is delicious on other cakes, too.

Nutrition Watch

Cocoa is chocolate without the cocoa butter, which contains the fat and cholesterol. One ounce of chocolate has 9 grams of fat. One ounce of cocoa has 3 grams.

In another bowl and using clean beaters, beat 4 egg whites until foamy. Gradually add ⅓ cup sugar, beating until stiff peaks form. Stir one fourth of egg whites into the batter. Gently fold in remaining egg whites just until blended. Divide the batter between the prepared cake pans.

Bake for 15 to 20 minutes or until a tester inserted in the center comes out clean. Let the cakes cool in their pans on a wire rack.

Make icing: In the top of a double boiler over simmering water or in a bowl that sits on a pot of simmering water, combine egg whites, sugar, and water. Beat for approximately 8 minutes or until the mixture is thickened and soft peaks form. Remove the pan from the heat; beat for another 1 to 2 minutes or until stiff peaks form. Sift cocoa into the icing; beat until it is thoroughly blended.

Place one cake layer on a cake platter. Spread some of the icing over the top. Place the second cake layer on top of the first. Ice the top and sides.

 **Nutrition per Serving**

Calories: 223   Fat (total): 7.5 g   Carbohydrate: 35 g
Protein: 3.8 g   Fat (saturated): 1 g   Dietary Fiber: 1.1 g
Cholesterol: 36 mg

Apple and Dried Cranberry Crisp

This Passover crisp tastes as delicious as the ones I make for the rest of the year. The topping is so crunchy and delicious.

Prep time: 15 minutes   •   Cook time: 40 minutes   •   Serves 8

Crisp

3 cups sliced peeled apples

⅓ cup granulated sugar

⅓ cup dried cranberries

¼ cup peach or apricot jam

3 TB. matzo meal

½ tsp. ground cinnamon

1 TB. lemon juice

Topping

½ cup matzo meal

½ cup packed light brown sugar

¼ cup chopped pecans

½ tsp. ground cinnamon

2 TB. Passover vegetable oil

2 TB. water

Position a rack in the center of the oven and preheat the oven to 350°F. Lightly coat an 8-inch square pan with cooking spray.

In a bowl, stir together apples, sugar, cranberries, jam, matzo meal, cinnamon, and lemon juice. Pour the mixture into the prepared pan.

Make topping: In a bowl, stir together matzo meal, brown sugar, pecans, cinnamon, oil, and water until crumbly. Sprinkle the mixture over the fruit mixture.

Bake for 40 minutes or until the top is golden. Serve warm.

 Nutrition Watch

One piece of matzo is approximately 110 calories and 0.5 grams of fat. Avoid egg matzo, which contains extra calories, fat, and cholesterol from the addition of the eggs.

 Nutrition per Serving

Calories: 243   Fat (total): 6.4 g   Carbohydrate: 45 g
Protein: 1.3 g   Fat (saturated): 0.5 g   Dietary Fiber: 2.0 g
Cholesterol: 0 mg

Cheesecakes and Cheese Pies

Everyone loves cheesecake so I had to include some special recipes to make during Passover. New Yorkers might try to convince you that Lindy's restaurant invented cheesecake, but that's not true. They may have made a perfect cheesecake, but this type of cake has a much longer history.

Actually early people of the Middle East hung soured cream in a bag and allowed the whey to drain away. This was then mixed with honey, egg yolks, sometimes lemon peel, and more cream and then baked. No doubt it wouldn't hold a candle to today's cheesecake, but nevertheless, it was cheesecake. The Jews carried the recipe with them as they immigrated to other countries. As with all recipes, it evolved over the years to what cheesecake is today. My cheese pie is merely a cheesecake baked in a pie shell.

Marble Mocha Cheesecake

This delicious cheesecake was in *Enlightened Home Cooking* and it remains one of my favorites. I created a brownie base that is delicious with the creamy cheese filling.

Prep time: 20 minutes • Cook time: 15 and 35 to 40 minutes • Chill time: at least 2 hours • Serves 12

Vegetable cooking spray

Crust

¾ cup granulated sugar

⅓ cup unsweetened cocoa

⅓ cup low-fat sour cream

¼ cup Passover vegetable oil

1 large egg

1 tsp. vanilla extract

⅓ cup matzo cake meal

2 TB. potato starch

Filling

1½ tsp. instant coffee granules

2 tsp. hot water

1⅔ cups smooth 5% ricotta cheese

⅓ cup light cream cheese, softened

⅓ cup low-fat sour cream

1 large egg

1 tsp. vanilla extract

¾ cup granulated sugar

1 TB. potato starch

Swirl

3 TB. semi-sweet chocolate chips

1 TB. water

Position a rack in the center of the oven and preheat the oven to 350°F. Lightly coat an 8-inch springform pan with cooking spray.

Make crust: In a bowl and using a whisk or electric mixer, combine sugar, cocoa, sour cream, oil, egg, and vanilla. In another bowl, stir together cake meal and potato starch; with a wooden spoon, stir the mixture into the cocoa mixture just until everything is mixed. Pour the mixture into the prepared pan. Bake for 15 minutes.

Meanwhile, make filling: Dissolve instant coffee in hot water. Place it in a food processor along with ricotta cheese, cream cheese, sour cream, egg, vanilla, sugar, and potato starch; purée until smooth. Pour it into the springform pan.

Make swirl: In microwavable bowl, combine chocolate chips and water. Microwave on medium-high for about 40 seconds or until chips begin to melt. Stir the mixture until it is smooth. Drizzle it over the cheesecake batter. Using a knife, swirl chocolate into the batter.

Continue to bake for another 35 to 40 minutes or until the cake is just slightly loose at the center.

Run a knife around the edge of the cake. Let it cool on a wire rack until it is room temperature. Chill for at least 2 hours.

To unmold the cake, release the spring and lift off the springform sides, leaving the cake on the pan bottom.

 Nutrition Watch

Most cheesecakes served at Passover are high in fat because they're made of 35 percent milkfat cream cheese and lots of whole eggs. By substituting ricotta for the cream cheese and using only 1 egg, you reduce the calories, fat, and cholesterol.

 A Piece of Advice

You can use 2 percent cottage cheese instead of the ricotta, but be sure to process it well to make the batter smooth.

Nutrition per Serving

Calories: 271
Protein: 7 g
Cholesterol: 54 mg

Fat (total): 11 g
Fat (saturated): 4.4 g

Carbohydrate: 36 g
Dietary Fiber: 1 g

Chocolate Cream Cheese Pie

This is a creamy chocolatey pie, with a firm crust thanks to the cake meal. Serve it with Vanilla Cream (see Chapter 16).

Prep time: 15 minutes • Cook time: 30 to 35 minutes • Chill time: at least 2 hours • Serves 12

Vegetable cooking spray

Crust

1 cup matzo cake meal

⅓ cup granulated sugar

2 TB. unsweetened cocoa

3 TB. water

3 TB. Passover vegetable oil

Filling

1½ cups smooth 5% ricotta cheese

2½ oz. light cream cheese, softened

¾ cup granulated sugar

¼ cup unsweetened cocoa

1 large egg

1½ TB. potato starch

⅓ cup low-fat sour cream

2 TB. semi-sweet chocolate chips

Position a rack in the center of the oven and preheat the oven to 350°F. Lightly coat a 9-inch pie plate with cooking spray.

 A Piece of Advice

Both good sources of protein, cottage cheese (2 percent milkfat) can replace the ricotta cheese. Purée it well until the curds are smooth, and add another 2 teaspoons potato starch. The sour cream can be replaced with plain low-fat yogurt.

Make crust: In a bowl, stir together cake meal, sugar, cocoa, water, and oil until everything is well mixed. Pat the mixture into the prepared pie plate.

Make filling: In a food processor, combine ricotta cheese, cream cheese, sugar, cocoa, egg, potato starch, and sour cream; purée until smooth. Pour it into the crust. Sprinkle with chocolate chips.

Bake for 30 to 35 minutes or until the filling is set. Let the plate cool on a wire rack. Chill for at least 2 hours.

 Nutrition per Serving

Calories: 220

Protein: 6.3 g

Cholesterol: 32 mg

Fat (total): 8.3 g

Fat (saturated): 3.4 g

Carbohydrate: 30 g

Dietary Fiber: 1.2 g

Cheesecake Squares

These cheesecake squares are moist and delicious. The crust tastes just like graham crackers.

Prep time: 15 minutes • Cook time: 15 to 20 minutes • Chill time: at least 1 hour • Serves 12

Base

1 cup matzo cake meal

⅓ cup granulated sugar

¼ cup water

1 TB. Passover vegetable oil

Filling

¾ cup smooth 5% ricotta cheese

¾ cup low-fat cottage cheese

½ cup granulated sugar

1½ TB. potato starch

1 large egg

1 tsp. vanilla extract

Glaze

2 oz. semi-sweet chocolate or ¼ cup chocolate chips

2 TB. water

Position a rack in the center of the oven and preheat the oven to 350°F. Lightly coat an 8-inch square baking dish with cooking spray.

Make base: In a bowl, stir together cake meal, sugar, water, and oil until combined. Press the mixture onto the bottom of a prepared dish.

Make filling: In a food processor, combine ricotta cheese, cottage cheese, sugar, potato starch, egg, and vanilla; purée until smooth. Pour it into the dish.

Bake for 15 to 20 minutes or until the center is slightly loose. Let it cool on a wire rack for 20 minutes before glazing.

Make glaze: In microwavable bowl, combine chocolate and water. Heat it on medium-high for 40 seconds or until chocolate begins to melt. Stir until it is melted. Spread it over the squares. Chill for 1 hour.

 A Piece of Advice

I like to use 1 percent or 2 percent milkfat cottage cheese. Be sure to process it well to make the batter smooth.

 Nutrition Watch

Regular cream cheese has 35 percent milkfat. By using ricotta cheese that has 5 percent milkfat and cottage cheese that has 1 percent to 2 percent milkfat, you can enjoy these squares without the fat, cholesterol, and calories.

 Nutrition per Serving

Calories: 155   Fat (total): 4.2 g   Carbohydrate: 24 g
Protein: 5.2 g   Fat (saturated): 1.8 g   Dietary Fiber: 0.5 g
Cholesterol: 24 mg

Sponge Cakes and Cake Rolls

Sponge cakes are light textured cakes that contain more eggs and less flour than other cakes. Because they contain no solid fat, they can be made ahead a time and refrigerated without hardening. A boon when you're busy preparing Passover meals. Because we're not allowed to use a chemical leavener during Passover, the leavening comes from stiffly beaten egg whites.

Cake rolls, also called jelly roll cakes, are thin sponge cakes that are baked in a special jelly roll pan. The cake is so moist than it can then be rolled without cracking around a luxurious, silken filling. What a spectacular dessert for a Passover Seder.

Apricot-Orange Sponge Cake with Orange Glaze

Passover sponge cakes are traditionally made with a large amount of egg yolks, oil, and egg whites beaten and then folded into the batter. My version uses two yolks, and most of the leavening power comes from the egg whites. Its combination of apricot and orange is wonderful. Serve with Mango Coulis (see Chapter 16) or top with sliced strawberries.

Prep time: 15 minutes • Cook time: 30 to 35 minutes • Serves 12

Cake

2 large egg yolks

1 TB. finely grated orange zest

½ cup orange juice

⅓ cup Passover vegetable oil

¼ cup orange juice concentrate

¾ cup + ½ cup granulated sugar (divided use)

⅔ cup matzo cake meal

⅔ cup potato starch

6 large egg whites

½ cup diced dried apricots

Glaze

1 TB. orange juice concentrate

¼ cup Passover confectioners' sugar

 **A Piece of Advice**

During Passover, you cannot use cream of tartar because it is made during alcohol distillation and contains baking soda, which is a leavening agent. I find that the whites will still beat well without the cream of tartar, but if you're having trouble try adding 2 teaspoons lemon juice.

Position a rack in the center of the oven and preheat the oven to 350°F. Use a 9-inch springform pan, not sprayed.

Make cake: In a large bowl and using a whisk or electric mixer, combine yolks, orange rind, orange juice, oil, orange juice concentrate, and ¾ cup sugar.

In another bowl, stir together cake meal and potato starch. With a wooden spoon, stir the mixture into the orange mixture just until everything is combined.

In a separate bowl and using clean beaters, beat egg whites until they are foamy. Gradually add ½ cup sugar, beating until stiff peaks form. Stir apricots and one fourth of egg whites into the cake batter. Gently fold in remaining egg whites just until blended. Pour the mixture into the pan.

Bake for 30 to 35 minutes or until a tester inserted in the center comes out clean. Let the pan cool on a wire rack. Loosen the spring and remove the sides of the pan, leaving the cake on the pan bottom.

Make glaze: Mix orange juice concentrate and confectioners' sugar until the mixture is smooth. Pour it over the cake.

Nutrition Watch

I have greatly reduced the fat and cholesterol of this sponge cake by using fewer egg yolks and more egg whites. The flavor is enhanced by the orange and apricot.

 Nutrition per Serving

Calories: 236
Protein: 3.3 g
Cholesterol: 35 mg

Fat (total): 7.0 g
Fat (saturated): 0.7 g

Carbohydrate: 40 g
Dietary Fiber: 1 g

Banana Roll with Chocolate Filling

This is a delicious and moist cake that you would never believe has so little fat and calories.

Prep time: 20 minutes • Cook time: 12 to 15 minutes • Serves 8

Vegetable cooking spray

Cake

1 ripe medium banana, mashed (⅓ cup)

½ cup + ½ cup granulated sugar (divided use)

1 large egg

1½ tsp. vanilla extract

¼ cup matzo cake meal

2 TB. potato starch

4 large egg whites

2 TB. Passover confectioners' sugar

Filling

¼ cup semi-sweet chocolate chips

2 TB. water

1 small ripe banana

Passover confectioners' sugar

Position a rack in the center of the oven and preheat the oven to 350°F. Line a 10-inch by 15-inch jelly roll pan with parchment paper and lightly coat the paper with cooking spray.

In a large bowl and using a whisk or electric mixer, beat mashed banana, ½ cup sugar, egg, and vanilla. In another bowl, stir together cake meal and potato starch. With a wooden spoon, stir the cake meal mixture into the banana mixture.

Nutrition Watch

Bananas are high in carbohydrate, low in fat, and rich in potassium and vitamin C.

A Piece of Advice

For a special presentation, after you dust the cake with Passover confectioners' sugar, arrange sliced bananas that have been rubbed with lemon juice to prevent browning on the cake.

In a separate bowl, beat egg whites until foamy. Gradually add ½ cup sugar, beating until stiff peaks form. Stir one fourth of egg whites into the cake batter. Gently fold in remaining egg whites just until combined. Pour the mixture into the prepared pan, spreading it evenly.

Bake for 12 to 15 minutes or until a tester comes out dry. Let the pan cool on a wire rack. Dust the cake with 2 tablespoons confectioners' sugar and invert it onto a clean tea towel. Remove the pan and peel off the parchment paper.

Make filling: Melt chocolate chips with water in microwave on high for approximately 40 seconds. Stir to melt it, and spread it over the surface. Thinly slice banana; scatter the slices over the cake. Starting from the short end, gently roll up the cake, with the help of the tea towel. Transfer it to a serving platter, seam side down. Dust with confectioners' sugar.

Nutrition per Serving

Calories: 200

Protein: 3.4 g

Cholesterol: 27 mg

Fat (total): 2.9 g

Fat (saturated): 1.5 g

Carbohydrate: 40 g

Dietary Fiber: 1.2 g

Chocolate Jelly Roll

This is a simple jelly roll cake lined with a creamy ricotta cheese filling and sprinkled with chocolate chips. Delicious!

Prep time: 20 minutes • Cook time: 12 to 15 minutes • Serves 8

Vegetable cooking spray

Cake

½ cup + ⅓ cup granulated sugar (divided use)

¼ cup unsweetened cocoa

¼ cup water

1 large egg

¼ cup matzo cake meal

2 TB. potato starch

3 large egg whites

2½ TB. Passover confectioners' sugar

Filling

1¼ cups smooth 5% ricotta cheese

⅔ cup Passover confectioners' sugar

1 tsp. vanilla

3 TB. semi-sweet chocolate chips

Position a rack in the center of the oven and preheat the oven to 350°F. Line a 15-inch by 10-inch jelly roll pan with parchment paper and lightly coat the paper with cooking spray.

Make cake: In a bowl and using a whisk or electric mixer, combine ½ cup sugar, cocoa, water, and egg. In another bowl, stir together cake meal and potato starch. With a wooden spoon, stir the mixture into the cocoa mixture just until everything is combined.

In another bowl, beat egg whites until foamy. Gradually add ⅓ cup sugar, beating until stiff peaks form. Stir one fourth of egg whites into the batter. Gently fold in remaining egg whites just until combined. Pour the mixture into the prepared pan, spreading it evenly.

Bake for 12 to 15 minutes or until a tester comes out dry. Let the pan cool on a wire rack.

Meanwhile, make filling: In a food processor, combine ricotta cheese, confectioners' sugar, and vanilla; purée the mixture until it is smooth. Stir in the chocolate chips.

Dust the cake with 2 tablespoons confectioners' sugar. Invert it onto a clean tea towel. Remove pan and peel off the parchment paper. Spread the filling over the surface. Starting from the short end, gently roll up the cake, with the help of the tea towel. Transfer the cake to a serving platter, seam side down. Sprinkle it with remaining confectioners' sugar.

 Nutrition Watch

Ricotta cheese is a wonderful substitute for cream cheese in baking. It contains only 5 percent milkfat and it's creamy and smooth.

 A Piece of Advice

Regular confectioners' sugar cannot be used during Passover because it contains cornstarch to prevent the sugar from getting lumpy. There is a confectioners' sugar that contains potato starch, which works well.

Nutrition per Serving

Calories: 258   Fat (total): 5.3 g   Carbohydrate: 45 g
Protein: 7.6 g   Fat (saturated): 3 g   Dietary Fiber: 1.3 g
Cholesterol: 38 mg

Brownies and Mandelbrot

With eight days of Passover, you're going to be cooking a lot of special meals. I always make several batches of brownies and mandelbrot before the holidays so that I can always have some sweet on hand for lunch, dinner, or when family and friends stop by. I've never served these cookies without raves from everyone.

 Nutrition Watch _____

I can buy brownies from a Passover bakery, and they are delicious but loaded with fat and calories due to the large amounts of oil and eggs used. My version is much healthier.

If you're not familiar with mandelbrot, do try them, as I actually prefer them to cookies. Mandelbrot is a Jewish version of biscotti. Since they are twice-baked, they are perfect for dunking into strong coffee or steeped tea.

Don't limit these recipes to just Passover; they are also wonderful for Sabbath and many other Jewish holidays throughout the year.

Brownies with Marshmallow and Chocolate Topping

I pack these brownies for my children's lunch during Passover week. All the other kids want their moms to have the recipe!

Prep time: 10 minutes • Cook time: 15 to 20 minutes • Serves 12

Vegetable cooking spray	1 large egg
¾ cup granulated sugar	1 tsp. vanilla extract
⅓ cup unsweetened cocoa	⅓ cup matzo cake meal
⅛ tsp. salt	1 TB. potato starch
⅓ cup low-fat sour cream	⅓ cup miniature marshmallows
¼ cup Passover vegetable oil	2 TB. semi-sweet chocolate chips

Position a rack in the center of the oven and preheat the oven to 350°F. Lightly coat an 8-inch square baking dish with cooking spray.

In a bowl and using a whisk or electric mixer, combine sugar, cocoa, salt, sour cream, oil, egg, and vanilla.

In another bowl, stir together cake meal and potato starch. With a wooden spoon, stir the mixture into the cocoa mixture just until everything is combined. Pour the mixture into the prepared dish.

Bake for 10 minutes or just until the brownies are slightly loose at the center. Sprinkle with marshmallows and chocolate chips. Bake for another 5 minutes. Let the pan cool on a wire rack.

 **A Piece of Advice**

Buy Passover marshmallows because the regular kind contains corn syrup, which is not to be used. If you only can find large marshmallows, use scissors to cut them into smaller pieces.

 **Nutrition per Serving**

Calories: 139
Protein: 1.6 g
Cholesterol: 20 mg

Fat (total): 6.3 g
Fat (saturated): 1.3 g

Carbohydrate: 19 g
Dietary Fiber: 1 g

Mocha Brownies

These are my adult version of brownies. They are moist and chocolaty and definitely hit the spot.

Prep time: 10 minutes • Cook time: 15 to 18 minutes • Serves 12

Vegetable cooking spray

¼ cup semi-sweet chocolate chips

¼ cup water

1 TB. strong brewed coffee

1 cup granulated sugar

¼ cup unsweetened cocoa

1 large egg

1 large egg white

¼ cup Passover vegetable oil

⅔ cup matzo cake meal

Nutrition Watch

You can substitute butter or margarine for the oil. Remember, whichever you choose, the amount of calories and fat is approximately the same; butter, though, contains saturated fat and cholesterol.

A Piece of Advice

If you don't have brewed coffee on hand, dissolve 1 teaspoon instant coffee in 1 tablespoon boiling water.

Position a rack in the center of the oven and preheat the oven to 350°F. Lightly coat an 8-inch square baking dish with cooking spray.

Combine chocolate chips, water, and coffee in a microwavable bowl. On medium-high, microwave for 40 seconds or until chips begin to melt. Stir the mixture until it is smooth.

In a large bowl and using a whisk or electric mixer, combine sugar, cocoa, egg, egg white, and oil. Add the chocolate mixture and with a wooden spoon, stir in the cake meal just until everything is combined. Pour the mixture into the prepared baking dish.

Bake for 15 to 18 minutes or until the center is still slightly loose. Let cool in the pan on a wire rack.

Nutrition per Serving

Calories: 160

Protein: 1.9 g

Cholesterol: 18 mg

Fat (total): 6.3 g

Fat (saturated): 1.2 g

Carbohydrate: 24 g

Dietary Fiber: 1.0 g

Coffee-Pecan Mandelbrot

When I was testing Passover desserts, I found that my favorite is the mandelbrot. I actually prefer them to regular cookies!

Prep time: 15 minutes • Cook time: 35 minutes • Makes about 30 cookies

Vegetable cooking spray

1½ TB. instant coffee granules

2 TB. hot water

¾ cup packed light brown sugar

½ cup granulated sugar

¼ cup Passover vegetable oil

1 large egg

1 large egg white

1½ cups matzo cake meal

½ cup potato starch

½ cup chopped pecans, toasted

Position a rack in the center of the oven and preheat the oven to 350°F. Lightly coat a large cookie sheet with cooking spray.

Dissolve instant coffee in hot water. In a large bowl and using a whisk or electric mixer, combine coffee, brown sugar, sugar, oil, egg, and egg white.

In another bowl, stir together cake meal, potato starch, and pecans. Stir the mixture into the coffee mixture just until combined. Divide it in half. Form two logs, each about 3 inches wide and 8 inches long. Transfer the logs to the cookie sheet.

Bake for 20 minutes. Remove the sheet from the oven and let the logs cool on the sheet for 5 minutes.

Transfer the logs to a cutting board. Slice them on the diagonal into ½-inch thick cookies. Place the cookies flat on the sheet. Bake for 15 minutes longer.

 Nutrition Watch

Egg white binds the cookie batter and lowers the fat and cholesterol in this recipe.

A Piece of Advice

If you don't have instant coffee, use 2 tablespoons strong brewed coffee.

 Nutrition per Serving

Calories: 88
Protein: 1 g
Cholesterol: 7 mg

Fat (total): 3.4 g
Fat (saturated): 0.3 g

Carbohydrate: 13 g
Dietary Fiber: 0.3 g

Chocolate Chip Mandelbrot

These cookies are wonderful after a heavy Passover meal. My children love them during the day with a glass of milk.

Prep time: 15 minutes • Cook time: 30 minutes • Makes about 30 cookies

Vegetable cooking spray

¾ cup granulated sugar

¼ cup Passover vegetable oil

2 large eggs

2 tsp. vanilla extract

1½ cups matzo cake meal

⅓ cup potato starch

⅓ cup semi-sweet chocolate chips

A Piece of Advice

If you can find other flavors of Passover chocolate chips, such as mint, orange, or white, try them, too.

Nutrition Watch

Feel free to substitute 1 egg with 2 egg whites in order to further lower the fat and cholesterol in these cookies.

Position a rack in the center of the oven and preheat the oven to 350°F. Lightly coat a large cookie sheet with cooking spray.

In a large bowl and using a whisk or electric mixer, combine sugar, oil, eggs, and vanilla.

In another bowl, stir together cake meal, potato starch, and chocolate chips. Stir the mixture into the sugar mixture until combined. Divide it in half. Form two logs, each about 3 inches wide and 8 inches long. Transfer the logs to the cookie sheet.

Bake for 15 minutes. Remove the sheet from the oven and let the logs cool on the sheet for 5 minutes. Transfer the logs to a cutting board. Slice them on the diagonal into ½-inch thick cookies. Place the cookies flat on the sheet. Bake for 15 minutes longer.

Nutrition per Serving

Calories: 75

Protein: 2.4 g

Cholesterol: 14 mg

Fat (total): 2.7 g

Fat (saturated): 0.6 g

Carbohydrate: 11.7 g

Dietary Fiber: 0.2 g

Orange Cranberry Mandelbrot

The combination of orange and dried cranberries is delicious in this light cookie.

Prep time: 15 minutes • Cook time: 30 minutes • Makes about 30 cookies

Vegetable cooking spray	1 TB. finely grated orange zest
¾ cup granulated sugar	2 tsp. vanilla extract
¼ cup margarine or unsalted butter	1½ cups matzo cake meal
¼ cup orange juice concentrate	½ cup potato starch
2 large eggs	½ cup dried cranberries

Position a rack in the center of the oven and preheat the oven to 350°F. Lightly coat a large cookie sheet with cooking spray.

In a large bowl and using a whisk or electric mixer, combine sugar, margarine, orange juice concentrate, eggs, orange rind, and vanilla.

In another bowl, stir together cake meal, potato starch, and cranberries. Stir the mixture into the sugar mixture until combined. Divide it in half. Form two logs, each about 3 inches wide and 8 inches long. Transfer the logs to the cookie sheet.

Bake for 15 minutes. Remove the sheet from the oven and let the logs cool on the sheet for 5 minutes.

Transfer the logs to a cutting board. Slice them on the diagonal into ½-inch thick cookies. Place the cookies flat on the sheet. Bake for 15 minutes longer.

 A Piece of Advice

Use orange juice concentrate for the most intense orange flavor. Keep a can in the freezer to use only for baking or cooking.

 Nutrition Watch

Dried fruit is a concentrated form of energy. Eat it in moderation because the calories are more dense than they are in fresh fruit.

 Nutrition per Serving

Calories: 73	Fat (total): 1.9 g	Carbohydrate: 13 g
Protein: 1 g	Fat (saturated): 0.4 g	Dietary Fiber: 0.4 g
Cholesterol: 14 mg		

The Least You Need to Know

- Be sure to observe the many religious requirements for ingredients used to prepare desserts during Passover.
- Don't confuse matzo cake meal with matzo meal. Cake meal is finer and produces a more tender dessert.
- Keep a small can of frozen orange juice concentrate in your freezer to add an intense orange flavor to your baking.
- Mashed ripe bananas add moisture and flavor to your baking without adding fat. Store overripe bananas in the freezer until you're ready to thaw, mash, and use.
- All of these Passover desserts are also wonderful for the Sabbath or other holiday meals.

Chapter 13

Other Divine Desserts

In This Chapter

- Buttery phyllo dough
- Very low-fat jelly roll cakes
- Light and airy gets it done

If you were to window shop at a popular bakery shop, you'd likely see any number of the spectacular desserts in this chapter on display—but more than likely they would be made with loads of butter and other high-fat ingredients. Sure, they'd taste fantastic, but they wouldn't be so wonderful for your health.

The recipes in this chapter are low in fat and cholesterol, yet they don't skimp on taste. By judicious use of small amounts of these high-fat ingredients, I've kept the rich flavor with a substantial cut in calories and fat.

These desserts are superb—a real feast for the senses yet low in fat. Don't be tempted to reserve them for special occasions, they're so easy to make that they can be used to jazz up a simple everyday meal.

Phyllo Desserts and Cream Cheese Pastries

Translated, the Greek word *phyllo* means "leaf." To cooks, phyllo means wonderful tissue paper-thin layers of delicate pastry dough that's used in Greece and other Middle Eastern countries around the Mediterranean, with an origin that can be traced back more than 2,000 years to Persia, Turkey, and Egypt. There is no recipe for the home cook to make phyllo; it requires a commercial machine to make the thin layers of dough. Fortunately it's easily found fresh or frozen most everywhere. You'll need to visit a Greek or Iranian market for fresh phyllo, but most supermarkets and grocery stores carry it frozen.

Thaw frozen phyllo at room temperature for a few hours or overnight in the refrigerator. When you open the box, you'll need to work quickly, unfolding the dough and removing the number of sheets you need. Immediately cover those layers with plastic wrap and a slightly wet towel. Refold the remaining dough, wrap it in plastic wrap, return it to the carton, and refrigerate. Don't try to refreeze phyllo dough, as it will become very brittle. Continue to work quickly when handling the phyllo; if it dries out, it can no longer be used.

Normally the layers of phyllo are brushed with melted butter, but you can keep the fat to a minimum when baking with phyllo by coating every other sheet with refrigerated butter-flavored cooking spray. Always spray the outer sheet so that it browns well while it bakes.

Phyllo desserts can be prepared in advance, sprayed with butter spray, covered tightly with plastic wrap, and frozen until ready to bake. Don't thaw before baking or the dessert will become soggy—just add 5 to 10 minutes extra baking time.

A Piece of Advice

Keep the phyllo in the freezer and leave the package at room temperature for a few hours or overnight in the refrigerator until it is thawed before using. Work quickly with phyllo and keep the sheets not being used covered with a tea towel. Rewrap unused phyllo and refrigerate. Use within a day or so.

Bake phyllo desserts on a cookie sheet lined with parchment paper that has been lightly coated with butter spray. Phyllo is ready when the crust becomes golden and crisp. Cut slices with a sharp or serrated knife.

Although I could have used phyllo for my Date Turnovers, I felt a cream cheese pastry dough did better justice to the marvelous date filling. The blend of flavors is superb and adding light cream cheese to the flaky dough makes it exceptionally easy to work.

Tropical Phyllo Strudel

Traditionally, strudel is a type of pastry made of many layers of very thin dough spread with a filling. It's rarely made at home because of the time and complexity it requires. Phyllo pastry from the refrigerator or freezer section of the supermarket is a wonderful substitute. The fresh tropical fruits in this strudel make it extra special. Serve with Mango Coulis (see Chapter 16).

Prep time: 20 minutes • Bake time: 25 to 30 minutes • Serves 8

Refrigerated butter-flavored cooking spray

2 cups fresh mango, diced (approximately 1 large mango)

2 cups diced fresh pineapple

⅓ cup dried cranberries

⅓ cup granulated sugar

¼ cup unsweetened coconut, toasted

1 TB. all-purpose flour

½ tsp. ground cinnamon

6 sheets phyllo pastry (if frozen, thawed)

Position a rack in the center of the oven and preheat the oven to 375°F. Lightly coat a large cookie sheet with cooking spray.

In a bowl, stir together mango, pineapple, cranberries, sugar, coconut, flour, and cinnamon.

On a work surface, layer one sheet of phyllo on top of the other. Spray the surface with cooking spray. Top with two more sheets of phyllo. Spray. Top with the last two sheets of phyllo. Spread the filling over the surface, leaving a 1-inch border on all sides. Starting at the short end, roll the phyllo several times away from you. Fold the left and right edges of phyllo in and over the filling. Continue to roll the strudel. Transfer it to the cookie sheet, seam side down. Spray the entire strudel.

Bake for 25 to 30 minutes or until it is golden and crisp.

Nutrition Watch

The fresh fruits in this strudel supply an abundance of vitamins and other nutrients, as well as containing very little to no fat. Mangoes and pineapple contain vitamins A and C.

 Nutrition per Serving

Calories: 164
Protein: 1.7 g
Cholesterol: 0

Fat (total): 2.8 g
Fat (saturated): 1.7 g

Carbohydrate: 33 g
Dietary Fiber: 2.4 g

Phyllo Strudel with Cherries

The combination of a cream-cheese filling and sour pitted cherries is delicious in this phyllo strudel. Serve it with frozen yogurt or Raspberry Coulis (see Chapter 16).

Prep time: 20 minutes   •   Bake time: 25 to 30 minutes   •   Serves 8

Refrigerated butter-flavored cooking spray

4 oz. light cream cheese, softened

¾ cup smooth 5% ricotta cheese

⅔ cup granulated sugar

2 tsp. all-purpose flour

1 tsp. vanilla extract

1 large egg

5 sheets phyllo pastry

⅔ cup canned pitted sour cherries, drained

Position a rack in the center of the oven and preheat the oven to 375°F. Lightly coat a large cookie sheet with cooking spray.

A Piece of Advice

Pitted sour cherries are not always easy to find. I usually use the ones that come unsweetened in a jar, not packed in heavy syrup.

Nutrition Watch

Cherries contain small amounts of vitamins and are a good source of potassium.

In a food processor, combine cream cheese, ricotta cheese, sugar, flour, vanilla, and egg; purée the mixture until it is smooth.

On a work surface, layer two sheets of phyllo—one on top of the other. Spray with cooking spray. Layer another two on top and spray again. Place the final sheet on top. Spread the cheese mixture over the surface, leaving a 1-inch border on all sides. Scatter cherries over top. Starting at the short end, roll the phyllo several times away from you. Fold the left and right edges of the phyllo in and over the filling. Continue to roll the strudel. Transfer it to a cookie sheet, seam side down. Spray the entire strudel with cooking spray.

Bake for 25 to 30 minutes or until the strudel is golden and crisp.

Nutrition per Serving

Calories: 191

Protein: 6 g

Cholesterol: 42 mg

Fat (total): 5.7 g

Fat (saturated): 3.1 g

Carbohydrate: 29 g

Dietary Fiber: 0.6 g

Baklava Pecan Phyllo Squares

Baklava, popular in Greece and Turkey, is a sweet dessert that usually consists of many layers of butter-drenched phyllo pastry, spices, and nuts, with lemon-honey syrup poured over the top. My recipe uses no fat. The filling is what makes this dessert so divine.

Prep time: 25 minutes • Bake time: 20 to 25 minutes • Serves 12

Refrigerated butter-flavored cooking spray

Honey Mixture

⅓ cup granulated sugar

¼ cup water

3 TB. honey

1½ TB. fresh lemon juice

Filling

½ cup Grape-Nuts cereal

½ cup golden raisins

½ cup chopped pecans, toasted

⅓ cup packed light brown sugar

½ tsp. ground cinnamon

4 sheets phyllo pastry (if frozen, thawed)

Position a rack in the center of the oven and preheat the oven to 350°F. Lightly coat an 8-inch square baking dish with cooking spray.

In a saucepan, combine sugar, water, honey, and lemon juice; cook the mixture over medium heat for 5 minutes.

In a bowl, stir together cereal, raisins, pecans, brown sugar, cinnamon, and 3 tablespoons of the honey mixture.

On a work surface, cut each phyllo sheet into quarters. Layer two squares in the prepared dish—one on top of the other. Lightly coat with cooking spray. Repeat the process until eight squares have been layered. Scatter the cereal-nut mixture over top. Layer the remaining phyllo squares on top, spraying after every other sheet. Spray the top.

Bake for 20 to 25 minutes or until the phyllo is golden. Reheat remaining honey mixture if necessary and pour it over the hot baklava. Let them cool in the baking dish on a wire rack.

 A Piece of Advice

Grape-Nuts cereal is a wonderful wheat and toasted barley cereal with virtually no fat. I like it because it gives a dessert the texture of chopped nuts without the excess calories or fat.

Nutrition Watch

If traditional baklava is drenched with butter, you can just imagine the calories and fat. One tablespoon of butter contains 100 calories and 11 grams of fat.

 Nutrition per Serving

Calories: 155
Protein: 1.6 g
Cholesterol: 0

Fat (total): 4.1 g
Fat (saturated): 0.4 g

Carbohydrate: 28 g
Dietary Fiber: 1.3 g

Phyllo Apple-Cheese Pie

This version of a phyllo apple pie with a cream-cheese filling makes a regular apple pie seem ordinary. I like to serve it warm, with sorbet or with Vanilla Cream (see Chapter 16).

Prep time: 30 minutes • Bake time: 35 to 40 minutes • Serves 12

Refrigerated butter-flavored cooking spray

Cheese Mixture

3 oz. light cream cheese, softened

½ cup smooth 5% ricotta cheese

⅓ cup granulated sugar

1 large egg

2 tsp. all-purpose flour

1 tsp. vanilla extract

Apple Mixture

4 cups peeled apples, diced (about 5 medium apples)

⅓ cup packed light brown sugar

1 TB. all-purpose flour

½ tsp. ground cinnamon

6 sheets phyllo pastry

 A Piece of Advice

Use a sweet, tasty, firm apple such as Mutsu, Royal Gala, Paula Red, or Spy. Avoid those that are too soft, such as McIntosh or Golden Delicious.

Nutrition Watch

Apples are a good source of vitamins A and C. Have one (with the peel on) during the day to supply some fiber and carbohydrate.

Position a rack in the center of the oven and preheat the oven to 350°F. Lightly coat a 9-inch springform pan with cooking spray.

In a food processor, combine cream cheese, ricotta cheese, sugar, egg, flour, and vanilla; purée the mixture until it is smooth.

In a bowl, stir together apples, brown sugar, flour, and cinnamon.

Place two sheets of the phyllo in the prepared pan, letting the excess hang over sides. Lightly coat with cooking spray. Place two more sheets in the pan, arranging them so the excess falls over different sides of the pan from first two sheets. Spray. Place the last two sheets of the phyllo in the pan. Place the apple mixture in the pan. Pour the cheese mixture over top. Fold the excess phyllo up and over top of the filling so it is completely enclosed. Spray again.

Bake for 35 to 40 minutes or until the phyllo is golden. Let it cool in the pan on a wire rack. To unmold, loosen the spring and lift off the sides of the pan, leaving the pie on the pan bottom.

 Nutrition per Serving

Calories: 138

Protein: 3.3 g

Cholesterol: 25 mg

Fat (total): 3.2 g

Fat (saturated): 1.6 g

Carbohydrate: 24 g

Dietary Fiber: 1 g

Date Turnovers

Turnovers are traditionally made with a lot of butter and flour. This dough uses some light cream cheese with a small amount of oil and butter. It has a wonderful depth of flavor and the texture is light and much lower in fat and calories. You'll find this pastry very easy to handle. Tuck these turnovers into your husband's lunchbox or offer them when you invite a friend for tea.

Prep time: 30 minutes • Bake time: 15 to 20 minutes • Serves 16

Vegetable cooking spray	1 cup all-purpose flour
Pastry	1 to 2 TB. water
2½ oz. light cream cheese, softened	**Filling**
¼ cup granulated sugar	3 oz. chopped pitted dates (⅔ cup)
2 TB. canola oil	½ cup fresh orange juice
1 TB. margarine or unsalted butter	1 tsp. finely grated orange zest

Position a rack in the center of the oven and preheat the oven to 375°F. Lightly coat a cookie sheet with cooking spray.

Make pastry: In a food processor, combine cream cheese, sugar, oil, and margarine; purée the mixture until it is smooth. Add flour and 1 TB. water. Pulse until the mixture is crumbly, adding more water as necessary. Form the dough into a ball and wrap in plastic wrap. Chill for 20 minutes.

Meanwhile, make filling: In a saucepan, combine dates, orange juice, and orange rind. Bring to a boil over medium-high heat; reduce heat and simmer for 5 to 8 minutes or until the liquid is absorbed. Mash the mixture until it is smooth. Let it cool while you prepare the dough.

Between two sheets of floured waxed paper, roll the dough to ⅛ inch thick. Using a 2-inch round biscuit or cookie cutter, cut out 16 circles. Re-roll scraps.

Place 1½ teaspoon date purée on each pastry circle, off center. Fold in half. Press the edges, using a little water to seal. Place the filled turnovers on the prepared cookie sheet. Repeat with the remaining filling and pastry.

Bake for 15 to 20 minutes or until the turnovers are golden. Cool on the cookie sheet on a wire rack.

 A Piece of Advice

I like to keep my dates in the freezer. I buy them at a bulk food store and use them as needed. Use scissors to cut dried fruit.

 Nutrition Watch

Dates are a good source of protein and iron. I enjoy them as a midday snack for a quick energy and complex carbohydrate boost.

Nutrition per Serving

Calories: 91
Protein: 1.4 g
Cholesterol: 2.5 mg

Fat (total): 3.3 g
Fat (saturated): 0.8 g

Carbohydrate: 14 g
Dietary Fiber: 0.6 g

Jelly Rolls

Jelly rolls are a thin layer of sponge cake that is rolled without cracking around a filling. When they first became popular in the mid-1800s, the filling was usually home-made jam or jelly, hence the name. My fillings are more scrumptious using chocolate, fruit, and all of the flavors of gingerbread. When cut, jelly rolls have an attractive pinwheel design of cake and filling. Jelly roll cakes are very low-fat so they can be enjoyed without guilt anytime.

Jelly rolls are baked in a 15-inch by 10-inch jelly roll pan. Line the pan with parchment paper and lightly coat the paper with cooking spray to avoid any sticking. Mix the wet ingredients first and then mix the dry ingredients so that they are ready to be added. Beat egg whites until they are foamy, adding the sugar gradually until stiff peaks form. Then add the flour mixture to the wet ingredients and mix just until the flour is incorporated. Fold in the whites just until they are blended. Do not over fold, or the egg whites will deflate. Spread the batter immediately evenly in the pan and bake it in the center of the oven for even baking.

While the cake is baking, prepare the filling. Many of the fillings in these recipes are based on ricotta cheese. Be sure to process the filling well to make the batter as smooth as possible. The fillings will roll more easily if they have been chilled.

> **Nutrition Watch**
>
> If you're looking for a cake with the lowest fat, calories, and cholesterol, your best selection is a jelly roll cake. It's one of the few cakes without any added fat. Beware of the fillings in commercial ones, though, because they usually contain whipping cream and buttery icings.

To test doneness, place a toothpick or tester into cake. The cake is ready if the tester comes out dry and clean. Cool the cake in the pan on a wire rack until it is room temperature. Sprinkle 2 tablespoons confectioners' sugar over the cake and then invert it onto a clean tea towel. The confectioners' sugar prevents the cake from sticking. Peel away the parchment paper, spread the filling onto the cake, and begin to roll, using the tea towel to assist. Roll gently until the whole cake is rolled; then carefully place it on a serving dish, seam side down. Chill.

If the cake cracks while rolling, it might not have been baked long enough and is still slightly wet, or it might have been baked too long and is too dry. Prevent cracks by checking the cake regularly with a tester a few minutes before the baking time is up. Cover any cracks with sprinkled confectioners' sugar or cocoa.

Banana Chocolate Roll

This jelly roll cake looks dramatic with its spiral design—white sponge roll, fudge filling, dotted with bananas!

Prep time: 30 minutes • Bake time: 12 to 15 minutes • Serves 8

Vegetable cooking spray

Cake

¾ cup mashed ripe bananas, about 2 medium

½ cup + ¼ cup granulated sugar (divided use)

1 large egg

1 tsp. vanilla extract

¾ cup all-purpose flour

½ tsp. baking soda

3 large egg whites

¼ tsp. cream of tartar

Filling

½ cup smooth 5% ricotta cheese

2 oz. light cream cheese, softened

⅓ cup granulated sugar

2 TB. unsweetened cocoa powder

2 TB. low-fat sour cream

2 TB. confectioners' sugar

1 small banana

Position a rack in the center of the oven and preheat the oven to 350°F. Line a 15-inch by 10-inch jelly roll pan with parchment paper and lightly coat the paper with cooking spray.

Make cake: In large bowl and using a whisk or electric mixer, beat mashed banana, ½ cup sugar, egg, and vanilla. In another bowl, stir together flour and baking soda.

In a separate bowl and using clean beaters, beat egg whites with cream of tartar until foamy. Gradually add remaining ¼ cup sugar, beating until stiff peaks form.

With a wooden spoon, stir the flour mixture into the banana mixture just until combined. Stir one fourth of egg whites into the cake batter. Gently fold in remaining egg whites just until blended. Pour the batter onto the prepared pan, spreading it evenly.

Bake for 12 to 15 minutes or until a tester comes out dry. Let the pan cool on a wire rack.

Make filling: In a food processor, combine ricotta cheese, cream cheese, sugar, cocoa, and sour cream; purée the mixture until it is smooth.

Dust cake with confectioners' sugar. Invert onto a tea towel. Remove pan and peel off parchment paper. Spread the filling over surface. Thinly slice the banana; scatter over cake. Starting from the short end, gently roll up the cake with the help of the tea towel. Transfer it to a serving platter, seam side down.

A Piece of Advice

For the best-tasting bananas for cooking, store over-ripe ones in the freezer. When you need them, just defrost them and use. To ripen bananas, place them in a perforated brown paper bag for a few days.

Nutrition Watch

Bananas are high in carbohydrate, low in protein and fat, and rich in potassium and vitamin C.

Nutrition per Serving

Calories: 257   Fat (total): 3.8 g   Carbohydrate: 49 g
Protein: 6.6 g   Fat (saturated): 2.1 g   Dietary Fiber: 1.6 g
Cholesterol: 37 mg

Apple Cinnamon Cream Roll

Taking a basic jelly roll recipe and adding different flavors and textures can create a wide variety of incredible desserts, like this one.

Prep time: 30 minutes   •   Bake time: 12 minutes   •   Serves 8

Vegetable cooking spray

Cake

½ cup packed brown sugar

⅓ cup unsweetened applesauce

1 large egg

½ tsp. ground cinnamon

⅔ cup all-purpose flour

½ tsp. baking powder

3 large egg whites

¼ tsp. cream of tartar

¼ cup granulated sugar

Filling

1 tsp. margarine or unsalted butter

1 cup peeled apple, diced (about 1 medium apple)

1 TB. packed light brown sugar

¼ tsp. ground cinnamon

¾ cup smooth 5% ricotta cheese

2 oz. light cream cheese, softened

⅓ cup granulated sugar

2 TB. confectioners' sugar

Position a rack in the center of the oven and preheat the oven to 350°F. Line a 15-inch by 10-inch jelly roll pan with parchment paper and lightly coat the paper with cooking spray.

Make cake: In a large bowl and using a whisk or electric mixer, beat brown sugar, applesauce, egg, and cinnamon. In another bowl, stir together flour and baking powder; with a wooden spoon, stir the mixture into the applesauce mixture just until it is combined.

Nutrition Watch _____

Jelly rolls are low in fat and calories because no fat is added to the batter. But be careful of the traditional ones, which are filled with whipping cream or butter icings.

In another bowl and using clean beaters, beat egg whites with cream of tartar until foamy. Gradually add ¼ cup sugar, beating until stiff peaks form. Stir one fourth of egg whites into the applesauce mixture. Gently fold in remaining whites just until blended. Pour the mixture onto the prepared pan, spreading it evenly.

Bake for 12 minutes or until a tester inserted in the center comes out clean. Let the pan cool on a wire rack.

Make filling: In a frying pan, melt margarine over medium-high heat; cook apples, brown sugar, and cinnamon for 3 minutes. Set aside to cool.

In a food processor, combine ricotta cheese, cream cheese, and sugar; purée the mixture until it is smooth. Stir in the apple mixture.

Dust the cake with confectioners' sugar, and invert it onto a clean tea towel. Remove the pan and peel off the parchment paper. Spread the filling over the surface. Starting from the short end, gently roll up the cake with the help of the tea towel. Transfer it to a serving platter, seam side down.

 A Piece of Advice

Use a firm, sweet-tasting apple for maximum flavor. Mutsu, Spy, Paula Red, and Royal Gala are good choices.

 Nutrition per Serving

Calories: 245
Protein: 6.6 g
Cholesterol: 38 mg

Fat (total): 4.3 g
Fat (saturated): 2.2 g

Carbohydrate: 45 g
Dietary Fiber: 0.8 g

Chocolate Chip Marble Roll

This is a marbled jelly roll, filled with a creamy cheese filling and dotted with chocolate chips.

Prep time: 30 minutes • Bake time: 12 to 14 minutes • Chill time: at least 1 hour • Serves 8

Vegetable cooking spray

Cake

2 large egg yolks

⅔ cup + ¼ cup granulated sugar (divided use)

⅓ cup 2% low-fat milk

1 tsp. vanilla extract

⅓ cup + ¼ cup all-purpose flour (divided use)

½ tsp. baking powder (divided use)

3 TB. unsweetened cocoa

3 large egg whites

¼ tsp. cream of tartar

Filling

1 cup smooth 5% ricotta cheese

1 oz. light cream cheese, softened

⅓ cup granulated sugar

1 tsp. vanilla extract

2 TB. semi-sweet chocolate chips

2 TB. confectioners' sugar

Position a rack in the center of the oven and preheat the oven to 350°F. Line a 15-inch by 10-inch jelly roll pan with parchment paper and lightly coat the paper with vegetable spray.

Make cake: In a bowl and using a whisk or electric mixer, beat egg yolks, ⅔ cup sugar, milk, and vanilla. Pour half the mixture into another bowl. In one bowl, using a wooden spoon, stir in ⅓ cup flour and ¼ tsp. baking powder. In the other bowl, using a wooden spoon, stir in remaining ¼ cup flour, cocoa, and ¼ tsp. baking powder just until mixed.

Nutrition Watch

One egg contains 75 calories, 6 grams of protein, 5 grams of fat, and 180 milligrams of cholesterol. Eggs are a healthy part of a diet if not consumed in excess.

A Piece of Advice

When folding egg whites into the batter, mix only until the whites are blended in. If you over fold, they'll lose their volume and the texture of the cake won't be as light.

In a third bowl and using clean beaters, beat egg whites with cream of tartar until foamy. Gradually add remaining ¼ cup sugar, beating until stiff peaks form. Fold half egg whites into the white batter and half into the brown batter just until blended.

Drop batters in mounds onto the prepared pan, alternating colors. Spread it evenly, swirling the two batters gently.

Bake for 12 to 14 minutes or until a tester inserted in the center comes out clean. Let the pan cool on a wire rack.

Make filling: In a food processor, combine ricotta cheese, cream cheese, sugar, and vanilla; purée the mixture until it is smooth. Stir in chocolate chips.

Dust cake with confectioners' sugar. Invert onto a tea towel. Remove pan and peel off parchment paper. Spread filling over surface. Starting from the short end, gently roll up the cake with the help of the tea towel. Transfer it to a serving platter, seam side down. Chill for 1 hour.

Nutrition per Serving

Calories: 265
Protein: 7.7 g
Cholesterol: 65 mg

Fat (total): 5.6 g
Fat (saturated): 3 g

Carbohydrate: 46 g
Dietary Fiber: 1.1 g

Orange Roll with Mandarin Cheese Filling

This is a light and refreshing dessert, especially after a heavy meal. With every mouthful, you get a piece of sweet mandarin orange.

Prep time: 30 minutes • Bake time: 10 to 12 minutes • Serves 8

Vegetable cooking spray

Cake

⅓ cup + ¼ cup granulated sugar (divided use)

2 tsp. finely grated orange zest

¼ cup fresh orange juice

1 large egg

⅔ cup all-purpose flour

½ tsp. baking powder

3 large egg whites

¼ tsp. cream of tartar

Filling

3 oz. light cream cheese, softened

⅔ cup + 2 TB. confectioners' sugar

2 TB. orange juice concentrate

1 tsp. finely grated orange zest

½ cup canned mandarin oranges, drained

Position a rack in the center of the oven and preheat the oven to 350°F. Line a 15-inch by 10-inch jelly roll pan with parchment paper and lightly coat the paper with cooking spray.

Make cake: In a large bowl, whisk together ⅓ cup sugar, orange zest and juice, and egg. With a wooden spoon, stir in flour and baking powder just until mixed.

In another bowl, beat egg whites with cream of tartar until foamy. Gradually add remaining ¼ cup sugar, beating until stiff peaks form. Stir one fourth of egg whites into the orange mixture. Gently fold in remaining whites just until blended. Pour the mixture onto the prepared pan, spreading it evenly.

Bake for 10 to 12 minutes or until a tester inserted in the center comes out clean. Let the pan cool on a wire rack.

Make filling: In a food processor, combine cream cheese, ⅔ cup confectioners' sugar, orange juice concentrate, and orange rind; purée the mixture until it is smooth. Stir in mandarin oranges.

Dust the cake with 2 tablespoons confectioners' sugar and invert it onto a clean tea towel. Remove the pan and peel off the parchment paper. Spread the filling over the surface. Starting from the short end, gently roll up the cake with the help of the tea towel. Transfer it to a serving platter, seam side down.

Nutrition Watch

Mandarin oranges are an excellent source of vitamin C and contain some vitamin A.

A Piece of Advice

You can use fresh mandarins, tangerines, or clementines when they are in season—peel them and remove all the seeds. Be sure that they are sweet!

 **Nutrition per Serving**

Calories: 203	Fat (total): 2.7 g	Carbohydrate: 40 g
Protein: 4.6 g	Fat (saturated): 1.4 g	Dietary Fiber: 0.7 g
Cholesterol: 33 mg		

Gingerbread Roll

Gingerbread flavoring is associated with a gingery taste, accompanied by molasses, coffee, or honey. Its distinct flavor makes for a unique jelly roll dessert.

Prep time: 25 minutes • Bake time: 10 to 12 minutes • Serves 8

Vegetable cooking spray

Cake

2 tsp. instant coffee granules

3 TB. hot water

⅔ cup packed light brown sugar

1 TB. dark molasses

1 tsp. vanilla extract

1 large egg

¾ cup all-purpose flour

½ tsp. ground cinnamon

¼ tsp. ground ginger

⅛ tsp. allspice

3 large egg whites

¼ tsp. cream of tartar

¼ cup granulated sugar

Filling

1 cup smooth 5% ricotta cheese

2 oz. light cream cheese, softened

½ cup packed light brown sugar

2 TB. dark molasses

2 TB. confectioners' sugar

Position a rack in the center of the oven and preheat the oven to 350°F. Line a 15-inch by 10-inch jelly roll pan with parchment paper and lightly coat the paper with vegetable spray.

 **A Piece of Advice**

There are three different kinds of molasses: extra light, dark, and blackstrap. Light comes from the first boiling, dark from the second, and blackstrap from the third. Dark is traditionally used in desserts.

Dissolve coffee in hot water. In a large bowl, whisk together coffee, brown sugar, molasses, vanilla, and egg. In another bowl, stir together flour, cinnamon, ginger, and allspice; with a wooden spoon, stir this mixture into the molasses mixture until mixed.

In another bowl, beat egg whites with cream of tartar until foamy. Gradually add sugar, beating until stiff peaks form. Stir one fourth of egg whites into the cake batter. Gently fold in remaining egg whites just until blended. Pour the mixture onto the prepared pan, spreading it evenly.

Bake for 10 to 12 minutes or until a tester inserted in the center comes out clean. Let the pan cool on a wire rack.

Make filling: In a food processor, combine ricotta cheese, cream cheese, brown sugar, and molasses; purée the mixture until it is smooth.

Nutrition Watch

Molasses contains iron, calcium, and phosphorus.

Dust the cake with confectioners' sugar and invert it onto a clean tea towel. Remove the pan and peel off the parchment paper. Spread the filling over the surface. Starting from the short end, gently roll up the cake with the help of the tea towel. Transfer it to a serving platter, seam side down.

Nutrition per Serving

Calories: 294
Protein: 7.6 g
Cholesterol: 40 mg

Fat (total): 4.4 g
Fat (saturated): 2.5 g

Carbohydrate: 56 g
Dietary Fiber: 0.4 g

Lemon Roll with Lemon Curd Filling

This double-hit of a lemon dessert makes lemon lovers like me think we're in heaven.

Prep time: 30 minutes • Bake time: 12 to 15 minutes • Serves 8

Vegetable cooking spray

Filling

¾ cup granulated sugar

3 TB. cornstarch

⅓ cup fresh lemon juice

⅓ cup water

1 oz. light cream cheese, softened

Cake

⅔ cup + ¼ cup granulated sugar (divided use)

2 tsp. finely grated lemon zest

¼ cup fresh lemon juice

1 large egg

¾ cup all-purpose flour

½ tsp. baking powder

3 large egg whites

¼ tsp. cream of tartar

2 TB. confectioners' sugar

Glaze

3 TB. confectioners' sugar

1 TB. fresh lemon juice

Position a rack in the center of the oven and preheat the oven to 350°F. Line a 15-inch by 10-inch jelly roll pan with parchment paper and lightly coat the paper with cooking spray.

Make filling: In a small saucepan off the heat, whisk together sugar, cornstarch, lemon juice, and water until smooth. Cook the mixture over medium heat, whisking constantly, for 2 to 3 minutes or until it has thickened. Remove the pan from the heat; whisk in cream cheese until it has dissolved. Transfer the mixture to a bowl. Cover the surface with a piece of plastic wrap. Let it chill while you prepare the cake.

Make cake: In a large bowl, whisk together ⅔ cup sugar, lemon zest, lemon juice, and egg. With a wooden spoon, stir in flour and baking powder until mixed.

In another bowl, beat egg whites with cream of tartar until foamy. Gradually add remaining ¼ cup sugar, beating until stiff peaks form. Stir one fourth of egg whites into the cake batter. Gently fold in remaining egg whites just until blended. Pour the mixture onto the prepared pan, spreading it evenly.

Bake for 10 minutes or until a tester inserted in the center comes out clean. Let the pan cool on a wire rack.

 A Piece of Advice

Use only freshly squeezed lemon juice when the recipe, like this one, depends on the lemon for its primary flavor. Bottled lemon juice is fine when a small amount is called for.

Dust the cake with confectioners' sugar and invert it onto a clean tea towel. Remove the pan and peel off the parchment paper. Spread the filling over the surface. Starting from the short end, gently roll up the cake with the help of the tea towel. Transfer it to a serving platter, seam side down.

Make glaze: Whisk confectioners' sugar and lemon juice together until smooth. Drizzle over lemon roll.

 Nutrition per Serving

Calories: 260
Protein: 3.8 g
Cholesterol: 29 mg

Fat (total): 1.4 g
Fat (saturated): 0.6 g

Carbohydrate: 58 g
Dietary Fiber: 0.5 g

Other Stunning Desserts

These desserts don't fit into the other categories, but they are too good to not include. I don't think I know anyone who doesn't love tiramisu; wouldn't moan with pleasure when they were presented with a perfectly executed baked Alaska; or have a look of amazement when served a charlotte, a molded dessert with a genesis that dates back to the Russian czars. These are lower-fat desserts to serve when you're wanting to impress—either family or friends.

Lemon Tiramisu

In *Enlightened Home Cooking*, I created a Chocolate Coffee Tiramisu that was luscious. You never knew it didn't contain mascarpone cheese. I adapted it to a Lemon Tiramisu that I think might be even better.

Prep time: 20 minutes • Chill time: at least 2 hours • Serves 12

Vegetable cooking spray

1¾ cups smooth 5% ricotta cheese

4 oz. light cream cheese, softened

½ cup + ⅓ cup + 3 TB. granulated sugar (divided use)

1 TB. finely grated lemon zest

⅓ cup + 2 TB. fresh lemon juice (divided use)

1 large egg yolk

3 large egg whites

¼ tsp. cream of tartar

½ cup boiling water

20 3-inch ladyfinger cookies

Lightly coat a 9-inch square cake pan or decorative serving dish with cooking spray.

In a food processor, combine ricotta cheese, cream cheese, ½ cup sugar, lemon zest, ⅓ cup lemon juice, and yolk; purée the mixture until it is smooth. Transfer it to a large bowl.

In another bowl, beat egg whites with cream of tartar until foamy. Gradually add ⅓ cup sugar, beating until stiff peaks form. Stir one fourth of egg whites into the ricotta mixture. Gently fold in remaining egg whites just until blended.

In a bowl, whisk together water, remaining 2 tablespoons lemon juice, and remaining 3 tablespoons sugar. Dip each ladyfinger in the mixture just enough to moisten it and place it in the bottom of the prepared baking dish. Pour half the ricotta-lemon mixture over ladyfingers. Repeat layers. Chill at least 2 hours.

 Nutrition Watch

Thanks to ricotta cheese and light cream cheese, there is little fat in this wonderful traditional Italian dessert. Mascarpone cheese has 14 grams of fat per 2 tablespoons; ricotta has only 3 grams of fat per 2 tablespoons.

 A Piece of Advice

Process the cheeses well until the batter is no longer grainy. Be sure to beat the egg whites and sugar well until all the granules are dissolved. Use only fresh lemon juice.

 **Nutrition per Serving**

Calories: 204   Fat (total): 6.3 g   Carbohydrate: 29 g
Protein: 7.8 g   Fat (saturated): 3.4 g   Dietary Fiber: 0.2 g
Cholesterol: 88 mg

Raspberry Charlotte

A charlotte is a classic molded dessert lined with sponge cake or ladyfingers and filled with a mixture of fruit, custard, and heavy cream. It's traditionally made in a special pail-shaped mold, but my version is made in a springform pan, which we all more likely have. This charlotte uses low-fat condensed milk and egg whites to get a delicious flavor and texture.

Prep time: 30 minutes • Chill time: at least 3 hours • Serves 12

Crust

3 TB. raspberry jam

2 TB. hot water

about 40 3-inch ladyfinger cookies

Filling

1 can (1¼ cups or 10 oz.) low-fat sweetened condensed milk

2 cups smooth 5% ricotta cheese

2 cups fresh or frozen raspberries

⅓ cup + ¼ cup granulated sugar (divided use)

1 TB. unflavored gelatin

3 TB. cold water

3 large egg whites

¼ tsp. cream of tartar

 **A Piece of Advice**

If you're using frozen berries, measure them while they're frozen, and then thaw and drain them well. Condensed milk is a mixture of cow's milk and sugar. It's heated until about 60 percent of the water evaporates, which results in a sticky, sweet mixture delicious for baking. The low-fat version is just as good, if not better.

Use an ungreased 8-inch springform pan. Make crust: In a small bowl, stir together jam and water. Brush ladyfingers with the mixture. Line the bottom of the pan with some of the ladyfingers. Break them to fit as necessary.

Make filling: In a food processor, combine condensed milk, ricotta cheese, raspberries, and ⅓ cup sugar; purée the mixture until it is smooth. In a small microwavable bowl, combine gelatin and water; let sit for 2 minutes. Microwave on high for 20 seconds. Stir it until it is smooth. With the motor running, add gelatin to food processor though feed tube. Transfer the mixture to a large bowl.

In another bowl, beat egg whites with cream of tartar until foamy. Gradually add remaining ¼ cup sugar, beating until stiff peaks form. Stir one fourth of egg whites into the ricotta-gelatin mixture. Gently fold in remaining egg whites just until combined. Pour the mixture into the pan. Place remaining ladyfingers against the wall of the pan with the flat part of the cookie facing out, pushing through the mousse filling. Chill for at least 3 hours. Unmold onto a serving plate.

 Nutrition Watch

Two tablespoons of regular condensed milk has 3 grams of fat; the low-fat version has only 1.5 grams of fat.

Nutrition per Serving

Calories: 279
Protein: 10 g
Cholesterol: 61 mg

Fat (total): 5.7 g
Fat (saturated): 3.2 g

Carbohydrate: 47 g
Dietary Fiber: 1.5 g

Baked Alaska

For this traditional dessert, frozen yogurt or sorbet replaces the ice cream, reducing the fat.

Prep time: 45 minutes • Bake time: 12 to 15 minutes plus 3 to 5 minutes • Freeze time: at least 2 hours • Serves 12

Vegetable cooking spray

Cake

1 large egg

⅓ cup + ¼ cup granulated sugar (divided use)

⅓ cup 2% low-fat milk

1½ tsp. vanilla extract

⅔ cup all-purpose flour

½ tsp. baking powder

⅛ tsp. salt

3 large egg whites

¼ tsp. cream of tartar

2 TB. confectioners' sugar

4 cups frozen yogurt or sorbet, any flavor, softened

Meringue Topping

3 large egg whites

1 cup granulated sugar

¼ cup water

¼ tsp cream of tartar

Position a rack in the center of the oven and preheat oven to 350°F. Line a 15-inch by 10-inch jelly roll pan with parchment paper and lightly coat the paper with cooking spray.

Make cake: In a bowl, whisk together egg, ⅓ cup sugar, milk, and vanilla. In another bowl, stir together flour, baking powder, and salt; with a wooden spoon, stir the mixture in the egg mixture.

In a separate bowl, beat egg whites with cream of tartar until foamy. Gradually add remaining ¼ cup sugar, beating until stiff peaks form. Stir one fourth of egg whites into the batter. Gently stir in remaining egg whites. Pour onto the prepared pan, spreading it evenly.

Bake for 12 to 15 minutes or until tester comes out dry. Let cool on a rack. Dust cake with confectioners' sugar. Invert onto clean tea towel. Remove pan and peel off parchment paper. Cut cake in thirds lengthwise, then in thirds crosswise to create nine squares. Cut each square on the diagonal to create two triangles.

Nutrition Watch

One-half cup of frozen yogurt has approximately 3 grams of fat, depending on the flavor; ½ cup of ice cream can have between 14 to 20 grams of fat. What a difference!

A Piece of Advice

To make this dish even more dramatic, use different flavors of yogurt or sorbet. Try 1 cup of four different flavors, totaling 4 cups. You can refreeze any leftovers, but this cake tastes best right out of the oven. You can always buy store-bought sponge cake if you don't have time to make your own.

Line a 6-cup bowl with plastic wrap, with a 6-inch overhang all around. Line it with some cake triangles placed end to end, trimming as necessary to cover the inside of bowl completely. Pack frozen yogurt into bowl. Place additional cake triangles on top to encase yogurt completely. Trim any bits that extend beyond the covering. Fold plastic wrap over the dessert. Freeze for at least 2 hours.

Preheat the oven to 450°F.

Make topping: In the top of a double boiler, mix egg whites, sugar, water, and cream of tartar. Beat with electric beater for approximately 7 minutes, until soft peaks form. Remove pan from heat and beat for 2 more minutes until mixture is stiff.

Remove bowl from freezer and remove plastic wrap. Invert cake onto pan and remove bowl. Using a spatula, spread topping over surface of cake. Bake for 3 to 5 minutes or until topping is golden. Serve immediately.

Nutrition per Serving

Calories: 228
Protein: 6.4 g
Cholesterol: 21 mg

Fat (total): 1.6 g
Fat (saturated): 0.9 g

Carbohydrate: 47 g
Dietary Fiber: 0.7 g

The Least You Need to Know

- Use small amounts of high-fat ingredients such as butter in desserts to keep the rich flavor.

- Work quickly with phyllo dough, taking care to prevent the thin pastry sheets from drying out and lightly misting every other layer with refrigerated butter-flavored cooking spray.

- Phyllo desserts are done when the pastry is golden brown and crisp.

- Avoid under baking or over baking a jelly roll, or it will likely crack as you roll it. Cover any cracks that do form with a dusting of confectioners' sugar or cocoa.

- Show-stopper desserts like tiramisu, baked Alaska, and charlotte don't have to be laden with fat and cholesterol; my lower-fat versions are worthy of your most special dinner guest.

Chapter 14

Muffins, Scones, and Loaf Cakes

In This Chapter

◆ Irresistible, home-style muffins for snacks and lunch-boxes

◆ Delectable scones—perfect for coffee or tea time

◆ Moist, light loaf cakes for dessert

Muffins and scones have become our new breakfast, but with their increasing popularity, we now seeing them served all day long. When they're filled with fruit, you're getting fruit and fiber all at once. Loaf cakes also have their place at breakfast, although they're more likely served for brunch, a coffee klatch, portable lunch, afternoon tea, or midnight snack.

I can't think of anything more inviting than freshly baked goods, and the wonderful thing about these is that they are so easy to make. Although technically quick breads, they fit perfectly into this dessert book because they are a light baked sweet without a lot of fuss.

Muffins and scones taste the best when they're still warm. I freeze them for later in a plastic freezer bag for up to 3 months. Warm them in a toaster oven at 350°F for 5 minutes. Loaf cakes are best served at room temperature. They can also be frozen, well wrapped, for up to 3 months.

Don't store muffins, scones, or loaf cakes in the refrigerator, because they become stale and dry faster. Leave them on the counter or in the freezer.

Marvelous Muffins

Muffins are one of the first foods we learned to make in cooking classes at school, but I dare say those muffins bore little resemblance to the gems in this chapter.

If you're one of those who think muffins are tricky to make, they're really not that difficult. You just have to follow the basic method of making any quick bread. Read the recipe before starting, making certain that all the ingredients are available or that you have ingredients that can substitute. For the best results, the butter, margarine, and eggs should be at room temperature. It's not necessary, though.

It is easy to over mix muffins and other quick breads. To avoid this, mix the batter only until most of the dry spots are gone when combining the dry and wet ingredients. A perfectly mixed batter will still have a few small dry spots, which will absorb moisture and disappear during baking.

Always lightly coat the muffin tins and loaf pans with vegetable cooking spray before filling or use paper liners. Some of the recipes make larger muffins than others. Just divide the batter among the 12 muffin cups accordingly, using standard 2½-inch muffin baking tins. I like to use an ice cream scoop when filling muffin tins so that I can deposit the batter into the muffin cup without spilling it all over the top of the muffin tin.

If you are putting a topping on your muffins, be sure to press it firmly into the batter or it might fall off as the muffin rises. Bake the muffins in a preheated oven with the rack set in the middle for even baking.

A bumpy top and a dense, moist interior are characteristics of muffins. Over baking is a common mistake. Watch the baking of these lower-fat muffins very carefully, because they have no excess fat that would tolerate excess baking. At least 5 minutes before the baking time is finished, insert a toothpick or cake tester to check for doneness. The tester should come out clean and dry. If it is still slightly wet, bake for just another 2 to 3 minutes and watch carefully. The muffins should be golden brown, firm to the touch, and come away easily from the sides of the pan. Once you've made a recipe, jot down any difference in baking time to that you'll know when it will be properly done next time.

Feel free to play with these recipes once you understand what you're doing—substituting different fruits and spices to make your own set of recipes.

Banana Bran Apricot Muffins

This variation on the standard bran muffin is outstanding. I pack these for my children's lunches.

Prep time: 15 minutes   •   Cook time: 15 to 18 minutes   •   Serves 12

Vegetable cooking spray

1 medium (⅓ cup) ripe banana, mashed

¾ cup granulated sugar

1 cup low-fat milk

¼ cup canola oil

1 large egg

1 tsp. vanilla extract

1 cup all-purpose flour

¾ cup natural bran

¾ cup chopped dried apricots

1 tsp. baking powder

1 tsp. baking soda

Position a rack in the center of the oven and pre-heat oven to 350°F. Lightly coat a 12-cup muffin pan with cooking spray.

In a large bowl and using a whisk or electric beaters, combine banana, sugar, milk, oil, egg, and vanilla.

In another bowl, stir together flour, bran, apricots, baking powder, and baking soda. With a wooden spoon, stir the mixture into the banana mixture just until everything is combined. Divide the mixture among the prepared muffin cups.

Bake for 15 to 18 minutes or until a tester inserted into the middle of a muffin comes out dry.

 Nutrition Watch

Bran is a good source of carbohydrates, calcium, phosphorus, and fiber. The best nutritional source is from natural bran, but bran buds and flakes are also a good source.

 A Piece of Advice

Freeze leftover bananas to use for baking. Just defrost and mash. Kitchen sheers make quick work when chopping dried apricots.

 Nutrition per Serving

Calories: 187   Fat (total): 5.5 g   Carbohydrate: 31 g
Protein: 3.4 g   Fat (saturated): 0.6 g   Dietary Fiber: 2.8 g
Cholesterol: 19 mg

Cappuccino Chip Muffins

The slight addition of coffee to your muffins perks them up. I love this as a late-morning snack.

Prep time: 10 minutes • Cook time: 15 to 18 minutes • Serves 12

Vegetable cooking spray

1 TB. instant coffee granules

2 TB. hot water

⅔ cup low-fat milk

¼ cup canola oil

1 large egg

1½ tsp. vanilla extract

¾ cup granulated sugar

1⅓ cups all-purpose flour

¼ cup semi-sweet chocolate chips

1½ tsp. baking powder

Nutrition Watch

I'm always asked what are the best oils to use. I only use those with the least amount of saturated fats and the highest amount of monounsaturated fats. Canola oil is my preference when I don't want the oil to add any flavor to what I'm baking. Olive and peanut oil are used when flavor from the oil is wanted.

Position a rack in the center of the oven and preheat oven to 350°F. Lightly coat a 12-cup muffin pan with cooking spray.

Dissolve the instant coffee in hot water. In a large bowl and using a whisk or electric mixer, combine dissolved coffee, milk, oil, egg, vanilla, and sugar.

In another bowl, stir together flour, chocolate chips, and baking powder. With a wooden spoon, stir the mixture into the coffee mixture just until everything is combined. Divide the mixture among the prepared muffin cups.

Bake for 15 to 18 minutes or until a tester inserted into the middle of a muffin comes out dry.

Nutrition per Serving

Calories: 171
Protein: 2.6 g
Cholesterol: 18 mg

Fat (total): 6.3 g
Fat (saturated): 1.2 g

Carbohydrate: 26 g
Dietary Fiber: 0.6 g

Banana Peanut Butter Jam Muffins

Forget the peanut butter and jam sandwiches. Try these great muffins. My kids devour them!

Prep time: 10 minutes   •   Cook time: 15 to 18 minutes   •   Serves 12

Vegetable cooking spray

1 large (½ cup) ripe banana, mashed

3 TB. smooth peanut butter

1 large egg

½ cup low-fat milk

2 TB. canola oil

1 tsp. vanilla extract

¾ cup granulated sugar

1¼ cups all-purpose flour

½ cup bran flakes cereal or corn flakes cereal

1½ tsp. baking powder

½ tsp. baking soda

3 TB. raspberry jam

Position a rack in the center of the oven and pre-heat oven to 350°F. Lightly coat a 12-cup muffin pan with cooking spray.

In a large bowl and using a whisk or electric mixer, combine banana, peanut butter, egg, milk, oil, vanilla, and sugar.

In another bowl, stir together flour, cereal, baking powder, and baking soda. With a wooden spoon, stir the mixture into the banana mixture just until everything is combined. Divide the mixture among the prepared muffin cups. Dollop a small amount of jam on top of each muffin.

Bake for 15 to 18 minutes or until a tester inserted into the middle of a muffin comes out dry.

Nutrition Watch

Peanut butter, when combined with a bread or grain, becomes a full protein—great for children who don't consume enough protein or who are vegetarians.

A Piece of Advice

I use only natural smooth peanut butter that consists only of peanuts and oil, usually peanut oil. Most commercial peanut butters also contain some sugar and a small amount of salt. Once opened, store natural peanut butter in the refrigerator for up to 6 months.

Nutrition per Serving

Calories: 187

Protein: 3.5 g

Cholesterol: 18 mg

Fat (total): 5 g

Fat (saturated): 0.7 g

Carbohydrate: 32 g

Dietary Fiber: 1.2 g

Chocolate Cheesecake Muffins

My children think I'm making Twinkies. These are divine treasures for young and old, with a creamy filling in every mouthful.

Prep time: 15 minutes • Cook time: 20 to 25 minutes • Serves 12

Vegetable cooking spray

1 cup granulated sugar

⅓ cup unsweetened cocoa

1 cup plain low-fat yogurt

¼ cup canola oil

1 tsp. vanilla extract

1 large egg

¾ cup all-purpose flour

1½ tsp. baking powder

2 oz. light cream cheese, softened

⅓ cup smooth 5% ricotta cheese

⅓ cup confectioners' sugar

A Piece of Advice

I usually make a double batch of these muffins and freeze them for school lunches and dessert. You can substitute low-fat cottage cheese for the ricotta cheese, but purée it well.

Nutrition Watch

Light cream cheese is 25 percent lower in fat than regular cream cheese. Use it carefully.

Position a rack in the center of the oven and preheat oven to 350°F. Lightly coat a 12-cup muffin pan with cooking spray.

In a large bowl and using a whisk or electric mixer, combine sugar, cocoa, yogurt, oil, vanilla, and egg.

In another bowl, stir together flour and baking powder. With a wooden spoon, stir the mixture into the cocoa mixture just until everything is combined. Divide half of the batter among the prepared muffin cups.

With clean beaters or in a food processor, beat cream cheese, ricotta cheese, and confectioners' sugar until the mixture is smooth. Divide the cheese mixture among the muffin cups. Top with the remaining batter.

Bake for 20 to 25 minutes or until a tester inserted into the middle of a muffin comes out dry.

Nutrition per Serving

Calories: 201
Protein: 4.2 g
Cholesterol: 24 mg

Fat (total): 7.1 g
Fat (saturated): 1.7 g

Carbohydrate: 30 g
Dietary Fiber: 1 g

Gingerbread Date Muffins

I've always enjoyed gingerbread cookies, so I took the flavoring and applied it to muffins. These may be even better than the cookies!

Prep time: 15 minutes   •   Cook time: 15 minutes   •   Serves 12

Vegetable cooking spray	⅔ cup chopped dates
¾ cup + 2 TB. granulated sugar (divided use)	1½ tsp. baking powder
⅔ cup plain low-fat yogurt	¾ tsp. ground cinnamon
3 TB. canola oil	¼ tsp. ground ginger
3 TB. dark molasses	⅛ tsp. allspice
1 large egg yolk	2 large egg whites
1 cup all-purpose flour	¼ tsp. cream of tartar

Position a rack in the center of the oven and preheat oven to 350°F. Lightly coat a 12-cup muffin pan with cooking spray.

In a large bowl and using a whisk or electric mixer, combine ¾ cup sugar, yogurt, oil, molasses, and egg yolk.

In another bowl, stir together flour, chopped dates, baking powder, cinnamon, ginger, and allspice. With a wooden spoon, stir the mixture into the molasses mixture just until everything is combined.

In a clean bowl and using clean beaters, beat the egg whites with the cream of tartar until they are foamy. Gradually add remaining 2 tablespoons sugar, continuing to beat until stiff peaks form. Fold the mixture into the batter just until combined. Divide it among the prepared muffin cups.

Bake for 15 minutes or until a tester inserted into the middle of a muffin comes out dry.

 Nutrition Watch

Molasses is rich in iron, calcium, and phosphorus.

 A Piece of Advice

Don't worry if you don't have allspice in your pantry. Try a bit of nutmeg or increase the amount of cinnamon. The most common molasses is dark molasses, which is what is used in most traditional North

 Nutrition per Serving

Calories: 156
Protein: 2.6 g
Cholesterol: 19 mg

Fat (total): 4.2 g
Fat (saturated): 0.5 g

Carbohydrate: 27 g
Dietary Fiber: 0.4 g

Apple Butter Streusel Muffins

Apple butter is a thick, dark-brown preserve made by slowly cooking apples, sugar, spices, and cider, which is then puréed and strained. It has a more intense flavor than applesauce.

Prep time: 20 minutes • Cook time: 18 to 20 minutes • Serves 12

Vegetable cooking spray

Topping

3 TB. packed light brown sugar

3 TB. Grape-Nuts cereal

2 TB. all-purpose flour

¼ tsp. ground cinnamon

1½ tsp. canola oil

1½ tsp. water

Muffins

⅔ cup granulated sugar

¼ cup packed light brown sugar

½ cup low-fat milk

⅓ cup apple butter

2 TB. canola oil

1 large egg

1 cup + 2 tsp. all-purpose flour (divided use)

1 tsp. baking powder

½ tsp. baking soda

½ tsp. ground cinnamon

¾ cup chopped peeled apples

 **A Piece of Advice**

If you don't have apple butter, use unsweetened applesauce that you've made by cooking firm sweet apples in a small amount of water until very soft, and then purée. I avoid McIntosh and Golden Delicious for cooking, and prefer Royal Gala, Spy, Mutsu, or Paula Red.

 **Nutrition Watch**

Apple butter is a great substitute for a topping over toast or breads—instead of butter or cream cheese. It has no fat or cholesterol.

Position a rack in the center of the oven and preheat oven to 350°F. Lightly coat a 12-cup muffin pan with cooking spray.

Make topping: In a bowl, stir together brown sugar, cereal, flour, cinnamon, oil, and water just until crumbly. Set the mixture aside.

Make muffins: In a large bowl and using a whisk or electric beaters, combine sugar, brown sugar, milk, apple butter, oil, and egg.

In another bowl, stir together 1 cup flour, baking powder, baking soda, and cinnamon. With a wooden spoon, stir the mixture into the apple butter mixture just until everything is combined.

In a small bowl, stir together apples and remaining 2 teaspoons flour; stir the mixture into the batter. Divide the batter among the prepared muffin cups. Sprinkle the topping evenly over the top.

Bake for 18 to 20 minutes or until a tester inserted into the middle of a muffin comes out dry.

 **Nutrition per Serving**

Calories: 181   Fat (total): 3.5 g   Carbohydrate: 35 g
Protein: 2.3 g   Fat (saturated): 0.4 g   Dietary Fiber: 0.8 g
Cholesterol: 18 mg

Cranberry Streusel Muffins

Who says that cranberries are only for the festive season? I keep a bag of frozen ones on hand. You don't need to thaw them.

Prep time: 15 minutes • Cook time: 18 to 20 minutes • Serves 12

Vegetable cooking spray

Topping

2 TB. quick-cooking oats

2 TB. all-purpose flour

2 TB. packed light brown sugar

¼ tsp. ground cinnamon

2 tsp. canola oil

1 tsp. water

Muffins

¾ cup granulated sugar

½ cup low-fat milk

¼ cup canola oil

1 large egg

1 tsp. vanilla extract

1 cup coarsely chopped cranberries

1⅓ cups all-purpose flour

2 tsp. baking powder

Position a rack in the center of the oven and preheat oven to 350°F. Lightly coat a 12-cup muffin pan with cooking spray.

Make topping: In a small bowl, stir together oats, flour, brown sugar, cinnamon, oil, and water until the mixture is crumbly. Set it aside.

Make muffins: In a large bowl and using a whisk or electric mixer, combine sugar, milk, oil, egg, and vanilla. With a wooden spoon, stir in the cranberries.

In another bowl, stir together flour and baking powder. With a wooden spoon, stir the mixture into the cranberry mixture just until everything is combined. Divide the mixture among the prepared muffin cups. Sprinkle the topping evenly over the top.

Bake for 18 to 20 minutes or until a tester inserted into the middle of a muffin comes out dry.

 A Piece of Advice

Because cranberries are so tart, I balance the flavor with a sweet cinnamon topping.

 Nutrition Watch

Cranberries are very high in vitamin C. Dried cranberries are a concentrated form of nutrients, carbohydrates, and energy.

 **Nutrition per Serving**

Calories: 181   Fat (total): 6.1 g   Carbohydrate: 29 g
Protein: 2.6 g   Fat (saturated): 0.6 g   Dietary Fiber: 0.9 g
Cholesterol: 18 mg

Superb Scones

There are few recipes for scones in early American cookbooks. It's only been recently that we've discovered scones, likely through our travels to England and Scotland where they are daily fare. Sweeter than biscuits, they require the same light hand. In Europe they are usually served for tea with clotted cream and jam. Here we forego the clotted cream, with good reason since it's high in fat, and only sometimes offer jam. You'll find scones wonderful for breakfast or brunch, but we've served them at tailgate parties and picnics with raves as a not-too-sweet dessert.

Take care when making scones: mix just until the flour is no longer lumpy and seems to be blended with the liquid ingredients. Scones can be shaped into perfect circles, by rolling or patting the dough into a large circle, then cutting the scones with a round biscuit cutter, reworking the scraps. You can also roll the dough into a circle and then cut it into pie-shaped triangles. Place the scones on the prepared baking sheet at least 1 inch apart. If you're in a hurry, just drop the dough from a spoon into clumps directly onto the baking sheet, again at least 1 inch apart. Follow the other baking cautions I've given for muffins.

Keep these recipes in mind the next time you plan a special party. You can split the scones and tuck in thinly sliced ham, turkey, or a special cheese for a lovely hors d'oeuvre.

Blueberry Sour Cream Scones

A scone is a Scottish quick bread that shares its name with the place where Scottish kings were once crowned. The original recipes were made from oats and baked on a griddle. Modern scones are flour-based and baked in the oven. These scones have blueberries, which makes them wonderful.

Prep time: 10 minutes   •   Cook time: 12 to 15 minutes   •   Serves 10

Vegetable cooking spray

½ cup granulated sugar

3 TB. cold unsalted butter

1 large egg

1 tsp. vanilla extract

1 cup all-purpose flour

1½ tsp. baking powder

⅓ cup low-fat sour cream

½ cup fresh or frozen blueberries

Position a rack in the center of the oven and preheat oven to 400°F. Lightly coat a baking sheet with cooking spray.

In a food processor, combine sugar, butter, egg, and vanilla; pulse on and off just until the mixture is crumbly. Add flour, baking powder, and sour cream; pulse on and off just until everything is combined. Stir in blueberries. Drop the batter on the baking sheet in 10 equal amounts.

Bake for 12 to 15 minutes or until the scones are golden. Serve them warm or at room temperature.

 **A Piece of Advice**

These scones are best with fresh berries. But if you're using frozen berries, measure them while they're still frozen; then defrost and drain them well. You can use raspberries as well. I sometimes serve these scones

 Nutrition per Serving

Calories: 139
Protein: 2.3 g
Cholesterol: 33 mg

Fat (total): 4.6 g
Fat (saturated): 2.7 g

Carbohydrate: 22 g
Dietary Fiber: 0.4 g

Apricot Orange Scones

The combination of orange and dried apricots makes for a distinctive breakfast quick bread. The citrus flavor is highlighted by the addition of orange zest and orange juice concentrate.

Prep time: 10 minutes • Cook time: 12 to 15 minutes • Serves 10

Vegetable cooking spray

½ cup granulated sugar

3 TB. cold unsalted butter

1 large egg

⅓ cup evaporated skim milk

2 TB. orange juice concentrate

2 tsp. finely grated orange zest

1 tsp. vanilla extract

1 cup all-purpose flour

⅓ cup diced dried apricots

1½ tsp. baking powder

⅛ tsp. salt

Nutrition Watch

Evaporated milk is canned unsweetened milk that has 60 percent of the water removed.

Vitamin D is added for extra nutritional value. The skim milk version has almost no fat, whereas the whole milk version has almost 8 percent fat.

Position a rack in the center of the oven and preheat oven to 400°F. Lightly coat a baking sheet with cooking spray.

In a food processor, combine sugar, butter, egg, evaporated milk, orange juice concentrate, orange rind, and vanilla; pulse on and off just until everything is mixed. Add flour, baking powder, and salt; pulse on and off just until they are combined. Stir in apricots. Drop the batter on the baking sheet in 10 equal amounts.

Bake for 10 to 12 minutes or until the scones are golden. Serve them warm or at room temperature.

Nutrition per Serving

Calories: 153
Protein: 2.9 g
Cholesterol: 31 mg

Fat (total): 4.1 g
Fat (saturated): 2.3 g

Carbohydrate: 26 g
Dietary Fiber: 0.7 g

Lovely Loaf Cakes

Loaf cakes, like muffins and scones, are easy to whip up, and they don't need to be frosted, making them great for eating out-of-hand from a lunch-box or at a picnic.

I use a 9-inch by 5-inch loaf pan for all my loaf cakes. Just follow the recipe carefully, step by step, always mixing the wet ingredients thoroughly and then adding the dry ingredients. At this point, don't over mix the batter, or the loaf cake will be tough and chewy. Use a cake tester to determine when the cake is done. The tester should come out clean and dry. If it is still slightly wet, bake for just another 2 to 3 minutes and watch carefully. The cake should be golden brown, firm to the touch.

These cakes freeze well so I frequently make a double batch, freezing one cake for later. This comes in handy when you have unexpected guests at the dinner table or people stop by for coffee or tea.

Cranberry Applesauce Loaf

Cranberries and applesauce make a great combination. The addition of cinnamon gives the loaf a real punch.

Prep time: 20 minutes   •   Cook time: 45 to 50 minutes   •   Serves 16

Vegetable cooking spray

Loaf

¾ cup granulated sugar

1 tsp. ground cinnamon

½ cup unsweetened applesauce

¼ cup canola oil

1 large egg

2 tsp. vanilla extract

½ cup plain low-fat yogurt

1⅓ cups all-purpose flour

1½ tsp. baking powder

½ tsp. baking soda

1 cup fresh or frozen cranberries

Topping

¼ cup quick-cooking oats

3 TB. packed light brown sugar

2 TB. all-purpose flour

¼ tsp. ground cinnamon

2 tsp. canola oil

1 tsp. water

Position a rack in the center of the oven and preheat oven to 350°F. Lightly coat a 9-inch by 5-inch loaf pan with cooking spray.

Make loaf: In a large bowl and using a whisk or electric mixer, combine sugar, cinnamon, applesauce, oil, egg, vanilla, and yogurt.

Nutrition Watch _____

Cranberries are very high in vitamin C.

In another bowl, stir together flour, baking powder, baking soda, and cranberries. With a wooden spoon, stir the mixture into the applesauce mixture just until everything is combined. Pour the mixture into the prepared loaf pan.

 A Piece of Advice _____

You can use either fresh or frozen cranberries. If you use frozen, there's no need to defrost them, since there is very little excess liquid.

Make topping: In a small bowl, stir together oats, brown sugar, flour, cinnamon, oil, and water until crumbly. Sprinkle the mixture over the batter.

Bake for 45 to 50 minutes or until a tester inserted in the middle comes out dry. Let the loaf cool in its pan on a wire rack. Unmold and cut into 8 slices. Cut each slice in half to serve.

 Nutrition per Serving

Calories: 146
Protein: 2.2 g
Cholesterol: 14 mg

Fat (total): 4.6 g
Fat (saturated): 0.5 g

Carbohydrate: 24 g
Dietary Fiber: 0.9 g

Fig Banana Loaf

Figs are a divine fruit with a soft flesh and many tiny edible seeds. I came up with this dessert when I tasted a similar recipe in a local coffee shop. But that one was filled with fat and calories!

Prep time: 25 minutes   •   Cook time: 50 minutes   •   Serves 16

Vegetable cooking spray

6 oz. (1¼ cup) dried figs, chopped

¾ cup water

¾ cup granulated sugar

1 large ripe banana, mashed (½ cup)

¼ cup canola oil

1 large egg

1 large egg white

2 tsp. vanilla extract

½ cup plain low-fat yogurt

1⅔ cups all-purpose flour

1½ tsp. baking powder

1½ tsp. ground cinnamon

½ tsp. baking soda

Position a rack in the center of the oven and pre-heat oven to 350°F. Lightly coat a 9-inch by 5-inch loaf pan with cooking spray.

In a small saucepan, combine figs and water. Bring to a boil; reduce heat to medium-low and simmer, uncovered, for 10 minutes, stirring occasionally. Remove the pan from the heat. Cool.

In a food processor, combine the fig mixture, sugar, banana, oil, egg, egg white, and vanilla; purée the mixture until it is smooth. Add yogurt, flour, baking powder, cinnamon, and baking soda; pulse on and off just until everything is combined. Pour the mixture into the prepared pan.

Bake for 50 minutes or until a tester inserted in the middle comes out dry. Let the loaf cool in its pan on a wire rack. Unmold and cut into 8 slices. Cut each slice in half.

Nutrition Watch

Figs are a good source of iron, calcium, and phosphorus. Great as a midday snack or dessert.

A Piece of Advice

Dried figs can be bought either in bulk or in a package. I often buy them in bulk and freeze them. Fresh figs are sensational and available from June through October.

Nutrition per Serving

Calories: 164
Protein: 2.8 g
Cholesterol: 14 mg

Fat (total): 4.1 g
Fat (saturated): 0.5 g

Carbohydrate: 29 g
Dietary Fiber: 1.9 g

The Least You Need to Know

◆ Luscious doesn't have to mean high in fat and cholesterol. With my precise use of low-fat cheeses and yogurt, excess eggs, heavy cream, and butter are not needed—and there's no loss of flavor or texture.

◆ Chocolate is high in saturated fat, but I get the intense taste of chocolate flavor with only a trace of saturated fat by using cocoa powder. Because you're counting on it for flavor, use the best cocoa powder that you can afford.

◆ Dried fruits add intense flavor to these desserts without a drop of fat. Buy them in bulk and keep them handy in your freezer so that in 30 minutes or less you can whip up a batch of muffins or scones, or a loaf cake.

Chapter 15

The Cookie Jar

In This Chapter

- ◆ Crisp or chewy drop cookies
- ◆ Festive rolled and pressed cookies
- ◆ Delicious biscotti
- ◆ Divine rugelach and crisps
- ◆ All other kinds of "cookies"

Cookies make me think of mothers and grandmothers and the aroma of baking cookies wafting from the kitchen. Maybe that's why I'm somewhat of a cookie maven, thinking that stopping for a glass of milk or a cup of coffee means cookies. I've reworked some of my very favorite recipes, lowering them in fat and making them more wholesome.

The kinds of cookies in this chapter are drop cookies, which are dropped by the spoonful onto a baking sheet; rolled, chilled dough cookies; pressed cookies; rugelach; biscotti; and meringue cookies.

Rolled and Drop Cookies

The dough for rolled cookies is easier to handle if it's first well chilled. Once rolled out, the cutters being used are then pressed into the dough to form the unique shapes, reworking any scraps. The cookies are then placed on the prepared baking sheet and baked until golden and slightly crisp. The cookies will continue to crisp as they cool.

When baking drop cookies, the dough is dropped by the spoonful directly onto the baking sheet at least 2 inches apart. These cookies are done when they have a golden bottom and the edges are brown. For a crisper cookie, bake a few minutes longer than the required time; for a softer, chewier cookie, bake to the minimum time specified. Place the baking sheet on a rack to cool for a few minutes, and then with a spatula place the cookies directly on the rack and let them cool until they are at room temperature before storing.

When making these cookies, you can substitute oil, unsalted butter, and margarine for one another. Oil gives a cookie a crispier texture, whereas butter gives it a softer texture. Use a whisk, electric mixer, or food processor to mix cookies.

Cookies are easy to make. With a little supervision from mom or dad, baking cookies is a great learning experience for young children, teaching them the basics of measuring, mixing, and following directions. Mix the wet ingredients first; then add the dry ingredients and mix just until the flour is incorporated. Do not over mix or the cookies will be tough. Use nonstick baking sheets sprayed with cooking spray, or line the sheet with parchment paper before spraying.

Nutrition Watch

In most cookie recipes, the primary ingredient is fat—either from butter, oil, or vegetable shortening. Most traditional recipes contain as much as 1 cup of fat. One tablespoon of fat contains approximately 120 calories and 14 grams of fat. I reduce the fat in my cookies by at least 50 percent.

I like to bake cookies in the center of the oven rather than on a bottom rack because cookies are more likely to burn at the bottom. The heat is more even in the center. Bake one sheet at a time; it takes a little longer than using two oven racks, but the results are much better.

Cookies are best eaten on the day they are baked. But if you want to store them, most will keep fresh for a few days at room temperature in an airtight container or box, and for a few weeks in the freezer.

To freeze cookies, wrap them in plastic wrap and then in foil, and place them in freezer bags. They're great if reheated in a 400°F oven for approximately 5 minutes. Do not store cookies in the refrigerator. Rolled or drop cookie dough can be frozen and then baked frozen. Add a couple of minutes to the baking time.

Don't insist on perfection when baking cookies—these are hand-made cookies, not cookies made by a commercial machine. Each one's supposed to look a little different and a bit rustic. Although lower in fat than their commercially baked cousins, these cookies are so delicious they'll disappear quickly. If for some reason you've baked too many and a few should become dried out, don't throw them away. Crumble the cookies and sprinkle on frozen yogurt or use as a yummy topping for fresh fruit.

Holiday Cut-Out Cookies

These are cookies that kids love to have a hand in making. Use cut-outs for the holiday season. For different colors, add a drop or two of food coloring and let the kids decorate them with sprinkles, sugar, cinnamon, chocolate chips, jam, and anything else they want.

Prep time: 30 minutes • Chill time: 20 minutes • Bake time: 15 to 18 minutes per sheet
• Makes about 30 cookies

Vegetable cooking spray

2 oz. light cream cheese

¾ cup granulated sugar

2 TB. canola vegetable oil

2 TB. margarine or unsalted butter

1 tsp. vanilla extract

1⅔ cups all-purpose flour

⅓ cup low-fat sour cream

Position a rack in the center of the oven and pre-heat the oven to 350°F. Lightly coat two baking sheets with cooking spray.

In a food processor, place cream cheese, sugar, oil, margarine, and vanilla. Purée until the mixture is smooth. Add flour and sour cream and pulse on and off until the mixture is crumbly. Remove it and form it into a ball. Wrap it with plastic wrap. Chill at least 20 minutes.

Between two sheets of floured waxed paper, roll the ball into a circle ⅛-inch thick. Using your favorite cookie cutters that are approximately 2 inches in diameter, cut out shapes and place them on the pre-pared baking sheets. If you like, sprinkle with your favorite topping. Re-roll the scraps and repeat.

Bake, one baking sheet at a time, for 15 to 18 minutes or until the cookies are light golden. Transfer to a wire rack to cool.

 Nutrition Watch _____

Traditional cut-out cookies are made primarily with butter or shortening and have a lot of calories, cholesterol, and fat. My version comes in at about 75 percent fewer calories and less fat than the traditional cookies—the light cream cheese replaces some of that fat.

 A Piece of Advice _____

You can make this dough in advance and freeze it. The cookies also freeze well after baking.

 Nutrition per Cookie

Calories: 58
Protein: 0.8 g
Cholesterol: 1.5 mg

Fat (total): 2.1 g
Fat (saturated): 0.4 g

Carbohydrate: 9 g
Dietary Fiber: 0.1 g

Chocolate Chip Cookies

Chocolate chip cookies are an all-time favorite. I add extra vanilla to boost the flavor. You'll never notice that the fat is reduced.

Prep time: 25 minutes • Bake time: 12 to 15 minutes per sheet • Makes about 24 cookies

Vegetable cooking spray

⅓ cup granulated sugar

⅓ cup packed light brown sugar

3 TB. canola oil

1 large egg

2 TB. light corn syrup

1 TB. vanilla extract

1 cup all-purpose flour

½ tsp. baking powder

⅛ tsp. salt

⅓ cup semi-sweet chocolate chips

 A Piece of Advice

I often make this batter in advance and form the cookies; then freeze them. You can bake the cookies right out of the freezer—makes a great quick, late-night treat.

Nutrition Watch

Traditional chocolate chip cookies have three times the fat and calories because of all the butter or shortening, eggs, and chocolate chips.

Position a rack in the center of the oven and preheat the oven to 350°F. Lightly coat two baking sheets with cooking spray.

In a large bowl, combine sugar, brown sugar, oil, egg, corn syrup, and vanilla.

In another bowl, stir together flour, baking powder, and salt. With a wooden spoon, stir the dry mixture into the wet ingredients until everything is combined. Stir in chocolate chips.

Drop by the tablespoonful onto the prepared baking sheets. Bake, one baking sheet at a time, for 12 to 15 minutes or until the cookies are golden. Transfer to a wire rack to cool.

 Nutrition per Cookie

Calories: 80
Protein: 0.9 g
Cholesterol: 8.9 mg

Fat (total): 2.7 g
Fat (saturated): 0.6 g

Carbohydrate: 13 g
Dietary Fiber: 0.3 g

Peanut Butter Chip Cookies

Peanut butter chips are sold in most grocery stores today. They make the difference in this cookie.

Prep time: 25 minutes • Bake time: 12 to 15 minutes per sheet • Makes about 36 cookies

½ cup packed light brown sugar

½ cup granulated sugar

1 large egg

1 tsp. vanilla

⅓ cup smooth peanut butter

3 TB. canola oil

¼ cup low-fat milk

1¼ cups all-purpose flour

½ tsp. baking powder

½ tsp. baking soda

¼ cup peanut butter chips

Position a rack in the center of the oven and preheat the oven to 350°F. Lightly coat two baking sheets with cooking spray.

In a large bowl and using a whisk or electric mixer, mix brown sugar, sugar, egg, vanilla, peanut butter, oil, and milk.

In another bowl, stir together flour, baking powder, and baking soda. With a wooden spoon, stir the flour mixture into the wet ingredients just until everything is combined. Stir in peanut butter chips.

Drop by the tablespoonful onto the prepared baking sheets. Bake, one baking sheet at a time, for 12 to 15 minutes. Transfer to a wire rack to cool.

 A Piece of Advice

Be sure to buy natural peanut butter, not commercial, which is loaded with sugar and hydrogenated fat. You can use regular chocolate chips instead of peanut butter chips in this recipe.

 Nutrition Watch

Peanut butter, when combined with a grain such as bread, is a complete protein—wonderful for vegetarians.

 Nutrition per Cookie

Calories: 72
Protein: 1.5 g
Cholesterol: 6 mg

Fat (total): 2.9 g
Fat (saturated): 0.5 g

Carbohydrate: 10 g
Dietary Fiber: 0.4 g

White Chocolate Chip Cookies

These chocolate cookies have white chocolate chips spread throughout, which melt into the cookies while they're baking. They're divinely delicious.

Prep time: 25 minutes • Bake time: 12 minutes per sheet • Makes about 30 cookies

Vegetable cooking spray

¾ cup granulated sugar

1 large egg

3 TB. canola oil

2 TB. water

1½ TB. light corn syrup

1 tsp. vanilla extract

1 cup all-purpose flour

¼ cup unsweetened cocoa

½ tsp. baking powder

⅓ cup white chocolate chips

A Piece of Advice

I often make this dough and freeze it to use later. Just remove the dough from the freezer and drop by tablespoonful on a baking sheet and bake.

Nutrition Watch

White chocolate is not chocolate at all because it contains no chocolate liquor. It's a mixture of sugar, cocoa butter, milk solids, lecithin, and vanilla. It has the same calories and fat as chocolate, though.

Position a rack in the center of the oven and preheat the oven to 350°F. Lightly coat two baking sheets with cooking spray.

In a large bowl and using a whisk or electric mixer, combine sugar, egg, oil, water, corn syrup, and vanilla.

In another bowl, stir together flour, cocoa, and baking powder. With a wooden spoon, stir the flour mixture into the wet ingredients just until everything is combined. Stir in chocolate chips.

Drop by the tablespoonful, spaced well apart, onto the prepared baking sheets. Bake one sheet at a time for 12 minutes or until the cookies are golden and slightly soft. Transfer to a wire rack to cool.

Nutrition per Cookie

Calories: 68
Protein: 0.9 g
Cholesterol: 7.5 mg

Fat (total): 2.3 g
Fat (saturated): 0.6 g

Carbohydrate: 11 g
Dietary Fiber: 0.4 g

Crisp Chocolate Oatmeal Cookies

I find that adding corn syrup to the batter makes a better-textured cookie. The oatmeal gives a crunchy texture.

Prep time: 20 minutes • Bake time: 12 to 15 minutes per sheet • Makes about 24 cookies

Vegetable cooking spray	1 tsp. vanilla extract
½ cup packed brown sugar	¾ cup quick-cooking oats
¼ cup granulated sugar	½ cup all-purpose flour
3 TB. canola oil	¼ cup unsweetened cocoa
2 TB. light corn syrup	½ tsp. baking soda
1 large egg	

Position a rack in the center of the oven and preheat the oven to 350°F. Lightly coat two baking sheets with cooking spray.

In a large bowl and using a whisk or electric mixer, combine brown sugar, sugar, oil, corn syrup, egg, and vanilla.

In another bowl, stir together oats, flour, cocoa, and baking soda. With a wooden spoon, stir the flour mixture into the wet ingredients until everything is combined. Drop by the teaspoonful, about 2 inches apart, onto the prepared baking sheets.

Bake for 12 minutes for a softer cookie, 15 minutes for a crisper cookie. Transfer to a wire rack to cool.

 Nutrition Watch

Oats are high in vitamin B1 and contain a good amount of vitamins B2 and E. Oatmeal is considered a low-glycemic food, which causes your blood sugar to rise slowly, which in turn keeps you feeling full longer.

A Piece of Advice

Use either quick-cooking rolled oats or old-fashioned oats in baking. Avoid instant oats, which can make the batter sticky.

 Nutrition per Cookie

Calories: 72
Protein: 1.1 g
Cholesterol: 8.9 mg

Fat (total): 2.2 g
Fat (saturated): 0.3 g

Carbohydrate: 12 g
Dietary Fiber: 0.6 g

Crispy Oatmeal Lace Cookies

These fine-textured cookies are fabulous right out of the oven. Use parchment paper because they tend to stick to the pan—even if it is well coated.

Prep time: 20 minutes • Bake time: 12 minutes per sheet • Makes about 18 cookies

Vegetable cooking spray

½ cup packed light brown sugar

3 TB. light corn syrup

1 large egg

2 TB. canola oil

1 TB. margarine or unsalted butter

1½ tsp. vanilla extract

1 cup quick-cooking oats

3 TB. all-purpose flour

½ tsp. baking powder

⅛ tsp. salt

Position a rack in the center of the oven and preheat the oven to 350°F. Line two baking sheets with parchment paper and lightly coat the paper with cooking spray.

In a bowl and using a whisk or electric mixer, combine brown sugar, corn syrup, egg, oil, margarine, and vanilla.

Nutrition Watch

Rolled oats are a great addition to baking. They give more volume without the added fat. They are high in vitamin B1 and offer a good amount of vitamins B2 and E.

In another bowl, stir together oats, flour, baking powder, and salt. With a wooden spoon, stir the oat mixture into the wet ingredients until everything is combined. Drop by the tablespoonful, 3 to 4 inches apart, onto the prepared baking sheets.

Bake one sheet at a time for 12 minutes or until the cookies are golden. Remove from the oven and transfer the paper (with the cookies) to a wire rack to cool. When completely cool, the cookies will come off the paper easily with a spatula.

Nutrition per Cookie

Calories: 75

Protein: 1.1 g

Cholesterol: 11 mg

Fat (total): 2.5 g

Fat (saturated): 0.3 g

Carbohydrate: 12 g

Dietary Fiber: 0.5 g

Crunchy Oatmeal Dried Cranberry Cookies

The combination of oatmeal, Grape-Nuts cereal, and dried cranberries makes a wonderfully crisp and light cookie. I love it with my coffee in the morning.

Prep time: 20 minutes   •   Bake time: 10 to 12 minutes per sheet   •   Makes about 24 cookies

Vegetable cooking spray

¾ cup packed light brown sugar

3 TB. canola oil

1½ TB. light corn syrup

1 large egg

1½ tsp. vanilla

½ cup all-purpose flour

½ cup quick-cooking oats

½ cup Grape-Nuts cereal

½ cup dried cranberries

1 tsp. baking powder

⅛ tsp. salt

Position a rack in the center of the oven and pre-heat the oven to 350°F. Line two baking sheets with parchment paper and lightly coat the paper with cooking spray.

In a large bowl and using a whisk or electric mixer, combine brown sugar, oil, corn syrup, egg, and vanilla.

In another bowl, stir together flour, oats, cereal, cranberries, baking powder, and salt. With a wooden spoon, stir the mixture into the wet ingredients just until everything is combined. Drop by the table-spoonful, spaced well apart, onto the prepared baking sheets.

Bake for 10 to 12 minutes or until the cookies are golden and still slightly soft. Cool them on the baking sheet for several minutes before transferring them to a wire rack.

Nutrition Watch

Grape-Nuts cereal is a tasty low-fat breakfast cereal made from wheat and toasted barley. It's ideal to use in baking because it adds a nut-like texture without the fat and calories of nuts.

A Piece of Advice

Use any dried fruit you like. Diced apricots, dates, cherries, or prunes go well with these cookies.

 Nutrition per Cookie

Calories: 83
Protein: 1 g
Cholesterol: 8.9 mg

Fat (total): 2.1 g
Fat (saturated): 0.2 g

Carbohydrate: 15 g
Dietary Fiber: 0.7 g

Peanut Butter and Jam Cookies

Who needs peanut butter and jam sandwiches when you can have these delicious cookies? The spiral effect makes these cookies very attractive.

Prep time: 20 minutes   •   Chill time: 20 minutes   •   Bake time: 18 to 20 minutes per sheet   •   Makes about 24 cookies

Vegetable cooking spray

¾ cup packed light brown sugar

¼ cup smooth peanut butter

3 TB. light corn syrup

2 TB. canola oil

1 large egg

1 tsp. vanilla extract

1⅓ cups all-purpose flour

2 TB. cornstarch

¾ tsp. baking powder

¼ cup raspberry jam

A Piece of Advice

Chilling the dough makes it easier to roll. But if you're in a hurry, drop the dough by the spoonful on a baking sheet, put a small amount of jam in the middle of each cookie, and bake 12 minutes or just until the cookies are lightly browned.

Nutrition Watch

Peanut butter is a highly nutritious snack for children and adults. Even though it contains 100 calories and 8 grams of fat per tablespoon, it is considered a healthy (monounsaturated) fat. Eat it in moderation.

Position a rack in the center of the oven and preheat the oven to 350°F. Lightly coat two baking sheets with cooking spray.

In a large bowl and using a whisk or electric mixer, combine brown sugar, peanut butter, corn syrup, oil, egg, and vanilla.

In another bowl, stir together flour, cornstarch, and baking powder. With a wooden spoon, stir the flour mixture into the peanut butter mixture just until everything is combined. Divide the dough into two balls and wrap them in plastic wrap. Chill for 20 minutes.

Between two sheets of floured waxed paper, roll one ball of dough into a rectangle ⅛-inch thick. Repeat with the other ball. Remove the top pieces of waxed paper. Spread jam evenly over both rectangles. Starting from the long end and using waxed paper to assist, roll each rectangle up tightly, jelly roll–fashion. Slice into ½-inch slices. Place, cut side down, on the prepared baking sheets.

Bake for 18 to 20 minutes or until the cookies are lightly browned. Transfer to a wire rack to cool.

Nutrition per Cookie

Calories: 99
Protein: 1.6 g
Cholesterol: 8.9 mg

Fat (total): 2.7 g
Fat (saturated): 0.3 g

Carbohydrate: 17 g
Dietary Fiber: 0.4 g

Biscotti

Biscotti are twice-baked Italian cookies that are increasingly popular here in America. It seems that they are popping up everywhere—served alongside coffee, espresso, or cappuccino at trendy restaurants; in striking packages at grocery and specialty foods stores; and in the cookie jar in homes throughout the country.

Just about everyone loves good biscotti and they can be made in an endless number of varieties. Made with any dried fruit, substituting whole-grain flours, or using different nuts, spices, and other flavorings, one can come up with dozens of variations on the theme.

Biscotti dough is first formed into logs and placed on a greased baking sheet. They are usually baked for approximately 20 minutes, brought out on a rack to cool for 5 minutes; then sliced into ½-inch slices, turned onto their sides, and baked again for 15 to 20 minutes. The longer the biscotti bake, the crisper they become.

Biscotti are the ideal gift cookie. They'll store for weeks in an airtight container and they pack well for mailing. Since they are low in fat, and can even be made entirely fat free, biscotti fit perfectly into today's healthier way of life.

White Chocolate Chip Biscotti

In my other cookbooks, I always include one or two biscotti recipes. I'm so thrilled that I can play with so many different flavors! The white chips melt into this cookie.

Prep time: 20 minutes • Bake time: 20 minutes plus 15 minutes • Makes about 30 cookies

Vegetable cooking spray

¾ cup granulated sugar

¼ cup margarine or unsalted butter, softened

1 large egg

2 large egg whites

2 TB. chocolate syrup

1 tsp. vanilla extract

1¾ cups all-purpose flour

¼ cup unsweetened cocoa

⅓ cup white chocolate chips

2 tsp. baking powder

Nutrition Watch

By using egg whites, you eliminate the fat and cholesterol from the yolk. In most recipes, I like to use 1 whole egg and substitute any other whole egg with 2 egg whites to reduce the fat and cholesterol.

A Piece of Advice

Chocolate syrup gives these cookies more chocolate flavor without added fat or cholesterol. You can use store-bought syrup or make the Chocolate Sauce in Chapter 16.

Position a rack in the center of the oven and preheat the oven to 350°F. Lightly coat two baking sheets with cooking spray.

In a food processor or bowl, combine sugar, margarine, egg, egg whites, chocolate syrup, and vanilla; process until the mixture is smooth.

With a wooden spoon, stir in flour, cocoa, chocolate chips, and baking powder just until everything is combined. Divide the dough in half. Shape each half into a log 12 by 4 inches. Place the logs well apart on a baking sheet.

Bake for 20 minutes. Remove the sheet from the oven. Let the logs cool on the sheet for 5 minutes. Transfer the logs to a cutting board. Slice them on the diagonal into ½-inch thick cookies. Place the cookies flat on the prepared baking sheets. Bake, one sheet at a time, for 15 minutes longer, until the biscotti are crisp and lightly browned.

Nutrition per Cookie

Calories: 61

Protein: 1.1 g

Cholesterol: 5.6 mg+

Fat (total): 1.9 g

Fat (saturated): 0.6 g

Carbohydrate: 9.8 g

Dietary Fiber: 0.4 g

Orange Pecan Biscotti

To get the most intense orange flavor, I use frozen orange juice concentrate, rather than orange juice. Keep a can in the freezer at all times just for baking and cooking.

Prep time: 20 minutes • Bake time: 20 minutes plus 15 minutes • Makes about 30 cookies

Vegetable cooking spray

1¼ cup granulated sugar

2 large eggs

¼ cup canola oil

5 TB. orange juice concentrate

2 tsp. finely grated orange zest

1½ tsp. vanilla extract

2 cups all-purpose flour

1½ tsp. baking powder

⅛ tsp. salt

⅓ cup chopped pecans, toasted

Position a rack in the center of the oven and preheat the oven to 350°F. Lightly coat a large baking sheet with cooking spray.

In a large bowl and with a whisk or electric mixer, combine sugar, eggs, oil, orange juice concentrate, orange rind, and vanilla.

With a wooden spoon, stir in flour, baking powder, salt, and pecans just until everything is combined. Divide the dough in half. Shape each half into a 12-inch by 4-inch log. Place the logs well apart on the baking sheet.

Bake for 20 minutes. Remove the sheet from the oven and let the logs cool on the sheet for 5 minutes. Transfer the logs to a cutting board. Slice them on the diagonal into ½-inch thick cookies. Place the cookies flat on the baking sheet. Bake for another 15 minutes or until they are crisp and lightly browned.

 A Piece of Advice

Toast nuts by heating in a dry skillet on a high heat for 3 minutes, or until they are browned. I do batches in advance and freeze them.

 Nutrition Watch

Nuts are a great source of protein and contain a fair amount of iron, phosphorous, and thiamine. They are high in calories and fat, but it's the good type of fat (unsaturated). Eat them in moderation.

 Nutrition per Cookie

Calories: 93

Protein: 1.6 g

Cholesterol: 14 mg

Fat (total): 3.2 g

Fat (saturated): 0.4 g

Carbohydrate: 14 g

Dietary Fiber: 0.4 g

Mocha Chip Biscotti

Coffee and chocolate go so well together. I enjoy these cookies as a late-morning snack, with a low-fat caffé latte.

Prep time: 20 minutes • Bake time: 20 minutes plus 15 minutes • Makes about 36 cookies

Vegetable cooking spray

2 tsp. instant coffee granules

¼ cup hot water

⅔ cup packed light brown sugar

¼ cup granulated sugar

⅓ cup canola oil

2 large eggs

2 tsp. vanilla extract

2⅓ cups all-purpose flour

⅓ cup semi-sweet chocolate chips

2 tsp. baking powder

Position a rack in the center of the oven and preheat the oven to 350°F. Lightly coat a large baking sheet with cooking spray.

 A Piece of Advice

If you have some left-over brewed coffee from break-fast, use ¼ cup instead of instant coffee.

 Nutrition Watch

The stronger you make the coffee, the less caffeine, so an occasional espresso is better for you than regular coffee.

Dissolve instant coffee in hot water. In a bowl and using a whisk or electric mixer, combine coffee, brown sugar, sugar, oil, eggs, and vanilla.

With a wooden spoon, stir in flour, chocolate chips, and baking powder just until everything is combined. Divide the dough in half. Shape each half into a 12-inch by 4-inch log. Place the logs well apart on a baking sheet.

Bake for 20 minutes. Remove the sheet from the oven and let cool for 5 minutes. Transfer the logs to a cutting board. Slice them on the diagonal into ½-inch thick cookies. Place the cookies flat on the baking sheet. Bake for 15 minutes longer or until they are crisp and lightly browned.

 Nutrition per Cookie

Calories: 76

Protein: 1.3 g

Cholesterol: 11.7 mg

Fat (total): 2.8 g

Fat (saturated): 0.5 g

Carbohydrate: 12 g

Dietary Fiber: 0.4 g

Rugelach

A traditional cookie for the celebration of Hanukkah, rugelach are melt-in-your-mouth bite-size crescent-shaped cookies that can have any number of fillings including raisins or other dried fruits, nuts, or jam. There's usually cream cheese in rugelach dough—in my recipes, low-fat cream cheese, of course.

Apricot Jam-Cranberry Rugelach

I get weak at the knees when I think about rugelach. They are crisp, buttery, and melt in your mouth. But I usually avoid them because traditional recipes are loaded with fat. Not these. They are creamy, yet light.

Prep time: 25 minutes • Chill time: 20 minutes • Bake time: 20 minutes •
Makes 20 cookies

Vegetable cooking spray	¼ cup plain low-fat yogurt
2 oz. light cream cheese	⅓ cup apricot or raspberry jam
½ cup granulated sugar	⅓ cup packed light brown sugar
¼ cup canola oil	⅓ cup dried cranberries
1½ cups all-purpose flour	½ tsp. ground cinnamon

Position a rack in the center of the oven and preheat the oven to 350°F. Lightly coat a baking sheet with cooking spray.

In a food processor, purée cream cheese, sugar, and oil until smooth. Add flour and yogurt; pulse on and off until the mixture is crumbly. Remove the dough from the food processor. Form it into two balls and wrap them in plastic wrap. Chill at least 20 minutes.

Between two sheets of floured waxed paper, roll one ball into a circle ⅛-inch thick. Spread half the jam over top and sprinkle with half the brown sugar, cranberries, and cinnamon. With a sharp knife, cut the circle into 10 wedges. From the wide, outside edge, roll each wedge toward the center; shape it into a crescent, and place it on the prepared baking sheet. Repeat with the remaining dough, jam, brown sugar, cranberries, and cinnamon.

Bake for 20 minutes or until the rugelach are golden brown. Transfer to a wire rack to cool.

 A Piece of Advice

If the jam is hard to spread, microwave it for 30 seconds to soften it.

Nutrition Watch

Dried cranberries are loaded with vitamin C and are a wonderful source of energy.

Nutrition per Cookie

Calories: 121   Fat (total): 3.4 g   Carbohydrate: 21 g
Protein: 1.5 g   Fat (saturated): 0.6 g   Dietary Fiber: 0.5 g
Cholesterol: 1.8 mg

Chocolate-Chocolate Rugelach

A Hanukkah tradition, these cookies can include a variety of fillings with a rich cream cheese dough. If you adore rugelach, wait until you try the double-hit of chocolate in these. Try not to eat the whole batch in one sitting!

Prep time: 25 minutes   •   Chill time: 20 minutes   •   Bake time: 15 to 18 minutes   •
Makes about 22 cookies

Vegetable cooking spray

1½ oz. light cream cheese

½ cup granulated sugar

2 TB. canola oil

2 TB. margarine or unsalted butter

1¼ cups all-purpose flour

3 TB. + 1 TB. unsweetened cocoa

¼ cup plain low-fat yogurt

½ cup packed light brown sugar

3 TB. semi-sweet chocolate chips

½ tsp. ground cinnamon

 Nutrition Watch

I always tell people not to deprive themselves of dessert. Just try to practice moderation. At least with these cookies, there is no room for guilt.

A Piece of Advice

If you prefer the wedge shape, follow the procedure in the Apricot Jam-Cranberry Rugelach recipe that's just before this recipe and add approximately 2 minutes to the baking time.

Position a rack in the center of the oven and preheat the oven to 350°F. Lightly coat a baking sheet with cooking spray.

In a food processor, purée cream cheese, sugar, oil, and margarine until the mixture is smooth. Add flour, 3 tablespoons cocoa, and yogurt; pulse on and off until the dough is crumbly. Remove it from the food processor. Form the dough into two balls and wrap them with plastic wrap. Chill at least 20 minutes.

In a small bowl, stir together brown sugar, chocolate chips, remaining 1 tablespoon cocoa, and cinnamon.

Between two sheets of floured waxed paper, roll one ball into an approximately 12-inch by 8-inch rectangle, ¼-inch thick. Sprinkle it with half of the filling. From the long end, roll it up tightly. With a sharp knife, cut the log into ½-inch thick slices. Place them on the prepared baking sheet. Repeat with remaining dough and filling.

Bake for 15 to 18 minutes or until the rugelach are golden brown on the bottom. Transfer to a wire rack to cool.

 **Nutrition per Cookie**

Calories: 103   Fat (total): 3.3 g   Carbohydrate: 17 g
Protein: 1.4 g   Fat (saturated): 0.9 g   Dietary Fiber: 0.6 g
Cholesterol: 1.3 mg

Crisps

These cookies are so thin and light; they are wonderful served alongside a bowl of summer berries or a scoop of frozen yogurt after a heavy winter meal. The thin batter is dropped by the spoonful onto the baking sheet, and then the cookies are quickly baked until golden and still slightly soft. They will become crisper as they cool.

Molasses Mocha Crisps

Molasses and coffee make a divine combination, especially in a cookie.

Prep time: 15 minutes   •   Bake time: 10 to 12 minutes per sheet   •   Makes about 24 cookies

Vegetable cooking spray

2 tsp. instant coffee granules

¼ cup hot water

3 TB. dark corn syrup

2 TB. canola oil

2 TB. dark molasses

1 TB. margarine or unsalted butter

½ cup packed dark brown sugar

¾ cup all-purpose flour

¼ tsp. ground cinnamon

¼ tsp. ground ginger

Position a rack in the center of the oven and preheat the oven to 350°F. Lightly coat two baking sheets with cooking spray.

Dissolve instant coffee in hot water. In a large bowl and using a whisk or electric mixer, combine coffee, corn syrup, oil, molasses, butter, and brown sugar.

 Nutrition Watch

Molasses contains iron, calcium, and phosphorus.

A Piece of Advice

You can substitute the instant coffee with strong brewed coffee left over from breakfast.

In another bowl, stir together flour, cinnamon, and ginger. With a wooden spoon, stir the mixture into the wet ingredients until everything is combined. Drop by the teaspoonful, spaced 3 inches apart, onto the prepared baking sheets.

Bake, one sheet at a time, for 10 to 12 minutes or until the cookies are golden and slightly soft. Transfer to a wire rack to cool.

Nutrition per Cookie

Calories: 61
Protein: 0.4 g
Cholesterol 0

Fat (total): 1.7 g
Fat (saturated): 0.2 g

Carbohydrate: 11 g
Dietary Fiber: 0.1 g

Lemon Poppy Seed Crisps

These lemon cookies are crisp and bursting with flavor. The addition of corn syrup gives the cookies a better texture, so the excess fat is not missed.

Prep time: 15 minutes • Bake time: 10 to 12 minutes per sheet • Makes about 30 cookies

Vegetable cooking spray

1 cup granulated sugar

3 TB. canola oil

1 TB. finely grated lemon zest

3 TB. fresh lemon juice

2 TB. light corn syrup

1 large egg

1 tsp. vanilla extract

⅔ cup all-purpose flour

¾ cup quick-cooking oats

1 tsp. poppy seeds

1 tsp. baking powder

⅛ tsp. salt

Position a rack in the center of the oven and preheat the oven to 350°F. Lightly coat two baking sheets with cooking spray.

In a bowl and using a whisk or electric mixer, combine sugar, oil, lemon zest and juice, corn syrup, egg, and vanilla.

In another bowl, stir together flour, oats, poppy seeds, baking powder, and salt. With a wooden spoon, stir the flour mixture into the wet ingredients until everything is combined. Drop by the tablespoonful, about 3 inches apart, onto the prepared baking sheets.

Bake, one sheet at a time, for 10 to 12 minutes or until the cookies are lightly browned. Transfer to a wire rack to cool.

 A Piece of Advice

For any recipe depending on lemon for the number-one flavor, as in this cookie, always use freshly squeezed juice. The flavor of the bottled version is inferior.

 Nutrition Watch

Lemons are an excellent source of vitamin C. Use soon after squeezing, or their vitamin power is reduced.

 Nutrition per Cookie

Calories: 90
Protein: 1.2 g
Cholesterol: 9.7 mg

Fat (total): 2.4 g
Fat (saturated): 0.3 g

Carbohydrate: 16 g
Dietary Fiber: 0.5 g

Beautiful "Cookies"

You'll likely recognize these cookies from your childhood. Because the word *cookie* comes from the Dutch word *koekje*, meaning "little cake," these cookies certainly qualify as they give the illusion of a little cake as you take your first bite. My children loved helping me bake these cookies and your kids will, too.

Marble Wafers

These cookies are beautiful to serve and delicious to eat. The two-tone look makes them appealing to kids as well.

Prep time: 15 minutes • Bake time: 10 to 12 minutes per sheet • Makes about 30 cookies

Vegetable cooking spray

¼ cup canola oil

2 TB. light corn syrup

1 large egg

2 tsp. vanilla extract

¾ cup + 2 TB. granulated sugar (divided use)

⅛ tsp. salt

½ tsp. baking powder (divided use)

1 cup all-purpose flour (divided use)

2 TB. unsweetened cocoa

Position a rack in the center of the oven and preheat the oven to 350°F. Lightly coat two baking sheets with cooking spray.

In a large bowl and using a whisk or electric mixer, combine oil, corn syrup, egg, vanilla, ¾ cup sugar, and salt. Divide the mixture in half.

To one half, add ¼ teaspoon of baking powder and ⅔ cup of flour; with a wooden spoon, stir until everything is combined.

To the other half, add remaining 2 tablespoons sugar; stir until everything is combined. Stir in cocoa, remaining baking powder, and remaining flour until combined.

 A Piece of Advice

Corn syrup gives this cookie a softer texture. Low-fat cookies can be dry or too crisp at times.

Take 1 teaspoon of each of the dark and the light dough; press them together and place them on the prepared baking sheets. Repeat with remaining dough.

Bake, one sheet at a time, for 10 to 12 minutes or until the cookies are lightly browned. Transfer to a wire rack to cool.

Nutrition per Cookie

Calories: 62

Protein: 0.7 g

Cholesterol: 7.1 mg

Fat (total): 2.1 g

Fat (saturated): 0.2 g

Carbohydrate: 10 g

Dietary Fiber: 0.2 g

Gingersnaps

The flavor of a gingerbread cookie is such a traditional one, with the most common ingredients being molasses and cinnamon. These gingersnaps are simple, yet addictive.

Prep time: 15 minutes   •   Bake time: 10 to 12 minutes per sheet   •   Makes about 30 cookies

Vegetable cooking spray	2 TB. canola oil
¾ cup packed light brown sugar	2 TB. dark molasses
½ tsp. ground cinnamon	1 large egg
¼ tsp. ground ginger	1 cup all-purpose flour
2 TB. margarine or unsalted butter	½ tsp. baking soda

Position a rack in the center of the oven and preheat the oven to 350°F. Lightly coat two baking sheets with cooking spray.

In a large bowl and using a whisk or electric mixer, combine brown sugar, cinnamon, ginger, margarine, oil, molasses, and egg.

In another bowl, stir together flour and baking soda. With a wooden spoon, stir the flour mixture into the wet ingredients until everything is combined. Drop by the tablespoonful, spaced well apart, onto the prepared baking sheets.

Bake, one sheet at a time, for 10 to 12 minutes or until the cookies are golden brown and still slightly soft. Transfer to a wire rack to cool.

A Piece of Advice

For spicier cookies, add a dash of nutmeg, allspice, and cloves.

Nutrition Watch

You can substitute 2 egg whites for the whole egg, if you want to reduce the fat and cholesterol from the yolk.

Nutrition per Cookie

Calories: 58	Fat (total): 1.9 g	Carbohydrate: 9.5 g
Protein: 0.7 g	Fat (saturated): 0.3 g	Dietary Fiber: 0.1 g
Cholesterol: 7.1 mg		

Mint Fudge Meringues

Another heavenly variation of a meringue cookie. The mint flavor is subtle and delicious.

Prep time: 15 minutes • Bake time: at least 60 minutes • Makes about 20 cookies

2 large egg whites

¼ tsp. cream of tartar

½ cup granulated sugar

2 TB. unsweetened cocoa

1½ tsp cornstarch

¼ tsp. mint extract

2 TB. semi-sweet mint chocolate chips

 Nutrition Watch _____

Meringues are the lowest fat cookies you can enjoy. There's never any oil or butter in them.

 A Piece of Advice _____

The longer that meringue cookies stay in the oven, the drier and chewier they become. You can leave them in the oven with the heat off—even as long as overnight.

Position a rack in the center of the oven and preheat the oven to 275°F. Line a baking sheet with parchment paper.

In a bowl and using a balloon whisk or electric mixer, beat egg whites until foamy. Add cream of tartar and beat until soft peaks form. Gradually add sugar, continuing to beat until stiff peaks form. Beat in cocoa, cornstarch, and mint extract. Fold in mint chocolate chips.

Drop by the tablespoonful onto the prepared baking sheet. Bake 1 hour or until the meringues are dry. Remove from the oven and transfer the paper (with the cookies) to a wire rack to cool. When completely cool, the cookies will peel off the paper easily.

 **Nutrition per Cookie**

Calories: 30

Protein: 0.4 g

Cholesterol: 0

Fat (total): 0.4 g

Fat (saturated): 0.3 g

Carbohydrate: 6.1 g

Dietary Fiber: 0.3 g

The Least You Need to Know

♦ When making cookies, you can substitute oil for unsalted butter or margarine or butter or margarine for oil. Oil gives the cookie a crispy texture; butter or margarine gives it a softer texture.

♦ Mix the wet ingredients first, and then the dry. When combining the two, don't over mix or your cookies will be tough.

♦ Cookies should be baked in the center of the oven for even baking and browning. When baking more than one sheet of cookies, do so one sheet at a time. It'll take you longer, but the results are worth the few extra minutes.

♦ All my cookies can be frozen with the exception of the meringue cookie. Even the dough can be made ahead and frozen for baking later.

♦ Biscotti and meringue cookies become crispier the longer they are baked.

Chapter 16

Sauces

In This Chapter

- Delicious, easy to make chocolate and caramel sauces
- Thick fruit purées called coulis
- Light lemon sauce, fruit glaze, or melted frozen yogurt sauce

Home cooks often overlook dessert sauces. The opposite is true with dessert chefs at fine restaurants—they offer a special sauce to complement most every dessert.

I feel that dessert sauces are a very individual choice. If you like an accompaniment to your dessert, select one that matches well. For example, strawberry or raspberry sauce always goes well with chocolate desserts or fruit-based desserts. Chocolate sauce goes well with chocolate, lemon, orange, or berry desserts.

Be inventive when using dessert sauces. They don't always have to go on top of the dessert. Sometimes you might want to spread a "puddle" of sauce on the dessert plate, and then place the dessert on top. Other times, decorate or "paint" the plate with decorative lines, squiggles, or dots of sauce and place the dessert alongside or on top. You might even want to experiment with two different sauces, such as raspberry coulis and mango coulis. Place each sauce in a small plastic squirt bottle and "paint" a design with the two contrasting colors and flavors.

One might think that sauces only came about with the introduction of *nouvelle cuisine*, but they actually can be traced back to ancient Greek and Roman cooking. The sauces in this chapter are all super easy to make; here's a few tips to insure success every time:

◆ If the sauce is used uncooked, make it at the last possible minute to get the best flavor. Cooked sauces can be kept refrigerated for weeks in an airtight container.

◆ When you're working with cornstarch, always add it to a cold base and mix until it is incorporated and the sauce is smooth. Then heat it on medium until it is slightly thickened. Be careful not to burn the sauce.

◆ If you are adding an egg to a sauce, always pour the hot sauce into the whisked egg and pour the mixture back into the saucepan, keeping it on a low heat and whisking constantly until the mixture is thickened. If not, you'll cook the egg. If the egg cooks or curdles, the heat was too high and you'll have to start again.

◆ When you're cooling a sauce, place some plastic wrap over the top to prevent a skin from forming.

◆ Cooked sauces usually thicken upon cooling. If you want a looser consistency, heat it gently in the microwave for approximately 20 to 30 seconds. You can also add a little milk or other liquid to the recipe.

Many desserts can be greatly enhanced with an appropriate sauce—providing a contract of flavors or colors, adding extra sweetness or tartness, or rounding out the flavors of the dessert.

Crème Anglaise

This light and creamy sauce is wonderful over bread puddings and pudding cakes. In fact, I serve it over any dessert that tastes best when it comes right out of the oven, such as phyllo desserts, soufflés, crisps, and cobblers.

Prep time: 2 minutes • Cook time: 10 minutes • Chill time: at least 30 minutes
• Makes about 1 cup

⅓ cup granulated sugar

1 large egg

1 tsp. vanilla extract

¾ cup 2% milk

In a bowl, whisk together sugar, egg, and vanilla.

In a small saucepan, heat milk over medium heat until it is steaming. Gradually add it to the egg mixture, whisking constantly. Return the mixture to the saucepan. Cook over low heat, stirring constantly, for 5 to 8 minutes or until it is slightly thickened. Do not boil.

Pour the sauce into a bowl. Place a piece of plastic wrap on the surface of the sauce. Chill for at least 30 minutes.

 **A Piece of Advice**

Be sure to stir this sauce constantly as it cooks, reaching around and into the corners of the pan so that the sauce is very smooth.

 **Nutrition per Tablespoon**

Calories: 27
Protein: 0.8 g
Cholesterol: 14 mg

Fat (total): 0.5 g
Fat (saturated): 0.2 g

Carbohydrate: 48 g
Dietary Fiber: 0

Chocolate Sauce

This is my basic low-fat chocolate sauce, which I love over almost any dessert. It goes well with other chocolate- and fruit-based desserts, as well as with cheesecakes, soufflés, jelly rolls, coffeecakes—just about any dessert!

Prep time: 2 minutes • Cook time: 6 minutes • Makes about ¾ cup

⅓ cup granulated sugar

3 TB. unsweetened cocoa

¼ cup light corn syrup

¼ cup water

Nutrition Watch

Cocoa gives the depth of flavor of solid chocolate in these sauces without the added fat.

In a small saucepan, whisk together sugar, cocoa, corn syrup, and water. Bring the mixture to a boil. Reduce the heat and simmer, stirring occasionally, for 5 minutes or until it is slightly thickened.

Pour the sauce into a bowl and cover.

 Nutrition per Tablespoon

Calories: 51
Protein: 0.3 g
Cholesterol 0

Fat (total): 0.2 g
Fat (saturated): 0.1 g

Carbohydrate: 12 g
Dietary Fiber: 0.5 g

Dark Chocolate Orange Sauce

This is a variation of my basic chocolate sauce with the addition of frozen orange juice concentrate and orange zest, which contribute an intense orange flavor.

Prep time: 2 minutes • Cook time: 6 minutes • Makes about 1 cup

⅓ cup granulated sugar

3 TB. unsweetened cocoa

¼ cup light corn syrup

¼ cup water

2 TB. orange juice concentrate

2 tsp. finely grated orange zest

In a small saucepan, whisk together sugar, cocoa, corn syrup, water, orange juice concentrate, and orange zest. Bring the mixture to a boil, stirring. Reduce the heat to low; simmer, stirring occasionally, for 5 minutes or until the sauce is slightly thickened. Pour it into a bowl and cover.

 Nutrition per Tablespoon

Calories: 40
Protein: 0.3 g
Cholesterol: 0

Fat (total): 0.1 g
Fat (saturated): 0.1 g

Carbohydrate: 9.5 g
Dietary Fiber: 0.4 g

Chocolate Raspberry Sauce

This is another variation of my basic chocolate sauce. The addition of raspberry jam gives this sauce a great flavor and texture.

Prep time: 2 minutes • Cook time: 5 minutes • Makes about 1 cup

⅓ cup granulated sugar

3 TB. unsweetened cocoa

¼ cup light corn syrup

¼ cup water

3 TB. red raspberry jam

In a small saucepan, whisk together sugar, cocoa, corn syrup, water, and jam. Bring the mixture to a boil, stirring. Reduce the heat and simmer, stirring occasionally, for 3 minutes or until the sauce is slightly thickened. Pour the sauce into a bowl and cover.

 A Piece of Advice

Be sure to purchase a seedless variety of jam. Some stores sell an imported seedless black raspberry jam that is also wonderful in this sauce.

 Nutrition per Tablespoon

Calories: 46   Fat (total): 0.1 g   Carbohydrate: 11 g
Protein: 0.2 g   Fat (saturated): 0.1 g   Dietary Fiber: 0.3 g
Cholesterol: 0

Caramel Sauce

This is a great sauce to serve over any dessert featuring apples or chocolate.

Prep time: 2 minutes • Makes about ¾ cup

½ cup packed light brown sugar

¼ cup evaporated skim milk

1½ TB. light corn syrup

2 tsp. margarine or unsalted butter

In a small saucepan, whisk together brown sugar, evaporated milk, corn syrup, and margarine. Cook over the lowest heat for 5 minutes, stirring constantly, or until the sauce is smooth and slightly thickened.

Pour the sauce into a bowl.

 Nutrition Watch

Evaporated skim milk takes the place of the traditional heavy cream in this delicious sauce, with a great reduction in fat grams.

Nutrition per Tablespoon

Calories: 52
Protein: 0.4 g
Cholesterol: 1.9 mg

Fat (total): 0.7 g
Fat (saturated): 0.4 g

Carbohydrates: 11 g
Dietary Fiber: 0

Vanilla Cream

This light, creamy sauce tastes fabulous over many of the pie and tart recipes in this book. It tastes like a light Devonshire cream.

Prep time: 3 minutes • Chill time: at least 30 minutes • Makes about ¾ cup

2 TB. granulated sugar

½ cup low-fat vanilla yogurt

1 oz. light cream cheese, softened

½ tsp. vanilla extract

In a food processor, combine sugar, yogurt, cream cheese, and vanilla; purée until the mixture is smooth. Pour the sauce into a bowl. Cover and chill for at least 30 minutes.

 Nutrition per Tablespoon

Calories: 23
Protein: 0.8 g
Cholesterol: 1.8 mg

Fat (total): 0.5 g
Fat (saturated): 0.3 g

Carbohydrate: 3.7 g
Dietary Fiber: 0

Nutrition Watch

A specialty of Devonshire, England, Devonshire cream—also known as clotted cream—is made by gently heating rich, unpasteurized milk until a clotted layer of cream forms on the surface. This thickened cream is then skimmed off and used as a topping for desserts. It's wonderful, but very high in fat. My recipe gives the illusion of Devonshire cream at a fraction of the calories and fat.

Strawberry Coulis

A coulis is a general term referring to a thick purée or sauce. This strawberry sauce is heavenly on any chocolate or fruit-based dessert.

Prep time: 3 minutes • Makes about 1 cup

8 oz. fresh or frozen strawberries

¼ cup confectioners' sugar

2 TB. water

If using frozen berries, thaw and drain well. In a food processor, combine berries, confectioners' sugar, and water; purée until the mixture is smooth. Pour into a small bowl.

 Nutrition per Tablespoon

Calories: 13
Protein: 0.1 g
Cholesterol: 0

Fat (total): 0.1 g
Fat (saturated): 0

Carbohydrate: 2.9 g
Dietary Fiber: 0.3 g

 A Piece of Advice

Other soft berries such as blueberries or blackberries can be used for coulis. If you wish to remove the seeds, wait until the mixture has been puréed, then strain it through a chinois, or a metal sieve with a very fine mesh.

Raspberry Coulis

This thick and rich-tasting sauce is wonderful over any chocolate dessert, soufflé, or fruit-based dessert.

Prep time: 2 minutes • Makes about 1 cup

8 oz. fresh or frozen raspberries

⅓ cup confectioners' sugar

2 TB. water

If using frozen berries, thaw and drain well. In a food processor, combine berries, icing sugar, and water; purée until the mixture is smooth. Pour into a small bowl.

 Nutrition per Tablespoon

Calories: 18
Protein: 0.1 g
Cholesterol: 0

Fat (total): 0.1 g
Fat (saturated): 0

Carbohydrate: 4.1 g
Dietary Fiber: 0.4 g

Mango Coulis

A mango sauce goes well over any fruit-based dessert, such as those with apricots or berries. It's also wonderful with any chocolate dessert.

Prep time: 2 minutes • Chill time: at least 30 minutes • Makes about 1 cup

1 large ripe mango, peeled, pitted, and diced   2 TB. fresh orange juice

3 TB. confectioners' sugar

In a food processor, combine mango, confectioners' sugar, and orange juice; purée until the mixture is smooth. Pour the sauce into a bowl. Cover and chill for at least 30 minutes.

 Nutrition per Tablespoon

Calories: 16   Fat (total): 0   Carbohydrate: 3.8 g
Protein: 0.1 g   Fat (saturated): 0   Dietary Fiber: 0.2 g
Cholesterol: 0

 A Piece of Advice

Try other fruits for coulis—peaches, plums, poached pears, papaya, blackberries, or cranberries (cooked in a small amount of water). Purée the fruit; then add the citrus juice and just enough sugar to taste. Coulis shouldn't be overly sweet—just enough to counter the tartness of the fruit.

Lemon Sauce

This citrus sauce is heavenly with chocolate desserts or lemon soufflés.

Prep time: 2 minutes   •   Cook time: 5 minutes   •   Chill time: at least 30 minutes
•   Makes about ¼ cup

½ cup granulated sugar

1½ TB. cornstarch

⅔ cup fresh orange juice

1 tsp. finely grated lemon zest

3 TB. fresh lemon juice

In a small saucepan off the heat, whisk together sugar, cornstarch, orange juice, lemon zest, and lemon juice until the mixture is smooth. Bring it to a boil. Reduce the heat and simmer, stirring occasionally, for 4 minutes or until the sauce is thickened. Pour the sauce into a bowl and cover. Chill for at least 30 minutes.

 Nutrition per Tablespoon

Calories: 44

Protein: 0.1 g

Cholesterol: 0

Fat (total): 0

Fat (saturated): 0

Carbohydrate: 11 g

Dietary Fiber: 0.1 g

Fruit Glaze

A fruit-decorated dessert always looks best if it is glazed before serving.

Prep and cook time: 1 minute   •   Makes about 3 tablespoons

2 TB. apple jelly or red currant jelly

1 TB. water

In small microwavable bowl, combine jelly and water. Microwave on high for 30 seconds. Stir until the mixture is smooth. Brush over berries or sliced fruit on top of a cheesecake or tart.

 A Piece of Advice

Experiment with other flavors of jelly or jam such as crab apple, sour cherry, quince, plum, apricot, or peach.

 Nutrition per Serving (on an 8-slice cake)

Calories: 14

Protein: 0

Cholesterol: 0

Fat (total): 0

Fat (saturated): 0

Carbohydrate: 3.5 g

Dietary Fiber: 0

Ready-to-Serve Sauce

This is the easiest sauce you can make. I often keep containers of frozen yogurt, ice, or sorbet on hand—usually chocolate, raspberry, lemon, and mango.

Prep time: 5 to 10 minutes • Makes about 1 cup

1 cup low-fat chocolate frozen yogurt or other
frozen yogurt or sorbet of your choice

Place the frozen yogurt in bowl. Let it stand until it has melted, stirring occasionally.

 Nutrition per Tablespoon

Calories: 15   Fat (total): 0.2 g   Carbohydrate: 0.2 g
Protein: 0.6 g   Fat (saturated): 0.2 g   Dietary Fiber: 0.2 g
Cholesterol: 0.6 mg

The Least You Need to Know

◆ Pick complementary flavors when matching sauces with desserts.

◆ Uncooked sauces need to be used right away; cooked sauces can keep refrigerated for several weeks.

◆ Be inventive with the placement of dessert sauces; they don't always have to be spooned on top.

Glossary

bain-marie   A water bath or a large open pan partially filled with hot water that holds a smaller pan of food so that the food is surrounded by gentle heat as it bakes.

baking sheet   A rigid heavy sheet of metal used to bake cookies, breads, scones, and so on.

baklava   A popular Middle Eastern sweet dessert that's made of layers of phyllo dough, spices, and nuts.

batter   An uncooked mixture that can be poured or dropped from a spoon.

beat   A rapid circular motion to incorporate air into a batter or dough.

boil   To cook until bubbling (212°F at sea level).

brûlée   The French word for "burned."

Bundt pan   Originally the trademark name of a tube pan with curved, fluted sides, the name now means a cake pan of that style.

canola oil   The market name for a bland-tasting cooking oil that's expressed from rape seeds. It's extremely popular because it is lower in saturated fat (about 6 percent) than any other oil and contains more cholesterol-balancing monounsaturated fat than any oil except olive oil.

caramelize   To cook sugar slowly until it turns to a liquid and its color changes to dark amber.

charlotte   A classic dessert made in a mold, usually pail-shaped.

chiffon cake   A cake made with oil instead of a solid shortening or butter.

citrus zester   A handy kitchen tool with five tiny cutting holes that produce thread-like strips of peel when the zest is pulled across the surface of a lemon, lime, or orange.

cooling rack   A network of closely arranged wires set on short legs to allow air circulation underneath a food as it cools.

dot   To scatter small bits or drops over a surface.

dust   To sprinkle a powdery ingredient, such as sugar or flour, over a surface.

drain   To pour off the liquid from a food.

flan   A baked custard coated with caramel.

fold   To gently combine two substances of different densities.

frosting   A sweet sugar-based mixture used to fill and coat cakes, cookies, and other pastries.

frothy   Showing a surface of tiny light, foaming bubbles.

garnish   An edible decoration on food to enhance the food's appearance.

glaze   A thin, glossy coating for food.

grate   To make thin shreds by rubbing a food against a coarse, serrated surface.

icing   *See* frosting.

jelly roll   A cake made from a thin sheet of sponge cake and spread with jam, jelly, or other sweet filling and rolled up.

kosher   Foods that conform to strict Jewish biblical laws that not only dictate what foods may be eaten, but also what kinds of foods can be combined. Commercial kosher products must be prepared under a rabbi's supervision.

lactose   The sugar in milk and milk products.

ladyfinger   Small light, delicate sponge cakes shaped like a fat finger.

mandelbrot   A Jewish crisp bread that is eaten as a cookie.

marbleize   To combine two or more colors or flavors of batter.

marmalade   A preserve containing small pieces of fruit zest (rind)

matzo   A thin, brittle, unleavened bread traditionally eaten during the Jewish Passover holiday.

matzo cake meal   Ground matzo used instead of wheat flour during the Jewish Passover holiday.

meringue A mixture of stiffly beaten egg whites and granulated sugar; sometimes stabilized by cream of tartar.

mocha A term used to describe a food that has been flavored with coffee.

mousse A rich, airy sweet dessert that is usually made from a fruit purée or a flavoring, such as chocolate, that gets its fluffiness from beaten heavy cream or egg whites.

phyllo Tissue-thin layers of pastry dough used in Greek and Near Eastern food preparation.

pit The stone or seed of a fruit.

pith The soft, bitter layer of white, spongy tissue that lies between the outer peel and flesh of citrus fruit.

poppy seed The very tiny dried, bluish-gray seeds of the poppy plant.

potato starch A gluten-free flour—made from cooked, dried, and ground potatoes—that's used in Jewish baking during Passover.

prick To make small holes in the surface of food.

purée Any food, usually fruits and vegetables, that is finely mashed to a smooth, thick mixture.

quick bread A bread that doesn't require rising time or kneading because it's leavened with baking powder or baking soda rather than yeast.

ramekin Individual baking dish that is 3 to 4 inches in diameter.

reconstitute To return a dried or dehydrated food back to its original consistency with the addition of water.

reduce To rapidly boil a liquid or sauce until some of it evaporates, resulting in a thicker consistency and a more intense flavor.

refresh To plunge a hot food into cold water to stop the cooking process and to cool it quickly.

salamander A kitchen tool used to brown the top of foods.

sauté To cook food in a small amount of oil or other fat.

seize A culinary term that applies to melted chocolate that becomes thick and lumpy.

sell date A system required by the Food and Drug Administration that dates foods to indicate freshness and shelf life.

sift To pass dry ingredients through a fine-mesh strainer to remove any lumps.

simmer To cook food gently at a temperature low enough that the surface shows little movement.

soy Made from soybeans.

spices Aromatic or pungent seasonings obtained from the bark, buds, fruit, roots, seeds, or stems of various plants or trees.

steam To cook food elevated over boiling water.

turnovers Circles or squares of pastry dough that are filled and then folded to form a triangle or semicircle before baking.

unleavened A term describing food that contains no leavener such as yeast, baking powder, or baking soda.

upside down cake A cake in which fruit, sugar, and spices are baked on the bottom. When the cake is done, it's flipped onto a plate so that the fruit and so on are now on the top.

water bath *See* bain-marie.

whip To beat ingredients, such as egg whites, to incorporate air and increase its volume.

whisk A kitchen utensil made from a series of looped wires that forms a three-dimensional teardrop shape held together with a long handle.

zest The outermost colored skin layer of citrus fruit, which contains the aromatic oils.

Appendix B

Resources

Most of the items for making these desserts are available at your supermarket or cookware store, but here's a list of where to mail-order supplies for your general baking and dessert-making needs.

cooking.com
www.cooking.com
—baking equipment and utensils, baking ingredients, food processors, electric mixers

Dean & DeLuca
560 Broadway
New York, NY 10012
1-800-221-7714
www.deandeluca.com
—baking supplies, utensils, chocolate

King Arthur's Flour Baker's Catalog
P.O. Box 876
Norwich, VT 05055
Phone: 802-649-5645
www.kingarthurflour.com
—baking equipment and supplies including flour, nuts and seeds, pure extracts, chocolate and cocoa

Maid of Scandinavia
3244 Raleigh Avenue
Minneapolis, MN 55416
1-800-328-6722
—baking supplies, utensils, chocolate

Paprika Weiss Importers
1572 Second Avenue
New York, NY 10028
212-288-6117
—poppy seeds, extracts, chocolate, baking utensils, nut mills

White Lily Flour Company
P.O. Box 871
Knoxville, TN 37901
615-546-5511
www.whitelily.com
—specialty flour

Williams-Sonoma
Mail Order Department
P.O. Box 7456
San Francisco, CA 94120
1-800-541-2233
www.williams-sonoma.com
—baking equipment and utensils, baking ingredients, fine chocolate and cocoa

Index